FASHIONING THE MODERN MIDDLE EAS

C000090318

Dress cultures

Series Editors: Reina Lewis & Elizabeth Wilson

Advisory Board: Christopher Breward, Hazel Clark, Joanne Entwistle, Caroline Evans, Susan Kaiser, Angela McRobbie, Hiroshi Narumi, Peter McNeil, Özlem Sandikci, Simona Segre Reinach

Dress Cultures aims to foster innovative theoretical and methodological frameworks to understand how and why we dress, exploring the connections between clothing, commerce and creativity in global contexts.

Reina Lewis: reina.lewis@fashion.arts.ac.uk
Elizabeth Wilson: elizabethwilson.auth@gmail.com

FASHIONING THE MODERN MIDDLE EAST

GENDER, BODY, AND NATION

Edited by
Reina Lewis and Yasmine Nachabe Taan

BLOOMSBURY VISUAL ARTS
LONDON • NEW YORK • OXFORD • NEW DELHI • SYDNEY

BLOOMSBURY VISUAL ARTS
Bloomsbury Publishing Plc
50 Bedford Square, London, WC1B 3DP, UK
1385 Broadway, New York, NY 10018, USA
29 Earlsfort Terrace, Dublin 2, Ireland

BLOOMSBURY, BLOOMSBURY VISUAL ARTS and the Diana logo are trademarks of Bloomsbury Publishing Plc

First published in Great Britain 2021

Selection, editorial matter, Introductions © Reina Lewis and Yasmine Nachabe Taan, 2021
Individual chapters © Their Authors, 2021

Reina Lewis and Yasmine Nachabe Taan have asserted their right under the Copyright,
Designs and Patents Act, 1988, to be identified as Editors of this work.

For legal purposes, the Acknowledgments on p. xiii constitute an extension of this copyright page.

Cover design: Adriana Brioso
Cover image: *Women on the Beach*, Digital Print on Canvas, 80 cm x 120 cm, 2012. (© Yasmine Nachabe Taan)

All rights reserved. No part of this publication may be reproduced or transmitted in any
form or by any means, electronic or mechanical, including photocopying, recording, or any
information storage or retrieval system, without prior permission in writing from the publishers.

Bloomsbury Publishing Plc does not have any control over, or responsibility for, any third-party
websites referred to or in this book. All internet addresses given in this book were correct at the
time of going to press. The author and publisher regret any inconvenience caused if addresses have
changed or sites have ceased to exist but can accept no responsibility for any such changes.

A catalogue record for this book is available from the British Library.

Library of Congress Cataloging-in-Publication Data
Names: Lewis, Reina, 1963- editor. | Taan, Yasmine, editor.
Title: Fashioning the modern Middle East : gender, body, and nation /
edited by Reina Lewis and Yasmine Nachabe Taan.
Description: London ; New York : Bloomsbury Visual Arts, 2021. | Series:
Dress cultures | Includes bibliographical references and index.
Identifiers: LCCN 2020036721 (print) | LCCN 2020036722 (ebook) | ISBN
9781350135215 (paperback) | ISBN 9781350135208 (hardback) | ISBN
9781350135222 (epub) | ISBN 9781350135239 (pdf)
Subjects: LCSH: Clothing and dress–Middle East. | Fashion–Middle East. |
Women–Clothing & dress–Middle East. | Middle East–Social life and customs.
Classification: LCC GT1380 .F37 2021 (print) | LCC GT1380 (ebook) | DDC 391.00956–dc23
LC record available at https://lccn.loc.gov/2020036721
LC ebook record available at https://lccn.loc.gov/2020036722

ISBN: HB: 978-1-3501-3520-8
         PB: 978-1-3501-3521-5
         ePDF: 978-1-3501-3523-9
         eBook: 978-1-3501-3522-2

Typeset by Integra Software Services Pvt. Ltd.
Printed and bound in India

To find out more about our authors and books visit www.bloomsbury.com and sign up for our newsletters.

CONTENTS

FIGURES

Figures

NOTES ON CONTRIBUTORS

Wilson Chacko Jacob is Professor of History at Concordia University in Montréal, Canada. In addition to several articles, he is the author of two historical monographs. His first book, *Working Out Egypt: Effendi Masculinity and Subject Formation in Colonial Modernity, 1870–1940* (2011), examines the global production of a regime of gender and sexuality. His second book, *For God or Empire: Sayyid Fadl and the Indian Ocean World* (2019), explores the global transformation of sovereignty through the lens of biography and through the recuperation of connected histories of the Middle East and South Asia.

Reina Lewis is Centenary Professor of Cultural Studies at the London College of Fashion, University of the Arts London, UK. An authority on the connections between religious cultures and fashion cultures, Reina is a frequent media commentator on modest and Muslim fashion. Her books include *Muslim Fashion: Contemporary Style Cultures* (2015); *Modest Fashion: Styling Bodies, Mediating Faith* (edited 2013); *Rethinking Orientalism: Women, Travel and the Ottoman Harem* (2004). Reina was consulting curator on the exhibition *Contemporary Muslim Fashions* for the Fine Art Museums of San Francisco in 2018—touring Museum Angewandte Kunst, Frankfurt, 2019; Cooper Hewitt Smithsonian Design Museum, New York, 2020.

Nancy Micklewright is currently an Andrew W. Mellon research fellow at the Metropolitan Museum of Art and a research associate at the Smithsonian, USA. Until 2019 she was Head of Public and Scholarly Engagement at the Freer and Sackler Galleries, Smithsonian. She is the author of *A Victorian Traveler in the Middle East: The Photography and Travel Writing of Annie Lady Brassey* (2003) and the editor, with Reina Lewis, of *Gender, Modernity and Liberty: Middle Eastern and Western Women's Writings; A Critical Sourcebook* (2006), as well as numerous articles. Her latest book project is *Dressing for the Camera: Fashion and Photography in the late Ottoman Empire*.

Yasmine Nachabe Taan is Associate Professor of art and design history and theory at the Lebanese American University. She has published a number of books in collaboration with Khatt Books, Amsterdam, with the aim to examine the development of Arab visual culture. Her recent curatorial work is *Traces of Drawings* (2019), an exhibition of more than a hundred drawings, studies, and sketches by Lebanese artists from the late nineteenth century to the mid-1990s at the NABU Museum. She is the author of *Reading Marie al-Khazen's Photographs: Gender, Photography, Mandate Lebanon* (Bloomsbury, 2020).

Afsaneh Najmabadi is Francis Lee Higginson Professor of History and of Studies of Women, Gender, and Sexuality at Harvard University, USA. Her book, *Women with Mustaches and Men without Beards: Gender and Sexual Anxieties of Iranian Modernity* (2005), received the 2005 Joan Kelly Memorial Prize from the American Historical Association. Her latest book, *Professing Selves: Transsexuality and Same-Sex Desire in Contemporary Iran* (2014) received the 2014 Joan Kelly prize from the American Historical Association for best book in women's history and feminist theory, and was a co-winner of the 2015 John Boswell prize, LGBT History, American Historical Association.

Mary Roberts is Professor of Art History, University of Sydney, Australia. Her scholarship addresses transcultural exchange between Europe and the Near East in the modern period, Ottoman visual culture, European art, debates about global histories of art, gender, orientalism, and material culture. Her books include *Intimate Outsiders: The Harem in Ottoman and Orientalist Art and Travel Literature*, (2007) and *Istanbul Exchanges: Ottomans, Orientalists and Nineteenth-Century Visual Culture* (2015, awarded 2016 AAANZ Best Book Prize). She has co-edited four books and been a Getty Scholar, YCBA, Clark Oakley, and CASVA senior fellow. Her forthcoming book is *The Threshold: Orientalist Interiors, Islamic art and the aesthetics of Global Modernities.*

Kirsten Scheid is Associate Professor of Anthropology at the American University of Beirut. She specializes in the anthropology of art and materiality, with a regional focus on Arab societies. She has published in the *International Journal of Middle East Studies, Museum Anthropology, Anthropology Now, and ARTMargins.* She co-curated "The Arab Nude: The Artist as Awakener" (Beirut 2016) and "Jerusalem Actual and Possible: the 9th Edition of the Jerusalem Show" (Jerusalem 2018). Scheid's research has been supported by the National Endowment for the Humanities, The Wissenschaftskolleg zu Berlin, the EHESS, and the Palestinian American Research Center. She has been a Clark Oakley Humanities Fellow (2019–2020).

Eve M. Troutt Powell is the Christopher H. Browne Distinguished Professor of History and Africana Studies at the University of Pennsylvania, USA. In addition to many articles, she is the author of *A Different Shade of Colonialism: Egypt, Great Britain and the Mastery of the Sudan* (2003) and *Tell This in My Memory: Stories of Enslavement from Egypt, Sudan and the Late Ottoman Empire* (2012) and is now working on a book about the visual culture of slavery in the Middle East.

ACKNOWLEDGMENTS

This book is part of a longstanding collaboration between we two editors and our institutions, the Lebanese American University and the London College of Fashion, UAL. Our first and deepest thanks go to Paul Yuille, Director of International at LCF, who brought us together to develop the research relationships underpinning the joint development of the Bachelor of Fine Arts in Fashion Design in collaboration with Elie Saab and the London College of Fashion

Our conversations led to the symposium *Modern Bodies: Dress, Nation, Empire, Sexuality and Gender in the Modern Middle East* held in Beirut in 2018 from which several of the chapters here emerged. We thank all the speakers who contributed to *Modern Bodies* and our wonderful audience interlocutors for building the rich dialogue that went on to inform this volume. For the smooth running of the event, we express gratitude to Janna Rais from LCF and Mary Kassab and Lina Abdun, from LAU; as also for the overall support of Professor Frances Corner—then Pro-Vice Chancellor at UAL and Head of College at LCF—and the Arab Institute for Women at LAU.

The authors in this book have contributed to a volume that is unusually wide ranging in intellectual, disciplinary, and geographical reach and they have each responded generously to our request that they write for readers outside as well as within their usual areas. The ensuing chapters are rich with ideas rendered vivid through their attention to visual and literary and media sources: we remain honored by the willingness of our expert authors to engage with our vision for the potential scope of this book.

All edited volumes come together in real time, and we are aware that during the writing of this volume several of our authors experienced major life events and losses; we especially appreciate the many extra miles they went to continue their participation.

We are grateful to Elizabeth Wilson, Series Co-Editor of Dress Cultures, and to Frances Arnold at Bloomsbury Visual Arts for their support and guidance on this book from its inception, as also to the excellent publishing assistance from Yvonne Thouroude and Rebecca Hamilton. Research assistance from Paul Bench and Vanessa Pope has been indispensable, and we thank them. Our deep thanks go to the anonymous readers, whose advice on the proposal and manuscript have immeasurably strengthened the volume.

The editors and publisher gratefully acknowledge the permission granted to reproduce the copyright material in this book. Every effort has been made to trace copyright holders and to obtain their permission for the use of copyright material. The publisher apologizes for any errors or omissions in the above list and would be grateful if notified of any corrections that will then be incorporated in future reprints or editions of this book.

CHAPTER 1

MAPPING MODERN BODIES IN THE MIDDLE EAST: INTRODUCTION

Reina Lewis and Yasmine Nachabe Taan

Introduction

This chapter introduces the reader to critical and historical terms used in the volume's discussion of fashion as key to understanding the development of modernity in the Middle East from the mid-nineteenth to mid-twentieth centuries. Our synoptic account covers significant changes in sovereignty in the context of competing European, Russian, and American imperial interests and the shifting power of Ottoman and Qajar Iranian imperial rule. We link historiographical approaches to multiple or "non-Western" modernities to the accelerating take-up of Western fashion and lifestyle commodities and related changes in Middle Eastern distributive trades. With sumptuary legislation remaining prevalent as a form of social order, our review of power elaborates the different forms of bodily governance across the region organized through the state, enacted by religious and ethnic communities, and exercised within the household. Our discussion of slavery explains the distinctions between the Islamicate and transatlantic models, and reveals how gendered and racialized relationships forged through slavery persisted into the twentieth century as a factor of household life and feature of the public consumptionscape. We delineate how codes of spatial segregation impacted on the organization of gender and sexuality for Muslims and non-Muslims alike. The awareness of European Orientalist stereotypes as a factor in changing attitudes to gender and sexuality across the region is considered in relation to the anti-degeneration drive of the Arab Awakening, or *al-Nahda*, and the shift in approaches to male and female beauty in Qajar Iran. With clothing operating as a marker of modernity, we outline state-mandated and individual processes in the selective adaptation of Western clothing styles for men alongside the changing significance of veiling and unveiling for women. As in Euro-America, moral concerns about women's consumption focused especially on fashion and, as we discuss, created changing opportunities for income generation. We match processes in fusion fashion to regional engagement with emerging international methods of modern art production and dissemination, including the take-up of photography in the imaging of modernity for self and other. We conclude with an outline of individual chapter contents.

Rendering Bodies Modern in the Middle East[1]

This volume demonstrates the many ways in which the dressed and undressed body played a central role in the formation and experience of modernities in the Middle East from the mid-nineteenth to mid-twentieth centuries. Our perspective regards modernity as multiple; investigates the interaction of several imperialisms; and foregrounds the diversity of regional experiences of post-imperial polities and nation-state formation.

We would like to thank Carolyn Goffman for her indispensable advice on components of this chapter.

As Mitchell argues, addressing processes of being modern in the Middle East automatically relocates the question of modernity within a global context.[2] The study of modernity in the Middle East—as for other "non-Western modernities"—re-interrogates framing categories such as "Western," "modern," and "civilized"; exploring the local and regional specificities of how individuals and groups adhered to, changed, challenged, and navigated these framing concepts.[3]

In a fashion context where very few garments survive, our authors combine analysis of extant vestments with visual and literary representations of clothed and unclothed bodies. Their multi-disciplinary interventions reveal dynamic relations between cultural, economic, and social histories, engaging scholarship from history of art, photography, visual culture, and material culture studies. The book thus navigates different research protocols, periodizations, and hierarchies of value attributed to primary sources. Inter alia, we evaluate the role of collecting, archiving, and curation in the telling of women's and gender history and histories of sexuality.

Our research melds regional and local contexts and histories onto theoretical paradigms developed (explicitly or implicitly) with other geographies in mind. Writing in the second decade of the twenty-first century, our authors—many themselves instrumental in the development of postcolonial theory, world history, and transnational fashion studies—reconsider orthodoxies emerging from first-round challenges to political, cultural, and scholarly Western-centrism.[4] Comparative, inter-, and multi-disciplinary research treads beyond conventional boundaries, just as our readers come from dissimilar perspectives. To help, each author provides contextual information setting the stage for modern bodies and hence for modernizing societies across the Middle East over nearly a hundred years.

Like its near comparators "Near East," and "Orient," the category of "Middle East" has over many years delimited and described the Arab world including Turkey and the Persian Gulf region for scholarship, colonialism, and imperialism, as also for market penetration. Alert to its ideological functioning, the term nonetheless remains a working category for those studying the region's lives and histories: for this book, the "Middle East" stretches across two continents to include territories in the countries now known as Egypt, Iran, Syria, Palestine, Lebanon, Turkey, and Sudan. Historiographically, our long durée permits us to track related processes of modernization and Westernization from their acceleration in the mid-1800s to their deployment in the shaping and representation of independent movements and nationalist cultures at the turn of the twentieth century. Within this, conventions of periodization vary by discipline, geography, and media.

The pre-history of this book's fashion periodization reaches back to the eighteenth century when the rapid turnover of style seen as emblematic of the "modern" fashion system began to embed in European fashion production and media, with worldwide ramifications. Contrary to earlier renditions of modern fashion as a property of Western experience, scholarship now demonstrates related changes to fashion style, production, and mediation appearing quickly across the Middle East.[5] Local dress cultures retained slower change cycles for longer, but engagement with imported Western fashions and textiles, and adaptations of conventional regional garments, are present from the eighteenth century. Our focus on the decades from the mid-nineteenth century captures an acceleration in impact across regional populations.

In fashion mediation, photography was in use in the Middle East soon after its invention in 1839, with growing take-up by local populations as affordability and availability increased.[6] For fashion distribution, we trace how regional norms of peddlers and bazaars servicing gender segregated societies adapted to the advent of specialist fashion shops and department stores. Changes in distribution modes for fashion and lifestyle commodities and services were part of larger changes in the spatial organization of societies, including places for the display of art.

Our chapters consider the fluctuating vistas in which dressed bodies became visible to observers within changing modes of gender segregation in household and public spaces. In an Islamicate region,[7] the cultural dominance of Islam structured social norms for Muslim and non-Muslim populations. In fashion terms, practices of veiling the face and obscuring the body with loose clothing functioned as indicators of social status (pre-Islamic in origin) rather than personal religious conviction; forms of class distinction for women in Armenian, Greek, and Jewish as well as Muslim communities.

Nonetheless, forms of affiliation based in religion did structure social classifications for women and men; at times determining place of habitation, clothing, occupation, and forms of governance. The predominance of non-Muslims in the distributive trades and forms of media such as photography provides an immediate riposte to the idea of the "Muslim world" as only inhabited by Muslims (then or now). Fashion does not operate outside of society, and the changes in political sovereignty brought about by imperial competition and the privations of war saw more Muslims and Muslim women finding employment in fashion and new ways to publicly present themselves as fashionable. Our volume offers insights into majority and minority populations through selected snapshots of regional significance and transnational consequence.

Authors focus on urbanized populations of the central Ottoman Empire and post-Ottoman Lebanon and Egypt, with one chapter on Iran and another on Sudan. Case studies analyze selected moments in which forms of dress and embodiment became critical indices within local, regional, and international debates about modernity and nation. Collectively we bring forth previously unseen primary sources and offer new readings of those better known, alert to the determining impact of social variations of religion, gender, sexuality, ethnicity, and race. Gaps in scholarship remain for our period and we regret that we could not secure chapters on territories such as Iraq, Saudi Arabia, and the Gulf. Some social groups are more represented in research than others. Accordingly, we are proud to include chapters that throw new light on experiences of slavery, contributing to scholarship on Islamicate slave societies.[8] We look forward to future research on how dress and undress factored in the formation and experience of rural, tribal, and peasant communities. And we anticipate further insights on the role of dress and changing attitudes to the body in modernizing apparatuses in health, education, prison, and the military.[9] For dress histories and histories of sexuality, we bring fresh information on elite women's practices of gender-cross dressing, and supply consumption studies with new ways to perceive local practices of transnational fashion, along with attention to everyday as well as special occasion wardrobe construction.

Our volume benefits from the digitized increase in primary sources.[10] Our decision to go wide in period and location reveals recurrences of places, historical persons and social roles, fashion developments, and primary sources. This results in a map of dress practices and fashioned subjects that we hope will provide new structures and methods for the broader understanding of the complex intra-imperial and transnational relations typical of the region and period.

Power: Governing the Body

Our comparative study covers a period in which sovereignty over territories changed dramatically in response to the conflicting relationships between European, Russian, and American imperial interests and the variable ability of Ottoman and Qajar Iranian imperial rule to withstand incursions from without and challenges from within. Dress and appearance were imbricated in the diverse structures of power inhering in the region and the different forms of resistance that met them. Legal frameworks seeking to control the movement of women's and men's bodies included methods of state governance sanctioned by the Ottoman and Iranian empires and post-Ottoman Egypt; replaced, adapted, or continued in the European mandates in Lebanon and Syria, and in post-Ottoman Turkey at the end of the First World War. Matched to this, and sometimes acting on behalf of the state, were the forms of governance enacted by religious and ethnic communities (with their own transnational affiliations). Finally, never least, were the gendered and sometimes racialized forms of household power exercised in societies organized on principals of gendered segregation: these impacted on social subjects of all religious affiliations. To understand how these types of governance produced gendered social subjectivities and afforded (regulated) social mobility requires comprehension of contemporary slavery and manumission, to which we turn later below.

State Governance

In state governance, our territories experienced tremendous flux across the time span of this book. Lebanon, for example, was part of Ottoman Syria before coming under French Mandate along with Syria at the end of the First World War. The legal boundaries of colonial civic order set a variety of gendered, class, and religious obstacles to people's full participation. In the case of Syria and Lebanon the mandate charter split legal authority between the state's jurisdiction over civil law and religious patriarchs' supervision of religious law, continuing a dual legal system rooted in the Ottoman era (still in place today).[11] In Mandate Syria and Lebanon, the reshuffling of social hierarchies after the First World War combined with the crisis of paternal privilege to give issues of gender centrality in conflicts over civil rights.

In contrast, Egypt, also formally part of the Ottoman Empire, had achieved quasi-independent status under Muhammad Ali (1805–48); entrenched further when his grandson Ismail secured the dynastic title Khedive. Invasion by the British during the Urabi revolt in 1881 brought Egypt under European control, while the Mahdi rebellion gained independence for Egyptian Sudan.[12] The development of Egyptian nationalism saw the articulation of aspirant identities—including the emerging *effendiyya* class of Arabic-speaking Egyptians—outside of Ottoman frameworks and also opposed to Western imperialism.[13] At the apex of the prevailing Turko-Circassian elite in Egypt, the Khedival family were related to the Ottoman imperial family by marriage and remained immersed in the social life of regional royal society. Their visits to their summer homes on the Bosphorous showcased the latest trends to Ottoman high society, with the Khedival ladies renowned as style leaders and early adopters of Western fashions.[14] The Khedivate ended when the British declared Egypt a protectorate at the start of the First World War.

Within the Iranian, Ottoman, and Egyptian state, as in Europe and North America, modernization showed quicker in urban than rural locations. In the Middle East, the selective adaptation of Western commodities and cultural forms—including fashion—was key to the articulation of modernity for individuals and rulers. Competing factions used fashion and lifestyle choices to communicate preferred versions of regional gendered modernity to domestic and foreign audiences. Port cities and border towns on key trading routes encountered foreign goods and behaviors soonest,[15] as did metropolitan cities and seats of power such as Alexandria, Cairo, Istanbul, Tehran, as also Tabriz and Isfahan.

Western fashion and lifestyle commodities were mostly adapted rather than straightforwardly adopted, used in a mélange of old and new, foreign and local goods.[16] This, Western observers often decried as ignorant tastelessness, expressing imperial nostalgia for the exoticized Orient of their imagination.[17] Middle Eastern commentators were also concerned with the social impact of Western goods and associated behaviors; whether regarded as routes to social and gender emancipation or signs of worrying moral decline. For all political views the appearance of women was a litmus test, fought over by states, religious communities, and families.

Western fashion and lifestyle commodities and services took on these valences in a social context where dress and appearance was already heavily indexed and disputed in relation to power and social distinction. Across Euro-America too, sumptuary legislation had demarcated and regulated social rank, occupation, religion, and (sometimes to a lesser extent) gender—though diminishing by the nineteenth century.[18] In the dispersed and heterogeneous Ottoman Empire, sumptuary legislation remained a central preoccupation because, as Madeline Zilfi explains, dress and appearance were the "principal delineator[s] of social place and relationships of power."[19] Ottoman rule required appearance ideally to serve as a transparent indicator of rank, religion, and social status until the centralized Tanzimat reforms (1839–71) removed the color-coded dress and distinctive headgear of minority population men. Sumptuary laws continued throughout our period, prompted by persistent concern about visual distinction, especially between Muslims and non-Muslims, and female respectability. The constant infractions against dress regulation were not regarded as insignificant matters of "mere" fashion: as a threat to the prevailing social order, incursions by women and non-Muslims, "society's preferred others, was a danger rather than just an annoyance,"[20] with poor Muslims agitated that non-Muslims enjoyed disproportionate relative advantage.

Religious Communities

For much of its existence, including the start of our period, the Ottoman Empire ruled over provinces where Muslims were a minority (especially while it retained European provinces). Islam was the official religion of the state, with the sultan as Caliph of all believers. Non-Muslim populations were accorded a degree of semi-autonomous self-governance in return for differential taxation and restrictions on forms of income generation and political representation. The Greek Orthodox Patriarch had authority over and was answerable for the behavior of his co-religionists; similarly the religious leader of Jews and Armenians. Restricted self-governance offered some advantages: often clustered in residential and trade enclaves, the implementation of imperial regulations by (male) community leaders might simultaneously shore up internal hierarchies and provide protection from collective punishment for real or perceived infractions.

For fashion, and for consumer culture more broadly, minority populations were central providers of services in distribution and manufacture (as traders, shopkeepers, milliners, tailors) and early adopters of Western lifestyle and fashion commodities. Benefitting (some thought unfairly) from external links with Western nations and transnational connections with co-religionists, the non-Muslim "Frankish" district of major cities—such as Pera in Istanbul—were long-established locations for acquiring novel goods and observing new trends.

The inequities encountered by minority populations cannot be underestimated, despite that the Ottoman model sometimes provided greater protection for religious minorities than Christian European polities. The ideal of social emancipation through social unity which gained traction in the pan-Ottoman idealism of Young Turk leadership in exile in Europe in the 1880s was overridden to devastating and deadly effect during the First World War as Turkish exclusionism led to deportations and massacres.[21] In Egypt, the role of minorities was as economically and socially important as in other Ottoman provinces, especially in the cotton and textile trade essential to Egypt's agricultural economy. Greeks, Armenians, Italians, and other Europeans who emigrated to Egypt during the late nineteenth and early twentieth century, were involved in all aspects from cultivation to factory finishing. Syrians and Jews who settled in great numbers during the nineteenth century were also active in factories and enterprises. The growing size of the local foreign minority population is a key factor in Egyptian social history for our period, particularly two major spheres of antagonism between local foreign minorities and Egyptian landowners. First, that local foreign minorities were exempt from paying taxes. Second, that landowners were largely dependent on credit and mortgage institutions—themselves also reliant on funds from Europe. Although local foreign minorities mostly resided in urban cities such as Alexandria, Cairo, Port Said, Ismailiya, and Suez, many local foreigners had ventured to remote villages; often Greeks, Jews, and Syrians working as moneylenders, merchants, and grocers. In the 1920s and 1930s these groups moved back to Alexandria, Cairo, and the larger provincial towns.[22] Influential in fashion and lifestyle trades and distribution, minorities had to a considerable extent Westernized the taste of the upper and middle Egyptian bourgeoisie.

In Iran, some of the main ethnic groups were also religious minorities in the context of Shi'a Islam as the state religion. This minoritized the majority of Kurds, Baluchis, and Turkmen who were Sunni Muslims, as also Armenian Christians. Many of the traditionally tribal groups became urbanized and culturally assimilated during the nineteenth and twentieth centuries. Across the region, Jewish and Christian communities were immersed in fashion trades such as tailoring and shoemaking. In 1930s the Pahlavi regime (1925–79) pursued an assimilationist policy of Persianization, imposing national homogeneity on a country where half of the population consisted of ethnic minorities.[23]

Throughout our region believers in Islam were demarcated by allegiance to local and tribal power structures and to spiritual leaders and modes of practice. For individuals and families, being Muslim and free did not necessarily guarantee superior status to the non-free or the non-Muslim. Across the Ottoman land mass, social class and closeness to sultanic power determined access to resources and to cultural capital. Neither did being Muslim prevent those living distant from the imperial center of Istanbul being positioned as exotic or primitive in forms of Ottoman Orientalism; provincial Muslims along with tribal communities and minority populations might be simultaneously valued as expressions of "folk" cultures and regarded as less civilized.[24] In the photographic costume album commissioned by Sultan Abdulhamit II in 1893 to present to the American government, the Ottoman populace is arranged into a hierarchical scale of modernity and tradition.[25] All were surveilled by and owed allegiance to the sultan.

Religion played a central role in the fashion cycle itself. Festivals and weddings were then—as now— important moments in fashion acquisition and display across social strata, with the fashions of royal and elite women especially noted. Muslim religious spaces served as consumption sites:[26] during Ramadan mosque courtyards hosted traders selling holy books and prayer beads as well as clothing and textiles. In the daily experiences of lived religion,[27] the clothing and management of the body was achieved through interaction with quotidian commodities and market relations.

In the Ottoman context social status was determined by forms of power linked to degrees of proximity to the sultan and his proxies, with roles that acted on the sultan's behalf also open to minority population members. All formal positions of public office within the imperial bureaucracy were held by men. Women operated parallel networks of patronage, with segregated female sociality a recognized route through which information travelled and power was exercised.[28] For men, marriage to royal princesses or women from within the imperial household could advance status. For women, brokering these marriages was a mechanism for exercising influence; mirrored across the empire in non-royal elite households. Central to this was slavery: until nearly the end of the empire, women in the imperial harem who might be "given" in marriage as a form of favor were themselves mostly of slave origin—except the daughters and sisters of the sultan—and were able to rise to positions of power.

Slavery: Transitional Generations

There is no denying the horrors of being an owned human commodity and the trauma and perils of the journey into slavery. And it is the case that there were several key distinctions between being a slave in the Islamicate context versus the experience of those enduring the transatlantic trade[29] (as contemporary Ottomans, Iranians, and sympathetic Western observers were keen to emphasize).[30] Formally, Islam routinized manumission; though like all regulations this was not always followed. Conceptualized as a potentially temporary status rather than a truth of a person's being, stigma did not necessarily inhere in the condition of having once been enslaved. Nor was slavery regarded as a state for which particular "races" had a propensity. Suppressed to some extent from the mid-nineteenth century, the Ottoman and regional slave trade continued albeit less publicly—including trade by women within elite households. To the bewilderment of Western visitors many royal and upper-class women had arrived in their households as slaves, and themselves purchased enslaved girls to be educated as suitable partners for male relatives or married to powerful officials to advance family interests.

Many of the historical subjects covered in this book were of the transitional generations who grew up with slaves and eunuchs, and manumitted slaves, as a component of lived experience; integral to families and households. We explore the role of social and personal relations of slavery in the making, dressing, and framing of bodies understood as modern.[31] It remains a necessary restorative project to find slave histories and bring to notice ways to see the enslaved body. Imbricated within these essential excavations is the historiographical urgency to find ways of understanding that the bodies of non-slave Middle Eastern subjects were equally and indelibly marked by their relationship to the state of slavery.

For most of our period Istanbul contained the highest density of slaves and manumitted persons, with regional variations such as the greater percentage of black slaves in Cairo.[32] Women made up the majority of the Ottoman slave population, most in a domestic context: serving as domestic labor (often African women) and as concubines (sometimes wives) with a racialized hierarchy of female beauty determining prices for women from Circassia, Georgia, and Abyssinia (Ethiopia). Male slave numbers decreased for agricultural and military labor,[33] and had waned outside the palace as a route to seniority in the sultan's service. Within the palace, education brought career opportunities.[34] Black eunuchs conventionally achieved power directly serving the sultan in the imperial household-office, and women slaves gained influence through concubinage (especially if they had a son), and as chief officers within the harem. Across the realm, enslaved (and manumitted) persons in senior roles exercised the delegated authority of the sultan; "[b]eing someone's slave did not mean being everyone's slave."[35]

In the Ottoman Empire and Egypt, the transition out of slavery occurred alongside other gendered transformations to family and social life. Our generations experienced—or witnessed—the shift away from a social norm of slave-owning, multi-generational, sometimes polygynous, and certainly multi-ethnic households. In many instances, new family models centered on versions of the companionate nucleated or "conjugalized" family,[36] sometimes in the new apartment buildings that came to characterize modern Middle Eastern metropolises. In others—such as Lebanon—it was the non-nuclear "native bourgeois family [that was] portended to possess the *qualities* of capitalist modernity."[37] While few Muslims were rich enough to have afforded polygynous marriage and concubinage,[38] the aspiration for new types of families inhabiting new types of homes was a way of living out in the present desires for future political and social emancipation which impacted broadly on Muslim and non-Muslim subjects. Becoming modern was an uneven and inconsistent process: polygyny might wane, but partners were chosen in consideration of family interests; families acquired apartments in the same building; eunuchs remained a recognizable part of the social fabric for a lifespan, of the cultural landscape for longer. And, as Eve Troutt Powell makes clear, the emotional patterns of being enslaved, living with slaves, and being the children of slaves or manumitted slaves did not disappear from the psychological patterning of the populace for quite some time.[39]

Spatialized Sartorial Power: Gender and Sexuality in Public and Private

Clothing played an integral part in spatialized gender segregation systems, with the veil in all its forms creating what Fatima Mernissi called a "portable harem" which allowed women to pass apparently unseen through gender-mixed spaces when they left the private, controlled, space of the household.[40] In fashion terms, the spatialized organization of gender and sexuality determined who saw which dressed body, how bodies were garbed, and how the garments that covered them were created and acquired.[41]

As feminist scholarship on the Middle East elaborates, rather than the sexualized prisons of the Western Orientalist imaginary harems were spaces of family life and female sociality. The women in gender segregated households (royal and elite palaces or humbler domiciles) lived in a space permeated by women visitors, relatives, and traders. Outside the home, women went to the *hamam* (baths), mosques and shrines, visited parks and beauty spots. In public, women's presence and behavior was scrutinized and regulated, including by neighborhood observers male and female.[42] Status-enhancing seclusion from the gaze of others to guarantee female respectability included sartorial means of face and body veiling, transportation modes such as closed carriages, and the living protective shield of eunuchs and the entourage of women slaves (whose "always 'exposable'" unveiled public presence protected the respectability of their owners, not themselves).[43]

With regional and temporal variations, women had a more prevalent direct public presence than is sometimes presumed.[44] Royal women's visibility in ceremonies and pageantry assisted imperial image-making;[45] non-elite women protested in the streets over food prices;[46] women of all classes demonstrated for nationalist and feminist causes.[47] Political consumption saw women lead boycotts of foreign goods produced by enemies of the state or support national economies by buying local in Iran, Egypt, and the Ottoman Empire.[48]

As Kate Fleet makes clear, consumption—both shopping and trading—brought different sorts of women into the Ottoman public domain, focusing political and social anxieties. Women's public presence in the marketplace was almost impossible to control yet had to be facilitated, because "a state unable to ensure the safety of its female population was a failing one."[49] Women's insistence on new fashion trends constantly flouted sumptuary legislation. Their appetite for novelty impacted on national trade balances (favoring imported European textiles) and on the welfare of local traders (faster trend cycles resulting in unsold inventory). Contravening sumptuary legislation was not without penalty; if elite women might sometimes ignore imperial decrees with impunity, tailors and traders might be punished—sometimes collectively—for transgressing regulations.[50] As Ottoman women's take-up of Western styles quickened in the late nineteenth and early twentieth century, no detail was too small to merit imperial state scrutiny. The appearance of Muslim women in on-trend tight-waisted jackets—regarded as non-Muslim apparel—prompted decrees from Sultan Abdulhamit II.[51]

The growing print media in the late nineteenth century reported moral panics about blurring sartorial distinctions between Muslim and minority populations, plus the deleterious impact of Westernized behavior on female morality.[52] Simultaneously, editorial and advertising visual content created opportunities to view European fashion. Print media informed on clothing to adorn the body (of women, children, and men) and the household items with which the modernized body should interact (sitting on Western style chairs to eat from individual place settings, rather than the shared receptacles of floor-based life). All this "further 'globalized'" women's consumption.[53] New relationships between body and garment were created by wearing Western garments and by incorporating European-style tailoring into conventionally loose-fitting Ottoman garments.[54] The experience of increasingly individuated fit was part of the processes by which were forged individuated modernizing subjects.

The Body of Modernity: Beauty, Health, Degeneration

For much of the Middle East, the fin de siècle witnessed a "liberal age"[55] with eclectic democratic movements, modernist movements in the arts and radical visions. In the Ottoman empire, including its Arab provinces, many in the elite identified with Sultan Abdülhamid II's modernization drive; articulating a sense of contemporaneity, of belonging to a modern and global age.[56] In Damascus, for example, walls and ceilings of courtyard mansions were adorned with paintings of Ottoman technological icons: steamships, locomotives, and bi-planes.[57]

In Beirut in 1863, Khalil al-Khuri, editor of the city's first privately funded newspaper *Hadiqat al-Akhbar*, hailed the coming of "the new age."[58] The previous year, this sense of being part of a distinctive modern moment had been identified as "*al-nahda al-'arabiyya*" (the Arab renaissance) by Jurji Zaydan in his journal *al-Hilal*. Wide-ranging social and linguistic reform efforts raised expectations among the well-educated that East, al-Nahda would revive the classical Arabic literary heritage. Across the Arabic speaking Middle East, the period saw an increase in printing presses and print media, translation projects, literary associations, and schools.[59]

Celebratory impetus to compose al-Nahda's new cultural canon was matched by anxiety about stagnation and degeneracy. Particularly, Joseph Massad argues, public moralists like Zaydan worried that Abbasid homoerotic love poetry and pederastic norms would affect contemporary Arab youth. The social and sexual "deviance" in the Arabic classics did not fit the image of Arabs that al-Nahda wanted to project. Rather, it confirmed Western stereotypes as produced by European "sex tourists" such as Gustave Flaubert and Victorian voyeurs like Richard Burton, translator of *The Arabian Nights*.[60] Prior Arab civilizations might prove a cultural reservoir to censor as much a source of inspiration to revive.[61] To counter a perceived tide of looming degeneracy—risked equally by extreme traditionalism and hyper-Westernization—jurist and liberal reformer Muhammad Abduh (1849–1905) constructed a modern Islam. Only the hybrid "thought space" between "imitation" and "estrangement," or Westernization, would emancipate modern Muslims from the totality of both.[62]

In Iran, from the late eighteenth century into the first decades of the twentieth century, modernity was shaped through the gendered re-articulation of nation and politics. As Afsaneh Najmabadi demonstrates, the nation was conceptualized as a brotherhood with homeland as female; a beloved and a mother.[63] This development was underwritten by a move away from early Qajar social and cultural concepts of human relations embedded in Sufi allegorical associations that did not necessarily distinguish beauty by gender. The love and the desire of adult men might be generated equally by a beautiful young man or young woman. By the end of the nineteenth century, a highly gender-differentiated portrayal of beauty emerged, along with a concept of love that naturalized male heteroeroticism and heterosexuality.[64] These major transformations in Qajar Iran can be seen as products of the Iranian interaction with Europeans dating back to the sixteenth century. We note that cultural hybridization was mediated not only through the increasing interactions between Iranians and European culture but also through interactions with the Ottoman Empire. Just as this cultural traffic transformed Iranian gender and sexual sensibilities, European gender and sexual mores were also changed through interactions with societies that Europe colonized or in which it exercised imperial influence. In Iran, as elsewhere in the Middle East, the adaptation of Western knowledge, goods, and behaviors met with caution in many quarters.

Iranian modernity—as elsewhere—came to be emblematized by companionate marriage. In Iran, the construction of marriage as a romantic rather than procreative contract disavowed male homoeroticism and homosexual practices. Instead, the idealized pairing was of modern citizen-man with his companionate wife, sufficiently educated to embody modern sensibilities and harness Western scientific childrearing for the nation. Feminists advocating modern marriages faced challenges from conservative clerics, as also from men unwilling to relinquish polygyny or easy divorce; both typical of modernist and counter-modernist discourse that retain currency in the contemporary politics of Iran and many other Islamic societies of the Middle East.[65]

Men's Clothing Change

Major social and political reforms saw centralized changes to Ottoman men's clothing across the long nineteenth century. When Sultan Mahmud II abolished the historically slave-recruited Janissary military corps in 1826 and established a conscription army he also replaced the distinctive Janissary uniform and headdress with Western style military uniforms. Leading by example, he altered the public attire of all men in state service who would now abandon caftans and loose trousers, or *şalvar*, for frock coats and trousers (except for the *ulema* [Islamic scholars]). Turbans would be replaced by the fez. Sumptuary legislation regulated the new presentation of Ottoman masculinity in public spaces and in workplaces: in private, at home, men were the guardians of sartorial scripts and household morality for all inhabitants.

Mahmud II's reforms inaugurated a lasting acceleration in the cycle of men's fashion change. Dandies might be pilloried for obsession with *alafranga* fashions, mocked in satirical novels at the turn of the twentieth century for slavishly adopting commodities (canes, cigarette cases, perfumes) showcased in seasonal Ramadan promotions.[66] Sometimes depicted as inappropriately effeminate, the dandified *alafranga* man also threatened to blur boundaries between Muslim and non-Muslim Ottomans and foreigners at a time when the multi-ethnic, multi-faith, multi-national household was altering as an elite norm.

When upper-class Iranian men began traveling to Europe in larger numbers in the nineteenth century, many became self-conscious about their looks and gradually adopted European clothing often retaining it on their return to symbolize progress.[67] In Iran the gap between the European model and the Muslim reality of society could be bridged by reclaiming the country's pre-Islamic heritage, understood to share a common ancestry with European culture.[68] As early as the middle of the nineteenth century, Mohammad Shah Qajar (1834–48) was presenting his implementation of European-style military uniforms as a re-adaptation of ancient Persian uniforms (engraved on the walls of Persepolis).[69] For Iranian modernists Europeanization could be coded as national particularism; a return to the true self rather than alienation. By the time Reza Shah began his rule (1925–41), this attitude had become prevalent among the educated elite of all political orientations, but it was he who harnessed the newly strengthened state to impose this view on the whole country.

One of his most enduring legacies is the problematization of dress in Iranian politics. A number of his policies had deep, sometimes traumatizing, effects on the everyday lives of Iranians. Following the example of Turkey, but unlike other Muslim governments in the Arab world, and in South and Southeast Asia, the Shah's state set out to standardize and Europeanize the appearance of its people. This policy paved the way for conflicts within society and between state and society that re-emerged after the Islamic revolution of 1979.

Before Reza Shah's accession, the gradual Westernization of menswear had encountered religiously motivated opposition. Nonetheless, wearing European suits spread down the social scale from the court and aristocracy to educated urbanites. The socio-political debate triggered by changes in men's clothing was nothing compared to the heat generated by sartorial change for women, most particularly when wearing a veil became obligatory after the Constitutional Revolution (1905–11). Now modernists found themselves not only opposed to religious strictures, as had been the case with men's European suits, but also to the patriarchal habits of Iranian society.[70]

Veiling and Unveiling: Making the Bodies that Reveal Modernity

In Iran, as across the region, progressive men wanted wives who could accompany them—appropriately dressed in Western fashion—to mixed gender events with foreigners to allay the Orientalist presumptions they knew informed the Western view. Not necessarily embracing the full scale of women's ambitions, male support for female emancipation as part of regional and national political emancipation was notably different to the opposition feminists faced in Euro-America into the twentieth century.[71] Middle Eastern feminists made strategic use of forms of unveiling to garner attention, though often misreported in the Western press. When Egyptian nationalist and feminist Hoda Shaarawi took off her veil in 1923, her hair remained covered: as increasingly common among her class milieu it was the face veil that she removed. Yet the Western media celebrated an "unveiling" as if total. Turkish Ottoman feminist Halide Edib similarly retained a headcovering,[72] just as other Muslim feminists retained forms of face cover.[73]

If the revealed female face, or hair, was totemic so too was the disposition of the rest of women's bodies important to state imaging. The lounging uncorseted odalisque iconized by Orientalist artists was replaced by women with the upright posture of the crinoline and bustle, with trends in regional outerwear changing accordingly.[74] Women's desire for fashion innovation corresponded with a desire for the freedoms of Western lifestyles, and conservative forces railed against both Western commodities and behaviors.

The public visibility of women was seized by progressive elites and new nation states to promote their modernization projects to internal and external audiences. By the early twentieth century, changes in body management previously hidden by protective outerwear were rendered unmissable: in photographs of bare-legged uniformed schoolgirls doing gymnastics in the early Turkish republic,[75] or adult women in beauty contests.[76] The bodies of boys and men also were re-envisioned as active and healthy to emblematize the vitality of the modern polity; whether body-building in post-Ottoman Egypt;[77] nudism on the beaches of Mandate Lebanon;[78] or co-ed dances as people practiced new ways of engaging bodily in spaces coded as public.

Modern and Transnational Consumption Practices in Fashion and Art

Regarding spaces of fashion consumption in the Middle East, concerns about women's public presence were amplified by moral concerns about what they might buy. Women's, and men's, experiences of shopping for fashion changed dramatically in our period as the existing regional transnationalism which had structured local distributive trades was recalibrated by the normalization of Western modern retail practice.

At the beginning of our period, affluent women of all religious backgrounds mostly purchased from home, served by women peddlers, merchants, and seamstresses often from Greek, Armenian, and Jewish minority population communities. Women traders were simultaneously welcomed and despised: circulating commodities, they also communicated news and created gossip. When respectable women did go out to shop, incursions into potentially dangerous retail space were carefully orchestrated: temporary seclusion was instigated for royal women visiting Istanbul's covered bazaar; non-royal elite women utilized veiling, servants, and slaves for a cordon sanitaire around their public shopping presence.[79] Consumption's moral contagion threatened gender and religious distinction, offering opportunities for mixing beyond family and across religious divides (more egregious for women than men).[80]

As in the West, fashion offered women employment and activated gendered moral panics. By the turn of the twentieth century, women shoppers from all communities were found in markets, in specialist fashion shops in the European quarters, and in the new department stores of the region's cosmopolitan cities.[81] Department stores inducted women into the newly developing norms of consumer society and—as in Paris, London, New York, and Sydney—triggered worries about women's unfettered consumption and unsupervised sociality.[82] West and East, anxieties about women consumers were matched by suspicions about the morals of the women who served them, with department stores educating "shop girls" in the desired performance of respectable femininity inside and outside the shop.[83] In the Middle East these concerns were mapped onto moralized divisions between minority and majority populations: Greek, Jewish, and Armenian young women whose influence as early adopters of foreign fashions might provide employment advantage nonetheless faced reputational risk through public labor.[84] So too did impoverished middle-class women of all backgrounds who repurposed accomplishment skills in embroidery to support their families during and after the First World War face scrutiny when selling to or working in stores.[85] Yet by the early years of the new Turkish republic, millinery schools were routinizing women's public labor in fashion as part of national modernization and development.[86]

Our authors focus on the role of individual, group, and state actors in all aspects of fashion to center Middle Eastern developments within critical approaches to global, diaspora, and "non-Western" fashion.[87] This melds scholarship in world histories that emphasize the multi-valency of global transmissions of commodities, style, and taste with foundational Middle Eastern consumption studies.[88] Our focus on dress and body cultures in Middle Eastern modernization emphasizes the significance of regional elite consumers as clients for the Euro-American fashion industry[89] and attends to how local distinction was created by mixing imported styles with home dress systems. The complexity of fusion fashion as lived modernity was not restricted to creating new garments; the fashion dexterity of moving simultaneously between new and existing fashion systems demonstrated "that adherence to Ottoman values and 'modernity,' that is awareness of French fashions, could be successfully cultivated by one and the same person."[90]

Similar fusion patterns of continuity and change applied to participation in international modes of modern art production and distribution. New artistic cultures were learned as part of adapted modern behaviors melded onto existing conventions of creation, acquisition, and display. Islamicate moralized structures of gendered space meant that—unlike the West where elite women had for centuries been memorialized in paint—it was unusual for respectable women from Middle Eastern elites (Muslim and otherwise) to pose for artists.

The engagement of the Ottoman court with Western portraiture did gather pace, with the imperial family exercising power as patrons to direct image making and control circulation. Despite that women's portraits were envisaged for private family or household consumption, protection was not guaranteed: while British artist Mary Walker adjusted her portrait of Fatma Sultan, daughter of Sultan Abdülmecid, to show a preferred French ensemble, Danish-Polish artist Elisabeth Jerichau-Baumann exhibited in Europe unsanctioned "fantasy" portraits of Ottoman-Egyptian princess Nazlı Hanım.[91]

Within the Middle East, modern behaviors of public art consumption required new dispositions for looking at art and being seen doing so. Where the department store brought attention to the reputational risks of women's ungoverned leisure outside the home, so too the development of art viewing as mixed gender public behavior imperiled individual and national reputation. As opportunities to demonstrate modernity to domestic and foreign audiences, the danger of failing to consume correctly risked a slide down the civilizational scale.

Sources: Visual Cultures, Art and Fashion Histories

The scarcity of surviving garments, including up to the mid-nineteenth century, increases researcher reliance on representations of garments.[92] Paintings, drawings, written accounts, and photographs gain special significance as our authors expand the corpus for cultural histories of visuality in the Middle East.[93]

As a new information communication technology and art form emerging in our period, photography features large. In use among the Iranian Qajar royal court from 1842,[94] photography quickly spread outside

Tehran and across social strata with studios opening across the country by the 1890s. This mirrors the Ottoman pattern, where photography was quickly embraced by many population segments as it became more available and affordable. Photographs in print media circulated fashion styles, while being photographed fashionably dressed allowed individuals to see themselves—and show themselves—as modern. In this volume Nancy Micklewright correlates the regional development of photography with the increased take-up of Western fashion among (in her case) the Ottoman female elite.[95] Small and portable, photographs could be shown and exchanged selectively; maintaining conventions of household privacy. Personal cameras brought image-making into family gatherings in Iran alongside an increase in use of studio photographers: if women rarely posed in studios with their family, fathers were eagerly photographed with their children, boys and girls.

Our authors contrast the elective use of painting and photography by the intellectual and artistic avant-gardes to the conscription of bodies into the visual construction of racialized and social difference for internal and external gazes. This includes the photographic capture of enslaved bodies in Egyptian Sudan and the role of masculine bodybuilding among the modernizing post-Ottoman Egyptian *effendiyya* class.

The Structure of the Book

The volume starts with Nancy Micklewright on photography's instrumental role in elite Ottoman women's quickening incorporation of Western fashions in the second half of the nineteenth century. As her costume diagrams demonstrate, the adaptation of European-style tailoring into loose-fitting Ottoman garment types brought garments closer to the shape of individual body. With photography and fashion regarded as signifiers of modernity by individuals and the state, self-imaging through photography amplified this effect of fitted clothing. The ability to visualize a changeable self along with the opportunity to alter or discard outmoded clothes became a central experience of embodied modernity.

Eve Troutt Powell analyzes powers of access and control in depictions of enslaved and manumitted black bodies in Egypt and Sudan. She sets Zaydan's 1892 historical novel about the Mahdist rebellion against photographs of Khartoum residents by French photographer Louis Vossion from 1881. For the novel's Egyptian male protagonist, performing racial indeterminacy is lifesaving; depicted as indigestible for British colonialist Gordon. The same desire for racial fixity underlies Vossion's photograph captioning, despite his visuals validating as familial the "inter-racial" relationships between notables and enslaved (or manumitted) black women with their "mixed race" children.

Reina Lewis focuses on enslaved, manumitted, and free subjects in the acquisition of fashion commodities and on fashion gifting in elite gendered clientage. She repositions royal and elite women's taste-making activities within material and affective connections that include the determining role of the free and unfree of all genders from diverse religious and racial communities. Applying circuit models of culture and of fashion-style-dress,[96] Lewis positions the exercise of social distinction through fashion shopping, styling, and wearing as differentially available to wide sections of Ottoman society, albeit surveilled and regulated.

Mary Roberts centers sartorial hybridity and the cross-cultural encounter as shared components of Western and Eastern modernity. Her focus on Constantine Guys' Istanbul sketches inserts Ottoman urbanity into the oeuvre of Baudelaire's painter of modern life, while revealing how engravers Orientalized images before European press publication. In contrast, Mary Adelaide Walker lost the battle against immortalizing in paint princess Nazlı Sultan's modern fusion fashion. With the sartorially hybrid body a characteristic of the contact zone, Roberts intervenes in presumptions that Orientalism inevitably depicts the Orient as out of the time of modernity.[97]

The body appears undressed in Kirsten Scheid's focus on the nude and nudism in 1930s Lebanon; two modernist renewal projects triggering local and international evaluation in civilizational terms. Artists and viewers cultivated new artistic dispositions; learning to enact modern art appreciation when viewing nudes, and training the self to resist physical arousal in making them: Moustapha Farrukh preparing for the life class with cold showers and study of the Quran. Scheid identifies these embodied behaviors as emotion practices, affective modern sensibilities characterized by hybridity.

Using a different kind of undressing, Wilson Chacko Jacob engages Foucault's concept of "bio-power" to unfold the gendered, sexualized, and classed trajectories of the quest for the *post*-Ottoman modern subject in Egypt. He focuses on the "spiritual" body of the *khawal*, the gender cross-dressed traditional native Egyptian male dancer popular in Egypt until the early nineteenth century. An exemplar of borderlessness disciplined in post-Ottoman Egypt, the *khawal* serves for Jacob as a *Sufi* and mystic figure that returns while transcending cultural, political, and historical boundaries.

Yasmine Nachabe Taan studies little-known photographs of Arab women engaged in gender cross-dressing in 1920s and 1930s Egypt, Lebanon, and Palestine. As photographers and photographic subjects, women's image-making challenged the institutions that regulated women's place in the Middle East and resisted Euro-American imagining of Arab cultures as frozen in time. Fashion projected secular modern womanhood for local and international audiences, breaking with religious, state, and family traditions to create a uniquely Arab version of the garçonne of Euro-American popular and fashion cultures.

Afsaneh Najmabadi examines previously unseen Iranian private family photographs, where the switch to Western-style wedding outfits evidences the conjugalization of the family; a process pervasive and uneven. Posing in Western bridal fashions for the studio wedding portrait became an important component in the aspirational imaging of modern self and family. Najmabadi combines family oral histories with image analysis to emphasize changes to family structure and personal relationships as processes: the wedding album consecrating the affective bridal couple may equally feature relations bound to them through polygyny, slavery, and manumission.

Conclusion

Being modern was an embodied and spatialized experience, delineated in the Middle East by regional codes of gender, ethnic, and religious distinction and segregation. By focusing on the dressed and undressed body in the context of free and unfree subjects, we freshly spotlight the mutually constitutive role of race, gender, and sexuality in the making of social subjectivities. As our authors show, claiming modernity involved the selective incorporation into daily life and politics of a collection of manners, habits, tastes, and ideas about gender, rationality, and authority understood to characterize the contemporary metropolitan West. As our studies elaborate, the traffic of transmitting modernity was two-way; images of Middle East modernities factored into the West's comprehension of its own processes of modern life. Our historical examples of global and transnational fashion bring new counterparts for contemporary critical studies of globalized fashion. We attend also to the (major and minor)[98] transnational forging of multiple modernities, evaluating how prevailing religious habitus are adapted within the interpenetrations of culture and community. Of course we focus especially on women's increasing public presence, but also in the context of new roles for male contemporaries. At work and at leisure for women and men, differentially, new modern behaviors were forged: in artistic and sports clubs; in creative arts practice and discerning consumption; by reading and contributing to print media; and through participation in the new technology of photography. Thus were conventional boundaries between public and private reformulated by participation in the activities and events that denoted modernity to self and to onlookers at home and abroad. As our authors show, the modern Middle East is revealed not simply by the wealth, professions, possessions, or the levels of education of its members, but also by the changeable and inconsistent, collective and individual ways by which women and men asserted their modernity through their bodies and their dress.

Notes

1   In addition to works cited on specific points, this introduction is particularly informed by the excellent scholarship of: Ebru Boyar and Kate Fleet, *A Social History of Ottoman Istanbul* (Cambridge: Cambridge University Press, 2020); Madeline C. Zilfi, *Women and Slavery in the Late Ottoman Empire* (Cambridge: Cambridge University Press, 2010); Palmira Brumett, "The 'what if' of the Ottoman Female: Authority, Ethnography, and Conversation," in *Ottoman Women in Public Space*, eds. Ebru Boyar and Kate Fleet (Leiden: Brill, 2016); Shiva Balaghi and Lynn Gumpert, eds., *Picturing Iran: Art, Society, and Revolution* (New York: I. B. Tauris, 2002); Mohamad Tavakoli-Targhi, *Refashioning Iran: Orientalism, Occidentalism and Historiography* (New York: Palgrave, 2001); Mai Ghoussoub and Emma Sinclair-Webb, eds., *Imagined Masculinities: Male Identity and Culture in the Modern Middle East* (London: Saqi Books, 2000); Lila Abu-Lughod, ed., *Remaking Women: Feminism and Modernity in the Middle East* (Princeton: Princeton University Press, 1998); As'ad AbuKhalil, "Gender Boundaries and Sexual Categories in the Arab World," *Feminist Issues* 15, nos. 1–2 (1997): 91–104; Margaret L. Meriwether and Judith E. Tucker, *Social History of Women and Gender in the Modern Middle East* (Boulder: Westview Press, 1999); Touraj Atabaki and Iran Heritage Foundation, *Iran in the 20th Century: Historiography and Political Culture* (London: I.B. Tauris, 2009); Talal Asad, *Secular Translations: Nation State, Modern Self, and Calculative Reason* (New York: Columbia University Press, 2018); J. A. Massad, *Desiring Arabs* (Chicago: The University of Chicago Press, 2007).

2   Timothy Mitchell, "The Stage of Modernity," in *Questions of Modernity*, ed. Timothy Mitchell (Minneapolis: University of Minnesota Press, 2000), 7. See also Keith David Watenpaugh, *Being Modern in the Middle East: Revolution, Colonialism, and the Arab Middle Class* (Princeton: Princeton University Pres, 2006) and Ilan Pappe, *The Modern Middle East: A Social and Cultural History*, 2nd edn (London: Routledge, 2010).

3   Watenpaugh, *Being Modern*, 11; see also Silvia Naef, "Visual Modernity in the Arab World, Turkey and Iran: Reintroducing the 'Missing Modern': Introduction," *Études Asiatiques: Revue de la Société Suisse – Asie 70*, no. 4 (2016): 1005.

4   See also Zeynep Çelik and Edhem Eldem, *Camera Ottomana: Photography and Modernity in the Ottoman Empire 1840–1914* (Istanbul: Koç University Press, 2015); Zachary Lockman, *Contending Visions of the Middle East: The History and Politics of Orientalism*, 2nd edn (Cambridge: Cambridge University Press, 2009); Reina Lewis, *Gendering Orientalism: Race, Femininity and Representation* (London: Routledge, 1996); Zeynep Çelik, "Colonialism, Orientalism, and the Canon," *The Art Bulletin* 78, no. 2 (June 1996); Jill Beaulieu and Mary Roberts, *Orientalism's Interlocutors: Painting, Architecture, Photography* (Durham: Duke University Press, 2002).

5   Suraiya Faroqhi, "Introduction, or Why and How One Might Want to Study Ottoman Clothes," in *Ottoman Costumes: From Textile to Identity*, eds. Suraiya Faroqhi and Christof K. Neuman (Istanbul: Eren, 2004).

6   Ali Behdad, *Camera Orientalis: Reflections on Photography of the Middle East* (Chicago: University of Chicago Press, 2016); Stephen Sheehi, *The Arab Imago: A Social History of Portrait Photography, 1860–1910* (Princeton and Oxford: Princeton University Press, 2016).

7   Marshal G.S. Hodgson, *The Venture of Islam: Conscience and History in a World Civilization*, 3 vols. (Chicago: University of Chicago Press, 1974), vol. 1.

8   Zilfi, *Women and Slavery in the Late Ottoman Empire*; Ehud R. Toledano, *The Ottoman Slave Trade and its Suppression: 1840–1890* (Princeton NJ: Princeton University Press, 1982); Beth Baron, "Liberated Bodies and Saved Souls: Freed African Slave Girls and Missionaries in Egypt," in *African Communities in Asia and the Mediterranean: Between Integration and Conflict*, eds. E. R. Toledano (Halle and Trenton, and Asmara, Eritrea: Max Plank Institute and Africa World Press, 2011); Eve Troutt Powell, *Tell This in My Memory: Stories of Enslavement from Egypt, Sudan and the Ottoman Empire* (Stanford: Stanford University Press, 2012).

9 See, for example, Zeynep Devrim Gürsel, "A Picture of Health: The Search for a Genre to Visualize Care in Late Ottoman Istanbul," *Grey Room* 72, (2018): 36–67.

10 Archival developments include the Feminist Library Istanbul, the Akkasah Center for Photography in Abu Dhabi, the Arab Image Foundation in Beirut, the National Library of France, and the Qajar Women online archive.

11 Elizabeth Thompson, *Colonial Citizens: Republican Rights, Paternal Privilege, and Gender in French Syria and Lebanon* (New York: Columbia University Press, 2000), 114

12 The Urabi revolt named after Colonel Ahmed Arabi (also spelled 'Urabi) who was an Egyptian nationalist and political leader.

13 Wilson Chacko Jacob, *Working Out Egypt: Effendi Masculinity and Subject Formation in Colonial Modernity, 1870–1940* (Durham: Duke University Press, 2011).

14 Kate Fleet, "The Powerful Public Presence of the Ottoman Female Consumer," in *Ottoman Women in Public Space*, eds. Ebru Boyar and Kate Fleet (Leiden: Brill, 2016).

15 Onur İnal, "Women's Fashions in Transition: Ottoman Borderlands and the Anglo-Ottoman Exchange of Costumes," *Journal of World History* 22, no. 2 (June 2011): 243–72.

16 Elizabeth B. Frierson, "Mirrors Out, Mirrors In: Domestication and Rejection the Foreign in Late-Ottoman Women's Magazines," in *Women, Patronage, and Self-Representation in Islamic Societies*, ed. Dede Fairchild Ruggles (New York: State University of New York Press, 2000).

17 Renato Rosaldo, *Culture and Truth: The Remaking of Social Analysis* (London: Routledge, 1993).

18 Giorgio Riello and Peter McNeil, eds., *The Fashion History Reader: Global Perspectives* (London: Routledge, 2010)

19 Zilfi, *Women and Slavery*, 46.

20 Ibid., 44.

21 Taner Akçam, *The Young Turks' Crime Against Humanity: The Armenian Genocide and Ethnic Cleansing in the Ottoman Empire*, (Princeton NJ: Princeton University Press, 2012); Donald Quataert, *The Ottoman Empire 1700–1922* (Cambridge: Cambridge University Press, 2000).

22 Marius Deeb, "The Socioeconomic Role of the Local Foreign Minorities in Modern Egypt, 1805–1961," *International Journal of Middle East Studies* 9, no. 1 (1978): 11–22.

23 Nikki Keddie, *Modern Iran: Roots and Results of Revolution* (London: Yale University Press, 2003).

24 Ussama Makdisi, "Ottoman Orientalism," *The American Historical Review* 107, no. 3 (June 2002): 768–96.

25 Çelik and Eldem, *Camera Ottomana;* Ali Behdad, "Mediated Visions: Early Photography of the Middle East and Orientalist Network," *History of Photography* 41, no. 4 (2017): 362–75.

26 Boyar and Fleet, *Social History*.

27 Meredith B. McGuire, *Lived Religion: Faith and Practice in Everyday Life* (Oxford: Oxford University Press, 2008).

28 Leslie Peirce, *The Imperial Harem: Women and Sovereignty in the Ottoman Empire* (Oxford: Oxford University Press, 1993); Reina Lewis, *Rethinking Orientalism: Women, Travel and the Ottoman Harem* (London and New York: I.B. Tauris, 2004).

29 Zilfi, *Women and Slavery*, ch. 3.

30 Grace Ellison, *An Englishwoman in a Turkish Harem* (1915; Piscataway, NJ: Giorgias Books, 2007); Fanny Davis, *The Ottoman Lady: A Social History from 1718–1918* (New York: Greenwood Press, 1986); Lewis, *Rethinking Orientalism*.

31 See also Carol Tulloch, *The Birth of Cool: Style Narratives of the African Diaspora* (London: Bloomsbury, 2016).

32 Zilfi, *Women and Slavery*, 130–31.

33 Toledano, *Ottoman Slave Trade*.

34 Gül İrepoğlu, *Topkapı Palace: The Imperial Harem: House of the Sultan* (Istanbul: Topkapı Palace Museum, 2012).

35 Zilfi, *Women and Slavery*, 15

36 Najmabadi, this volume.

37 Stephen Sheehi, "A Social History of Early Arab Photography or a Prolegomenon to an Archaeology of the Lebanese Imago," *International Journal of Middle East Studies* 39, no. 2 (May 2007): 175–206, 191 (original emphasis).

38 Already rarer than contemporaries realized, Alan Duben and Cem Behar, *Istanbul Households: Marriage, Family and Fertility, 1880–1940* (Cambridge: Cambridge University Press, 1991).

39 Troutt Powell's *Tell This* detects in the memoirs of Halide Edib and Hoda Shaarawi the haunting fear that their mothers may have been concubines.

40 Fatima Mernissi, *Beyond the Veil: Male-Female Dynamics in Muslim Society*, 2nd edn (London: al Saqi Books, 1985).

41 Marie Grace Brown. *Khartoum at Night: Fashion and Body Politics in Imperial Sudan*. Stanford: Stanford University Press, 2017.

42 Janet L. Abu-Lughod, "The Islamic City – Historic Myth, Islamic Essence, and Contemporary Relevance," *International Journal of Middle East Studies* 19 (1987): 155–76.

43 Fleet, *Extremes of Visibility*, 128.

44 Fleet, *Public Presence*.

45 Ebru Boyar, "An Imagined Moral Community: Ottoman Female Public Presence, Honor and Marginality," in *Ottoman Women in Public Space*, eds. Ebru Boyar and Kate Fleet (Leiden: Brill, 2016).

46 Fleet, *Powerful Public Presence*.

47 Margot Badran, *Feminists, Islam, and Nation: Gender and the Making of Modern Egypt* (Princeton, NJ: Princeton University Press, 1995).

48 Fleet, *Powerful Public Presence*.

49 Ibid., 108.

50 Zilfi, *Women and Slavery*, 90–91.

51 Boyar and Fleet, *Social History*, 302.

52 Nora Şeni, "Fashion and Women's Clothing in the Satirical Press of Istanbul at the End of the 19th Century," in *Women in Modern Turkish Society*, ed. Şirin Tekeli (London: Zed Books, 1995).

53 Fleet, *Powerful Public Presence,* 117.

54 Micklewright, this volume.

55 Baron, B. (2005). The "Ladies' Demonstrations". In Egypt as a Woman: Nationalism, Gender, and Politics, 107–134. Berkeley; Los Angeles; London: University of California Press.

56 Jens Hanssen, *Fin de Siècle Beirut: The Making of an Ottoman Provincial Capital* (Oxford: Clarendon Press, 2005), 279.

57 Ibid., 268.

58 Ibid.

59 Ibid., 269.

60 Hanssen, *Fin de Siècle*, 277.

61 Massad, J., *Desiring Arabs*, 9–11, 57–60.

62 Samira Haj, *Reconfiguring the Islamic Tradition: Reform, Rationality, and Modernity* (Stanford: Stanford University Press, 2009), quoted in Hanssen *Fin de Siècle,* 277.

63 Afsaneh Najmabadi, *Women with Mustaches and Men Without Beards: Gender and Sexual Anxieties of Iranian Modernity* (Berkeley and Los Angeles: University of California Press, 2005), 1.

64 Ibid., 4.

65 Parvin Paidar, *Women and the Political Process in Twentieth-Century Iran* (New York: Cambridge University Press, 1995).

66 Boyar and Fleet, *Social History*, 302–07.

67 Mohamad Tavakoli-Targhi, "Imagining Western Women: Occidentalism and Euro-Eroticism," *Radical America* 3, no. 24 (July–September 1994): 73–6.

68 Houchang E. Chehabi, "Staging the Emperor's New Clothes: Dress Codes and Nation-Building under Reza Shah," *Iranian Studies* 26, no. 3/4 (Summer–Autumn, 1993): 209–29.

69 Mohamad Tavakoli-Targhi, "Refashioning Iran: Language and Culture during the Constitutional Revolution," *Iranian Studies* 23, 1/4 (1990): 83.

70 Chehabi, *Staging*, 76.

71 Ellison, *An Englishwoman*. See also Lewis, *Rethinking Orientalism*.

72 Lewis, ibid.

73 Marilyn Booth, *May Her Likes be Multiplied: Biography and Gender Politics in Egypt* (Berkeley: University of California Press, 2001); Badran, *Feminism, Islam and Nation*.

74 Reina Lewis and Nancy Micklewright, eds., *Gender, Modernity and Liberty: Middle Eastern and Western Women's Writings: A Critical Sourcebook* (London: I. B. Tauris, 2006)

75 Ruth Woodsmall, *Moslem Women Enter a New World* (New York: Round Table Press, Inc., 1936).

76 Holly Shissler, "Beauty is Nothing to Be Ashamed of: Beauty Contests as Tools of Women's Liberation in Early Republican Turkey," *Comparative Studies In South Asia, Africa, and the Middle East* 24, no. 1 (2004): 109–26.

77 Jacob, *Working Out Egypt*.

78 Scheid, this volume

79 Leyla Hanımefendi, *The Imperial Harem of the Sultans: Memoirs of Leyla (Saz) Hanımefendi* (1922; Istanbul: Peva Publications, 1994).

80 Zilfi, *Women and Slavery*, 57–58.

81 Fleet, *Public Presence*, 99

82 Mica Nava, *Visceral Cosmopolitanism: Gender, Culture and the Normalisation of Difference* (Oxford: Berg, 2007); Susan Porter Benson, *Counter Cultures: Saleswomen, Managers, and Customers in American Department Stores, 1890–1940* (Champaign: University of Illinois Press, 1986); Bill Lancaster, *The Department Store: A Social History* (Leicester: Leicester University Press, 2000).

83 Gail Reekie, *Temptations: Sex, Selling in the Department Store* (St. Leonards, NSW: Allen & Unwin, 1993).

84 Nancy Reynolds, *A City Consumed: Urban Commerce, the Cairo Fire, and the Politics of Decolonization in Egypt* (Stanford: Stanford University Press, 2012).

85 Irfan Orga, *Portrait of a Turkish Family* (London: Victor Gollancz Ltd, 1950); Demetra Vaka (Mrs. Kenneth Brown), *The Unveiled Ladies of Stamboul* (Boston and New York: Houghton Mifflin Co., 1923).

86 Woodsmall, *Moslem Women.*

87 Leslie W. Rabine, *The Global Circulation of African Fashion* (Oxford: Berg, 2002); Victoria L. Rovine, *African Fashion, Global Style: Histories, Innovations, and Ideas You Can Wear* (Indiana: Indiana University Press, 2015); M. Angela Jansen and Jennifer Craik, eds., *Modern Fashion Traditions: Negotiating Tradition and Modernity through Fashion* (London: Bloomsbury, 2016); Parminder Bhachu, *Dangerous Design: Asian Women Fashion the Diaspora Economics* (London: Routledge, 2004).

88 See Ruggles, *Women, Patronage, and Self-Representation;* Donald Quataert, ed., *Consumption in the Ottoman Empire* (New York: State University of New York Press, 1999).

89 Alex Aubry, "Beyond Orientalism: A Journey Through Two Centuries of Muslim Patronage at the Paris Haute Couture," in *Contemporary Muslim Fashions*, eds. Jill D'Alessandro and Reina Lewis (San Francisco: Fine Arts Museums of San Francisco, 2018).

90 Faroqhi, *Ottoman Costumes*, 32, drawing on Nancy Micklewright, "Late Nineteenth-century Ottoman Wedding Costumes as Indicators of Social Change," *Muqarnas* 6 (1989): 161–74.

91 Mary Roberts, this volume; Mary Roberts, *Intimate Outsiders: The Harem in Ottoman and Orientalist Art and Travel Literature* (Durham, NC: Duke University Press, 2007); Zeynep İnankur, "Mary Adelaide Walker," in *The Poetics and Politics of Place: Ottoman Istanbul and British Orientalism*, eds. Zeynep İnankur, Reina Lewis, and Mary Roberts (Seattle: University of Washington Press, 2011); On Nazlı Hanım, see Mary Roberts, "Nazlı's Photographic Games: Said and Art History in a Contrapuntal Mode," *Patterns of Prejudice* 48, no. 5 (2014): 460–78.

92 Faroqhi, *Ottoman Costumes*; Micklewright, this volume.

93 Julie Codell and Joan Del Plato, eds., *Orientalism, Eroticism, and Modern Visuality in Global Cultures* (London: Routledge, 2018)

94 Mohammad Reza Tahmasbpour, "Photography during the Qajar Era, 1842–1925," in *The Indigenous Lens: Early Photography in the near and Middle East,"* eds. Markus Ritter and Staci G. Scheiwiller, trans. Reza Sheikh (Berlin and Boston: De Gruyter Inc., 2017).

95 Micklewright, this volume.

96 Paul Du Gay, Stuart Hall, Linda Janes, Anders Koed Madsen, Hugh Mackay, and Keith Negus, *Doing Cultural Studies: The Story of the Sony Walkman*, 2nd edn (1997; Milton Keynes: Open University, 2013); Susan Kaiser, *Fashion and Cultural Studies* (London: Bloomsbury, 2012).

97 Linda Nochlin, "The Imaginary Orient," in *The Politics of Vision. Essays on Nineteenth-Century Art and Society*, ed. Linda Nochlin (New York; Harper and Row, 1989).

98 Françoise Lionnet and Shu-mei Shih, eds., *Minor Transnationalism* (Durham, NC: Duke University Press, 2005).

CHAPTER 2

FASHION AND THE CAMERA: ISTANBUL IN THE LATE OTTOMAN EMPIRE

Nancy Micklewright

Introduction

In the late Ottoman Empire dress and photography were signifiers of modernity and identity. Both were deployed by the government and individual actors to communicate specific images of the empire or of themselves and to claim identities. This chapter begins by presenting some of the research challenges involved in studying historic dress, and then introduces the use of photography in nineteenth-century Istanbul. The text goes on to interrogate these two key modes of visual culture, fashion, and photography via a series of case studies. Each of the four case studies brings an image or set of images into conversation with relevant garments. The first case study presents a pre-photographic image of Ottoman women's dress by the British artist Thomas Allom, together with an example of traditional dress as it appeared in the first decades of the nineteenth century, as a kind of benchmark for the change which had already begun slowly taking place. Next, there is an analysis of early examples of the transition from a traditional robe or *entari* to a dress in the European tradition through a close look at tailoring and garment construction. Family snapshots illustrating the dress of the emerging professional class, and the relationship of those garments to contemporary European fashion are addressed in the third case study. The final case study focuses on Fehime Sultan, a daughter of Murad V, who is known to us through photographs, her own garments, and the historical record. This material provides a rare opportunity to bring diverse categories of information together to understand the impact of royal women on fashion and culture more generally in late Ottoman Istanbul. Taken as a group these pairings highlight specific issues, for example the indexicality of the images, the changing circumstances of clothing production, and the circulation of fashion images in the fashion world of nineteenth-century Istanbul women. The chapter expands on current work in fashion history, gender, and Ottoman social history.

Fashion and Photography in the Nineteenth century

In the last decades of the Ottoman Empire, photography and fashion shared a complex relationship. While the dress of the elite[1] women of Istanbul had always changed as new fabrics and accessories reached the city, the pace of change picked up dramatically in the second half of the nineteenth century. Similarly, photographic

I am most grateful to the editors of this volume, Dr. Reina Lewis and Dr. Yasmine Nachabe Taan for including me in the Beirut conference, *Modern Bodies: Dress, Nation, Empire, Sexuality and Gender in the Modern Middle East*, and for their insightful editing of my work in this volume. I am also very grateful to Vazken Davidian, Zeynep Simavi, and Heghnar Watenpaugh for their help in obtaining images, and I thank Barış Kıbrıs, Pera Museum, and Lale Görünür, Sadberk Hanım Museum for their assistance in obtaining permission to use material from those collections. I would also like to thank Leila Karaman for her help in on this project.

Transliteration in this chapter is based on the system recommended by the *International Journal of Middle East Studies* with diacritics in proper names and article/book titles in the footnotes kept in their original format.

images, while present in Istanbul since the 1840s, became increasingly pervasive as the medium became easier to use and cameras more readily available. Both fashion and photography were understood as signifiers of modernity and identity, and both could be changed at will: just as a garment could be easily tried on and discarded if it did not suit, so a photograph could be discarded and replaced when the identity displayed in the image was no longer accurate. Dress and photography were both deployed by the government and a range of individual actors as a means of communicating and disseminating specific images of the empire or of

Figure 2.1 *Dame du Serail, c.* 1810. Ankara, Ethnographical Museum, 8283, f.191.

themselves and to claim identities. The fashion and photography economies, while distinct from each other, intersected at many points—dissemination of new fashion trends being perhaps the most obvious example—and extended across social and ethnic divisions within Ottoman society.

The long nineteenth century was a time of dramatic change in the Ottoman Empire; dress[2] and photography were at the same time constitutive and reflective of these changes. Representations of Ottoman women separated by about 100 years or so as seen in Figures 2.1 and 2.2, encapsulate the transformation at the heart

Figure 2.2 Fehime Sultan, photographer unknown, 1912. Istanbul, Topkapı Sarayı, 17/435.

of this project. Virtually nothing links the two images illustrated here except for the fact that they are both depictions of women from the same place, the Ottoman court. The mode of representation in the two images is different, the dress is different, the manner in which the images would have circulated is different, the relationship between the garment and its representation is different—these differences merit careful attention not only because they tell us so much about these two modes of representation and self-presentation, but also about how Ottoman society had changed over the time period bracketed by these images. In the pages that follow, we will look closely at a series of such images and the garments they depict to understand the fashion changes and begin to unpack the way in which fashion and photography worked together to communicate identity and construct meaning.

Ottoman Dress Histories: Research Challenges

Studying historic dress presents some unique challenges. While this is the case in nearly all cultural contexts to some extent, here I am specifically describing the Ottoman situation. First among these challenges is the absence of actual examples of dress until quite late in the historical record. While the study of dress is not alone in confronting a scarcity of source material, it is a significant aspect of research on fashion, dress, and the body. There are only a handful of garments before the nineteenth century that survive, and those which do survive come from very specific, typically elite contexts as is the case in most geographical and cultural locations where non-elite clothing was either worn until it fell apart or not considered worth saving. By the time we get to the nineteenth century the situation has improved slightly, but there is still a relatively limited sample of extant garments.

Given these circumstances, any study of Ottoman dress must rely heavily on images of people wearing clothes.[3] In earlier centuries, these consist of drawings, manuscript illustrations and single figure paintings; in the nineteenth century, photographs and European style paintings join this list. All of these present serious issues of interpretation. Apart from the matters of artistic license and skill, both of which affect the accuracy of representation, the intended audience for the image, the access the artist may have had to the dress or the contexts in which it was worn, the purpose for which the image was created, and a myriad other factors must be considered before accepting the information apparently presented regarding dress in a painting or photograph. Again, this is not an issue that is limited to the study of dress, but it is a central one nonetheless.

Separated in time by two centuries, Figures 2.3 and 2.4 are each representative of their period in terms of medium and painting style, and are indicative of the challenges involved in using such images to document dress history.[4] In the earlier painting of two standing figures (Figure 2.3) dated c. 1560–70, there is some effort made to indicate three dimensionality by painting folds in the fabric, for example, but in general the figures are quite flat and the garments resemble paper doll outfits more than actual garments.

The artist of the eighteenth-century painting (Figure 2.4) on the other hand, was interested in conveying the human form beneath the garments worn by the subject, thus the gaps in the robe over the woman's torso where the fabric is straining against her figure. Light and shadow reveal the drape and texture of the fabric.

Looking at these two paintings for what they tell us about women's dress, there are significant changes, which are also visible in other representations from the same periods. The woman from the sixteenth-century painting wears the three garments that comprised women's dress in that period: *şalvar*, straight, loose-fitting trousers gathered at the ankle; *gömlek*, a long-sleeved, round-neck underdress usually of light fabric, often trimmed with gold embroidery; and an *entari* or robe fastened at the front with a row of frogs. In this period the *entari* could be either full or hip-length, as it is in Figure 2.3. The outfit was completed with a small pill box hat, or *takke*, a belt or sash, and slippers. The eighteenth-century figure wears an outfit made up of the same

Figure 2.3 Standing figures, artist unknown, *c.* 1560–70. Istanbul, Topkapı Sarayı, H.2168, fol. 35a.

Figure 2.4 *Portrait of a Woman of the Court*, Rafael Manas, mid-eighteenth century Istanbul. Suna and İnan Kıraç Foundation Orientalist Paintings Collection, Pera Museum.

basic elements; *şalvar*, *gömlek*, *entari*, and a fourth piece, the *yelek*, or vest. The *yelek* was also present in the sixteenth century, although not in our example. However, while the basic vocabulary of costume elements is the same, each is somewhat different than two centuries earlier. The *gömlek* is no longer full length, the sleeves are narrow, and it was worn tucked into the *şalvar*. The *şalvar* are wider and made of figured fabric, not plain. The *entari* is nearly full length, as is the vest. The pill box hat has been replaced by a scarf wound around a small cap.

These two images, and others like them,[5] are useful up to a point for understanding what Ottoman women were wearing, especially when read in combination with other images. But they are limited in their value: we know little about what the artists knew of women's dress; specific details of fabric, trim, and construction must be assumed to be of secondary importance to the artist and thus not particularly reliable; it is not clear whether these depictions are particular to distinct social or ethnic groups, and so on.

By the early nineteenth century, the manuscript illustrations of previous centuries which had been the primary means of illustrating dress were supplemented by printed books which included lithographs based on traveler's drawings, and in some cases, the earlier manuscript illustrations. In addition to this greater range of visual sources regarding dress, there are many more garments surviving from the nineteenth century than earlier.[6] Both of these allow us to trace the transformation in women's dress in nineteenth-century Istanbul with more detail than is possible for previous centuries. The mid-century addition of photographs to the visual record of fashion adds a key new source of information to this study.

Photography in Istanbul

How does that story of fashion change appear in the photographic record of Istanbul? During the same decades that women were experimenting with aspects of European fashion, photography arrived in Istanbul. Nearly simultaneous announcements of the invention of photography were made in Paris and London during 1839 and covered widely in the press. News of the invention reached the Ottoman capital almost immediately afterwards. By 1845 we know that residents of Istanbul were having their portraits made because an Italian photographer named Naya was advertising cheap daguerreotypes in Ottoman Turkish, so clearly his advertisement was directed at a local audience in Istanbul.[7]

The photographers who first arrived in the Ottoman capital and in the other cities of the empire such as Cairo and Beirut were interested in creating photographs of antiquities and local sights to be sent back to Europe for sale. But it was not long before a local interest in consuming photographs and participating in photographic practices emerged in these cities; shops were soon providing images for the growing tourist market as well as for local residents and the Ottoman government. While the images that were produced for a tourist audience have limited value for understanding local fashion or indeed most aspects of local life, the photographs taken at the behest of local residents are an invaluable resource.[8]

The analysis of surviving examples of photographic projects commissioned by the Ottoman government and private individuals provides detailed evidence of how photography was practiced in Istanbul by the last decades of the nineteenth century.[9] We know that taking pictures of public events like parades was commonplace, as was the staging of events such as practice drills for the camera. Complex photographs involving large numbers of people all posing at the direction of the photographer indicate a level of familiarity and acceptance of the photographic medium on the part of the diverse subjects pictured in such images. While many of the most well-known photographic studios were concentrated in the European or "Frankish" quarters of Pera and Beyoğlu, business records indicate that photographer's shops were spread across the city, thus providing access to the diverse religious and ethnic populations of many different neighborhoods.[10] The photographers themselves were using techniques and attempting effects very similar to their counterparts in other cities of Europe and North America.

Photographic portraiture took hold easily in Istanbul, as it did in many other cities around the globe in the mid-nineteenth century. The large universe of surviving images includes portraits made in commercial studios, or in other spaces, by professionals and by amateur photographers. The photograph illustrated in Figure 2.5 demonstrates many of the challenges in working with this material. Who is the sitter, what are the

Figure 2.5 Woman wearing a *bindallı* dress, photographer and date unknown, collection of the author.

circumstances of the image, and who was the photographer? What can we learn from the internal evidence of the photograph; perhaps the pose or the clothing, her ethnicity, or social class? Can details of the backdrop, the props, or the carpet help to identify the photographer, or at least the studio? Does the context of the collection in which the photograph now resides provide any useful information? And perhaps most vexing, in the absence of any specific information about the image, how can we use it?

Picturing Fashion

This chapter began with the claim that two key modes of visual culture, fashion and photography, shared a relationship in the late Ottoman context. So far they have been discussed separately from one another, but now I would like to turn to a consideration of a series of case studies, each of which bring together an image or set of images with relevant garments. These case studies have been selected to highlight specific issues, for example the indexicality of the images, the changing circumstances of clothing production, or the way in which fashion information circulated, and they are presented in varying levels of detail, reflecting the work-in-progress nature of this project.

Events in history rarely line up neatly. In this case, there is a disjuncture between the two histories I am choosing to examine. From the point of view of fashion history, the trajectory of rapid change begins in the 1820s, but photography, the primary mode of fashion illustration for the period under review, wasn't invented until 1839. So this project begins with a prequel, at least in terms of the photographs, by looking at one of the many illustrations of Ottoman women's dress that preceded the age of photography.

As we discussed above, the nature of the evidence for the study of dress is always at the forefront of any costume project, and the representations of dress in the Ottoman context before photography raise specific issues around the matter of access and accuracy. Thomas Allom (1804–72), whose work is illustrated in Figure 2.6 was an English architect and artist, known primarily for his topographical illustrations. Arriving in Istanbul in 1834, he then traveled through Anatolia, Syria, and Palestine, producing drawings that illustrated two books, *Constantinople and the Scenery of the Seven Churches of Asia Minor* by Robert Walsh, published in 1838, and *Costume and Character in Turkey and Italy*, which appeared in nine editions between 1839 and 1845.[11] Allom's twenty illustrations, eight of which were of Ottoman subjects, were accompanied by text written by Emily Reeve.

There is no evidence that Allom had any privileged access to the interiors of Ottoman Muslim homes. The setting in which the figures in our image are placed is a generic domestic interior familiar from other published engravings of the period and one which Allom could have encountered in a visit to Greek or Armenian residents of the city. Allom's representations of dress reside mostly at the level of the imagination, but nonetheless, the costume worn by the figures in the illustration bears a certain similarity to the garment pictured in Figure 2.7.

In Figure 2.6 we see the *şalvar*, *entari* with very long sleeves, and *cepken* familiar from surviving examples. Less accurate is the lace trim around the necklines of the two most prominent figures, and the headdresses worn by those same figures present rather unlikely creations.

The elaborate outfit illustrated in Figure 2.7 provides a good idea of what wealthy women in Istanbul were wearing in the first decades of the nineteenth century—unfortunately, in the absence of the very rare documentary evidence that occasionally accompanies garments, it is difficult to establish firm dates for most garments, hence the approximate dating.

The three-piece outfit is comprised of a sheer round-necked, long-sleeved undershirt (*gömlek*), not visible in Figure 2.6, *şalvar* and *entari*. The *şalvar* are extremely full and so long that they were typically tied below

Figure 2.6 *The Odalique or Favorite of the Harem, Constantinople,* Thomas Allom. Published in *Character and Costume in Turkey and Italy* (London, Fisher, Son and Co. 1939, and later editions).

Figure 2.7 *Üçetek entari*, nineteenth century. Büyükdere, Vehbi Koç Foundation, Sadberk Hanım Museum, SHM 11940-K.504.

the knee to allow them to billow down. The *entari* worn in this period is divided into three skirts by a long slit at each side and is known as *üçetek* (literally, three skirts). The sleeves of the *üçetek* were long, with long slits to allow the excess length to fall over the arms, and the robe was held closed with a belt, sometimes with a series of frogs along the bodice. The edges of the *entari* were finished with a braided or crocheted trim, and the garment is so long that the skirts trail on the floor. Accessories included socks, slippers, a belt or sash, and headgear, which was often ornamented with jewels or feathers. This particular set of garments is at the very pinnacle of fashion and expense; other women would be seen wearing the same basic elements, made up of less costly fabric, more modest decoration, and more restrained dimensions, depending on their resources.

Both Allom's illustration (Figure 2.6) and the costume pictured in Figure 2.7 serve as a kind of baseline for the change that takes place over the course of the next century or so. Until the advent of portrait photography in Istanbul, visual information circulating about women's dress was based primarily on conjecture, in the case of illustrations produced by foreign artists such as Allom or hindered by the limitations of artistic skill and license in the case of paintings produced by Ottoman artists. The circulation of such images was dependent on the mode of production, with published travel accounts enjoying wide popularity in Europe, and illustrated manuscripts and albums being seen by only very limited audiences. It is unlikely that either the travel books or the illustrated manuscripts would have been available—in the case of the manuscripts—or of interest—in the case of the travel accounts—to the Ottoman women whose dress was displayed in them, so neither of these pre-photographic modes for representations of dress were significant factors in disseminating fashion information among the women of Istanbul.

In terms of fashion, the multi-garment outfit with exaggerated proportions, the lavish use of soft fabric that draped well, the elaborate trim at all of the edges of the outer garment and multiple accessories was the epitome of fashion in the 1820s. This ensemble already demonstrated the influence of French fabrics in its construction—and indeed Ottoman fashion had always been in conversation with European modes to some extent[12] but in the main, the Istanbul fashions of the 1820s demonstrated a close connection to women's dress of the preceding century described above. This is the backdrop against which fashion begins to change.

Early Experimentation in Fashion Change

While we do not know the original owner of this set of garments, we can surmise that she was a wealthy member of the elite, perhaps associated with the royal court and married to a high-ranking member of the political hierarchy. It is likely that in terms of social standing, the woman who wore this outfit was very similar to Fehime Sultan, the woman shown in the 1912 photograph seen earlier (Figure 2.2), who was a daughter of the Ottoman sultan, Murad V. The transformation in the dress of wealthy women that these two illustrations reveal, and indeed of Ottoman women more generally, that can be traced over the course of the nineteenth century did not happen overnight. Rather, it was the result of a series of gradual changes as women began experimenting with what they learned of European dress from magazines and newspapers, the foreign women with whom they came into contact, and the foreign goods which were becoming available.[13]

This initial fashion experimentation took a variety of forms and was quite subtle. One example of such experimentation can be seen in the comparison of two short jackets, illustrated via drawings as these display details of construction more clearly (Figure 2.8). This kind of short jacket, or *cepken*, would have been worn over an *entari*. The example at the top shows the traditional shape and construction method: the main body of the jacket is made from a single piece of fabric folded over the shoulders with a round neck, and long gussets added at the sides for fullness. The sleeves are each a single piece of fabric, seamed under the arms. There are no cuffs and no collar. The jacket at the bottom is from the Topkapı Sarayı collection and forms one piece of

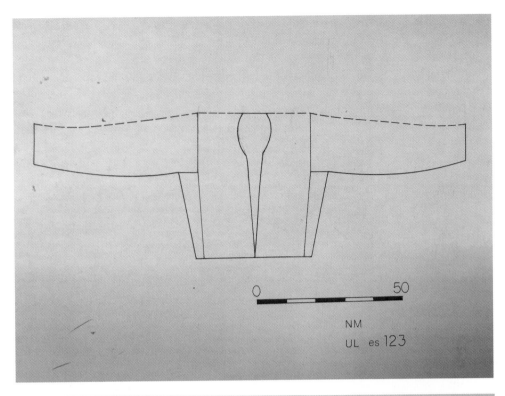

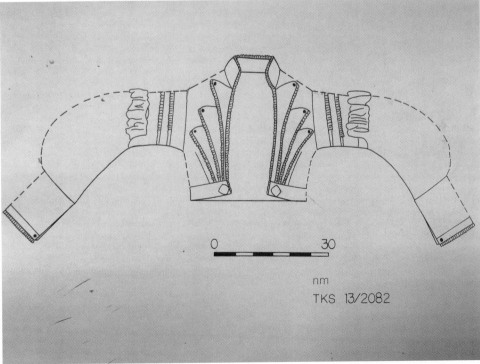

Figure 2.8 *Top*: *Cepken*, nineteenth century, private collection, drawing by the author. *Bottom*: *Cepken*, *c.* 1820s. Istanbul, Topkapı Sarayı collection, 13/2082, drawing by the author.

a three-part outfit that also included *şalvar* and an *entari*. The jacket is now tailored, with set in sleeves, cuffs, and collar, the pleated and ruffled ornament is novel, and the details of cut and ornamentation are closely related to British dress fashions of the 1820s. The basic elements of the ensemble—*şalvar, entari, cepken*—are unchanged, but the details of one garment are completely different. It is a striking experiment, but one that does not challenge norms of modesty or disrupt the overall structures of the typical ensemble.

Another transitional garment is illustrated in Figure 2.9. Based on its dimensions, fabric choice, and construction details, this *entari* is a much more modest garment than that shown in Figure 2.7, providing

Figure 2.9 *Üçetek entari*, nineteenth century. Istanbul, Yapı Kredi Museum Collection.

intriguing evidence of how fashion experimentation extended beyond the elite women who might have worn the Topkapı Sarayı outfit discussed previously.[14] The modifications made to this *entari* are small but telling: the sleeves now end in cuffs and were intended to conform to the actual length of the wearer's arms, and gathers were added on either side of the robe to add a shaped waist to the contours of the garment.[15]

These changes signal that the owner of this garment was watching European fashions and had realized a key difference between that mode and the traditional dress of Ottoman women. Consider the garment illustrated in Figure 2.7: there is no tailoring for the individual shape of the wearer. That outfit is meant to be a loosely fitting series of garments, held on by ties and sashes. The impact of the outfit is in the lavish use of expensive fabric and the layering of different fabrics, colors, and patterns. European dress of the same period was of course completely different. It depended on its impact for precise tailoring to fit the body exactly, with specific measurements for the individual who would be wearing the garment. Waist, shoulders, wrists, and hem length were all carefully measured and visible. The *entari* in Figure 2.9 shows us an attempt on the part of a dressmaker or her patron to adapt what she was seeing of European fashion to the local dress. Apart from tailoring changes similar to the two examples illustrated by Figures 2.8 and 2.9, at this relatively early stage of transition other kinds of modifications would have been seen in accessories—stockings instead of socks, shoes imported from Europe, and the adoption of gloves and parasols.[16]

Acceleration of Change: The Dress

While like elements from one tradition—stockings, shoes, newly styled jacket—were substituted for those from local tradition, and small changes such as cuffs signaled an awareness of completely new tailoring modes, soon more substantial design changes began to be made. While it is impossible to assign specific dates to these changes, travelers' accounts, surviving garments, paintings, and photographs all indicate that by the 1860s or so, extensive changes had taken place. One of these was the adoption of the dress, replacing the *entari*, but still sometimes worn together with *gömlek* and *şalvar*. Our second case study presents one such early dress, the *bindallı* dress (Figure 2.10) and a photographic portrait (Figure 2.5) of an unknown woman wearing a dress similar to the example illustrated in Figure 2.10.

Bindallı dresses were worn for weddings, both by the bride and others, and for other special occasions. Their name, *bindallı*, means thousand branches and describes the embroidered decoration which was generally an elaborate design of plant motifs, often growing out of vases or arranged in garlands, executed in a couched technique using gold or silver wrapped thread over cardboard. The dresses were typically made in dark-colored velvets, in maroon, purple, dark rose, or navy.

As the example illustrated in Figure 2.10 reveals, the basic structure of the garment is closely related to the *entari*, and was in fact known as the *biretekli entari*, or single-skirted *entari*.[17] The long central opening has evolved into a round neck with a shorter front opening at the bodice. The side slits in the skirt have been eliminated, thus the name "single-skirted." The robe of traditional Ottoman women's dress has become a dress, but not exactly a closely fitted garment. There are set in sleeves, gathers at each side to mark the waist and it was often worn belted, but it was still a long way from a tailored dress in the British or French tradition. Yet this kind of dress is the first example of an outer garment which would have been donned over the head and which was semi-fitted to the body. Worn throughout Anatolia for weddings by both brides and guests, *bindallı* dresses survive in large numbers and can be seen in provincial museum collections across Turkey as well as in major collections. One intriguing feature of these garments which aided in their wide distribution was the fact that since they were not closely fitted, they could be purchased ready-made and shipped outside of the major cities.

Figure 2.10 *Bindallı entari*, late nineteenth century. Büyükdere, Vehbi Koç Foundation, Sadberk Hanım Museum, SHM 2606-K.24.

Bindallı garments continued to be worn for weddings as fashions evolved. No longer a one-piece dress, the early twentieth-century *bindallı* outfit became a skirt and blouse resembling European fashions much more closely in its construction and closely tailored for the wearer. Examples of such wedding outfits have survived in both the traditional dark velvets, but also in pastel satins, which had already begun to be popular for wedding dresses in European fashion. From there it was a short step to wedding outfits for the elite women of Istanbul that were indistinguishable from those worn by their counterparts in Europe at the same time.[18]

Looking at the photograph (Figure 2.5), we see a closely cropped image of a woman wearing a *bindallı* dress, one hand at her metal belt, the other holding out her skirt to display the elaborate embroidery. The garment itself is a beautiful example of a *bindallı* dress, heavily embroidered, with lace trim at the cuffs and around the round neck and front opening. The woman wears a close-fitting necklace of gold coins around her neck and a white bridal veil with crocheted edging that frames her face. She is standing slightly angled away from the picture frame, apparently looking out of the frame at someone to her left.

While the photograph (Figure 2.5) provides a clear record of the dress and the other elements that were worn in this bridal outfit, there is unfortunately virtually no other documentary evidence that can be gleaned from the picture. Purchased at the Ortaköy flea market in the early 1980s, it is a modern re-photographing of an older image and much of the original detail has been lost. The close cropping has eliminated the backdrop and floor which often provide evidence of a photographer's studio. There is no studio signature visible but given that such information would have increased the value of even a modern reprint, it seems likely that the original was also lacking such information.

As photography became more accessible in the last decades of the nineteenth century, it became more common for wedding couples to have their pictures taken to mark the occasion. Typically such images present the bridal couple in a photographer's studio setting, standing stiffly next to each other facing the camera, usually looking rather nervous. In our photograph, on the other hand, only the bride is shown, looking very comfortable in front of the camera and displaying her dress. In the absence of any context for the image, we can only speculate about the circumstances of the photograph: was it an outtake following the shooting of the more traditional wedding image to allow the bride to show off her beautiful dress? Or was it made for a dressmaker to show prospective clients a specific *bindallı* model, or how the dress could be worn and accessorized? We know that such dresses could be purchased ready-made so perhaps this is an example of an innovative marketing tool. Or was it intended for the tourist market, to appeal to visitors interested in local customs and dress? While not an erotic image, there is certainly an element of display, of both garment and figure, in how the photograph is composed which suggests such an intention for the photograph.[19]

Ottoman wedding dresses and wedding photography are particularly fruitful areas for an investigation of fashion evolution and of the relationship between fashion and photography. With the possible exception of unique children's garments such as receiving gowns or circumcision outfits, wedding dresses are the garments most likely to be preserved and could often be the single most expensive outfit a woman ever wore. Similarly, a wedding was the one occasion that could bring members of nearly all social classes to the photographer's studio. Those images too tended to be saved more than others—and perhaps passed down from mother to daughter[20]—although since they do not necessarily end up in public collections they are more difficult for researchers to access. While this brief discussion here has introduced the topic, a fuller investigation of the evolution of the *bindallı* wedding dress and wedding photography in the late Ottoman context will have to wait for another occasion.

Family Snapshots

Bindallı garments are particularly valuable examples of nineteenth-century dress because they were worn by women from a range of social classes, thus allowing a glimpse into the fashion history of women outside of court circles. Our third case study presents a similar opportunity, through the examination of a group of fifty-nine snapshots dating to the turn of the century. The group pictured in the snapshots seems to be a family, perhaps with some friends, who enjoyed being the subjects of snapshots for a family member who was an amateur photographer—and most likely a member of the military.[21] My interest in these images was initially piqued by their photographic creation of a parody of the harem scene typically produced in the studios of commercial photographers, in this case set in their own home, with family members posing for the camera in ad hoc and inaccurate costumes. This set of snapshots is extremely valuable for what it can tell us about how people in Istanbul interacted with photography, as well as their familiarity with the stereotypical views of their culture which were depicted in the photographs.[22]

However, the photographs as a group also have a great deal to tell us about fashion, which allows us to date these pictures to the period of 1890–1910. They also give us a glimpse into the kinds of clothes the women of this military family chose. Taken over a relatively short period of time—we know this because the people in the photos haven't aged and in some cases are wearing the same clothes in multiple snapshots—and including about twenty different people on a few separate occasions, this set of snapshots is a rare opportunity to see how women, most likely Muslim and part of the city's growing bourgeoisie, interacted with fashion, particularly in the ten views that clearly show women in their indoor clothing.[23]

While some of the snapshots are very clear, others are more difficult to read and it is hard to identify faces in some cases. There seem to be eight different women in the pictures ranging in age from perhaps late teens to middle age. The two women pictured in Figure 2.11 can be seen in four views, always wearing the same outfits. The older of the two, on the bottom left in the photograph, wears a light-colored blouse with a high neck and leg-of-mutton sleeves, closed down the bodice by a row of small buttons, and a dark skirt. The younger woman, in the back right of the group, has on a dark dress with the same stylish sleeves. Her dress otherwise appears rather plain, although the dark fabric makes it difficult to see any ornamentation. Other women in the photos demonstrate a similar range of clothing, with variations in fabric, degree of embellishment, and design, depending on individual taste, age, and perhaps the occasion. A second example (Figure 2.12) shows a younger woman seated at a table, wearing a lace-trimmed, tucked blouse, together with a plain skirt and wide belt. Her outfit creates a less formal and more "fashion forward" impression than the clothing of the two women pictured in Figure 2.11. Based on their silhouettes it is clear that all three of these women were wearing the corsets required to produce the very small waistlines that European fashion demanded in this period.

The everyday clothing worn by the women in these snapshots is not what typically ends up in a museum costume collection, but the Sadberk Hanım Museum contains numerous examples of garments of similar design, although executed in a much more lavish style and most likely intended for special events. One of these is pictured in Figure 2.13. The skirt and blouse, dated to the early twentieth century, have the same profile as the clothes worn in Figures 2.11 and 2.12, with a high neck, leg-of-mutton sleeves, boned bodice, and long gored skirt. This example is made of a voided velvet with a cream pile on a green background and thin linear designs of red flowers. The elaborate fabric is further ornamented with appliqued lace and blue silk flowers. Both the skirt and blouse have a label inside which reads "A. Elefteropoulo Robes & Manteaux Constantinople" and the outfit is thought to have been purchased ready-made.[24]

Advertisements for stores selling ready-made clothing and accessories imported from Europe and dressmaker's advertisements for their shops began appearing in the French and English language press in

Figure 2.11 Untitled snapshot (a group raising glasses) *c.* 1890–1910. Getty Research Institute, Los Angeles (96.R.14 (CD7)).

Istanbul in the last decades of the century, and by the late nineteenth/early twentieth century the women of Istanbul would have had numerous shopping options for their clothing purchases. Many women, particularly women of the court, would have continued to have their clothing made by seamstresses who came to their homes with pattern books and fabric samples thus sparing their elite clients the need to go shopping in public. The Topkapı Sarayı holds a number of dressmakers' orders notebooks, beginning from the late eighteenth century, that record details of the purchases made by women of the court from individual dressmakers who produced clothing for them;[25] the custom of a dressmaker visiting the house for a week or two several times a year to sew clothing for the women and girls of the family persisted in Istanbul among wealthy families at least into the 1980s.[26]

Figure 2.12 Untitled snapshot (seated woman) *c.* 1890–1910. Getty Research Institute, Los Angeles (96.R.14 (CD7)).

Royal Women

While it is so far not possible to match the clothing worn by the women in the Getty snapshots (Figures 2.11 and 2.12) with surviving garments, our final case study presents one of the rare occasions in fashion history when it is possible to make secure connections with garments, their wearer, and a photographic record. The photograph (Figure 2.2) is one that has fascinated me ever since it was first published in 1993, which is

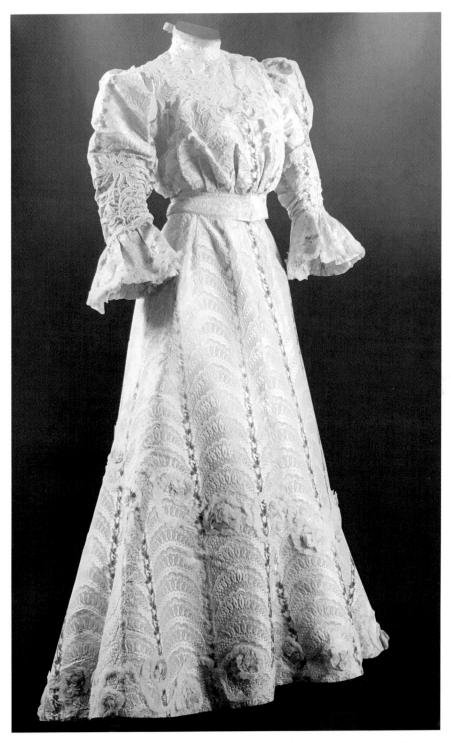

Figure 2.13 Skirt and blouse, early twentieth century. Büyükdere, Vehbi Koç Foundation, Sadberk Hanım Museum, 15392-K.996 a, b.

when I believe it came to the attention of a wider audience than private collectors.[27] In the photograph, the subject, Fehime Sultan, faces the camera directly and signals clearly that music is extremely important to her by placing her hand on the music that is displayed on the piano. The setting is modern, even luxurious with the piano, other furniture, and the large palm in the background. Her dress is very much of the moment, elegant and in keeping with current fashion. There is no visible connection to the traditional dress that a woman of her position would have worn fifty years previously. There is a second photograph from this same occasion, presumably taken by the same photographer. In the second version, Fehime is seated at the piano, as if playing, although it is clear from the way her skirt is arranged, and her pose, that the image was carefully composed.

Fehime Sultan was born in 1875, the only child of Murad V's fourth wife, and one of his seven children. Her father, Murad V, was put on the throne in 1876 following the deposition of his uncle Abdulaziz, and reigned only ninety-three days.[28] Following his deposition, Murad, who died in 1904, and his family lived, carefully watched over, in various palaces until the abolition of the caliphate in 1924, at which point they were exiled. Fehime Sultan was married twice, first in a marriage arranged for her by her uncle when she was twenty-six, and then, following a divorce, to a military officer in 1910. She adopted his two children but did not have any of her own. In 1924 she went to Nice, without her husband or children, and died there of tuberculosis in 1929 at the age of fifty-four.[29]

Like most members of the Ottoman royal family, Fehime was educated in the palace. In her case, she developed a strong interest in music, no doubt influenced by her father who was apparently a prolific and at least somewhat talented composer. She was also, according to one source, a very strong supporter of the Nationalist Movement—Committee of Union and Power—which forced Sultan Abdulhamid to establish a constitutional government in 1908 and which had effective control over the government, beginning in about 1913.[30] In support of the movement, Fehime Sultan composed a piano sonata, *Pour la Constitution*, in 1911, and it is almost certainly that work which is commemorated in these two photographs.[31]

There are two garments in the Topkapı Sarayı collection which are connected with her. Like many royal women, Fehime Sultan had a reputation for enjoying expensive fashion which seems to be supported by what she is wearing in Figure 2.2. As discussed above, royal women generally were a large and influential segment of the Ottoman elite, connected by family and marriage across Ottoman high society, so understanding their patterns of dress gives us essential information about the fashion economy of the late Ottoman period in general. Many of them were also enthusiastic consumers of photographic portraiture, so there is a wealth of documentation of their fashion choices.[32] For Fehime, in addition to the two photographs already mentioned, at least three other images of her have so far come to light and there could well be more.

The dress pictured in Figure 2.14 resembles the one that Fehime Sultan is wearing in Figure 2.2. Each is designed to create the impression of a multi-piece outfit, but the Topkapı Sarayı dress, at least, is a one-piece garment that relies on the complex construction and the use of multiple fabrics to give the impression of a robe overlaying a blouse and skirt. A cursory review of surviving examples of French fashion in the period preceding the outbreak of the First World War reveals gowns with comparable profiles and equally elaborate combinations of luxurious fabrics and trimming. The House of Worth, which created the dress in Figure 2.14, was known for such creations.[33] We know that some wealthy Ottoman women traveled to Paris to buy clothes and fashion accessories, but given Fehime Sultan's restricted movements for much of her life, it is more likely that her dress was either ordered from Paris or made for her by a dressmaker well acquainted with the latest modes.

Figure 2.14 Dress, House of Worth, *c.* 1911. New York, Metropolitan Museum of Art, 1982.304.

Conclusion

Ottoman women of Istanbul, aspects of whose lives are recorded in travelers' accounts, in their own writing, in legal documents, in various genres of visual representation and through their surviving clothing, understood the power of dress in constructing their identity. Similarly, the Ottoman interaction with photography as a means of self-representation evolved from a limited engagement with portraiture in the first decades after the technology reached the city, to a sophisticated understanding of the power of photography to create and disseminate identity. Studying these two bodies of material together allows a richer and more nuanced understanding of how each of these modes of social expression were embraced over a critical period in the transformation of Ottoman society. As we have moved through the long nineteenth century, garment by garment and image by image, these have revealed a consistent attentiveness to innovation, experimentation, and creativity in adopting new modes of dress and of self-presentation by women of the late Ottoman Empire.

Notes

1 In its most general meaning, especially for our purposes, "elite" means wealthy. It is wealthy women who would typically have had access to information about European fashion and who would have had the means to experiment with new dress styles and accessories. Since they would have owned more extensive wardrobes, their clothing would not have been worn until it was too tattered to save, and thus the history of dress is always better supplied with examples of the dress of the wealthy than of other members of society.

   In the Ottoman context, elite women were also those who had some connection to palace circles. Over the course of the nineteenth century as the Ottoman government developed a more systematic bureaucracy, high-level members of both the government and the military, as well as members of the royal family shared many connections through marriage, particularly through the daughters of the sultans and their descendants.

   Ottoman society was multi-ethnic and multi-religious, but palace circles were almost exclusively Muslim. Non-Muslim women, primarily members of the Greek and Armenian communities, had greater access to European visitors. Coming from minority communities in which a great deal of wealth was concentrated, Greek and Armenian women in particular embraced new fashion in somewhat different ways than their Muslim counterparts. These distinctions are important, complex, and take us beyond the limits of this paper, which focuses primarily on the dress worn by wealthy Muslim women in Constantinople.

2 The use of the terms "dress," "costume," and "fashion" in scholarship has changed over time according to the context of the garments or clothing practices being studied. In the past few decades, "dress" has come to be used as an all-inclusive term to describe clothing and body adornment across cultures, see Charlotte Nicklas and Annebella Pollen, *Dress History: New Directions in Theory* (New York: Bloomsbury Academic, 2015), 2. In a European context, costume has meant dressing up for a special event in clothing that was somehow different from everyday wear, but in the study of dress in other parts of the world, costume was used as an overarching term to describe clothing more generally, reflecting perhaps the dominance of a Euro-American perspective in this scholarship. As the boundaries dividing the study of dress in Euro-American areas and other parts of the world have broken down, the use of these terms has evolved to reflect these developments. Fashion continues to imply change in clothing habits, connected to large and complex social and economic systems. Key reference works for the definition of these terms remain Valerie Cumming, C.W. Cunnington, and P. E. Cunnington, *The Dictionary of Fashion History* (Oxford: Berg Publishers, 2010), and Nicklas and Pollen, *Dress History*, as above.

3 Another critical body of sources for the study of women's dress in the Ottoman context is written material: travelers' accounts—particularly those written by women—legal documents of various kinds, the foreign language, and local press, Ottoman women's writing, and more. While all those have informed this work, they are not specifically referenced here.

4 A detailed discussion of these differences in style and the reasons underlying them is outside the bounds of this chapter. However, the subject has been addressed by a number of scholars. A key reference work for the history of Turkish painting remains Günsel Renda, *A History of Turkish Painting* (Seattle: University of Washington Press, 1989).

5   Other eighteenth-century artists whose work is considered important for understanding how women dressed are Abdülcelil Çelibi, known as Levni, and Abdullah Buhari, both prolific producers of single figure studies and other work. Another important source of costume imagery through the early nineteenth century are the so-called costume manuscripts that were produced in large numbers and circulated widely. These are complex sources which have begun to receive renewed attention from researchers. See Gwendolyn Callaço, "Dressing a City's Demeanour: Ottoman Costume Albums and the Portrayal of Urban Identity in the Early Seventeenth Century," *Textile History* 48, no. 2 (2017): 248–67, and her 2020 dissertation.

6   The most significant collections of women's dress from the Ottoman Empire can be found in the Topkapı Sarayı collection, the Sadberk Hanım Museum, Sariyer, the Uluumay Museum of Folk Costumes and Jewelry, Bursa, and the Ethnography Museum of Ankara. Ethnically specific collections of dress from the Ottoman period can be found in the Benaki Museum, Athens, the Museum of Traditional Greek Costumes in Kalamata, and the Israel Museum in Jerusalem, among others. There are small numbers of costume pieces scattered in collections in Europe and North America, primarily collected by travelers or foreign residents during their stays in the Ottoman Empire.

7   Naya's advertisement is reproduced in numerous publications on early photography in Istanbul. For one example, see Engin Cizgen, *Photography in the Ottoman Empire* (Istanbul: Haşet Kitabevi A.Ş., 1987).

8   There is a growing body of scholarship on the history of photography in the Ottoman Empire and a wide divergence of opinion on how the Ottoman interaction with photography should be understood and what the large body of surviving images can tell us about the subjects they depict. For a range of approaches to this literature, see Zeynep Çelik and Edhem Eldem, *Camera Ottomana: Photography and Modernity in the Ottoman Empire, 1840–1914* (Istanbul: Koç University Press, 2015), 18–19; Nancy Micklewright, "Alternative Histories of Photography in the Ottoman Middle East," in *Photography's Orientalism*, eds. Ali Behdad and Luke Gartlan (Los Angeles: The J. Paul Getty Trust, 2013), 75–92; Nancy Micklewright, "Picturing the 'Abode of Felicity' in 1919. A Photograph Album of Istanbul," in *Seeing the Past—Envisioning Islamic Art and Architecture: Essays in Honor of Renata Holod*, ed. D. Roxburgh (Leiden: Brill, 2014), 250–78; Bahattin Öztuncay, *The Photographers of Constantinople: Pioneers, Studios and Artists from 19th Century Istanbul*, 2 vols (Istanbul: Aygaz, 2003); Wendy Shaw, "Modernism's Innocent Eye and Nineteenth-Century Ottoman Photography," *History of Photography* 33, no. 1 (2009): 80–93; and Stephen Sheehi, *The Arab Imago: A Social History of Portrait Photography, 1860–1910* (Princeton and Oxford: Princeton University Press, 2016), among others.

9   For examples of such works and a longer discussion of the way in which photography was practiced in late Ottoman Istanbul, see Micklewright, "Alternative Histories," in Behdad and Gartlan, *Photography's Orientalism* (Los Angeles: Getty Research Institute, 2013), 75–92.

10 William Allen, "Sixty-five Istanbul Photographers, 1887–1914," in *Shadow and Substance: Essays in the History of Photography*, ed. Kathleen Collins (Bloomfield Hills: The Amorphous Institute Press, 1990), and Çelik and Eldem, *Camera Ottomana*, 18–19.

11 WorldCat lists nine editions published between 1839 and 1845. Emma Reeve is listed as co-author on two 1839 and two 1845 editions, and Emily Reeve is named on two 1839 editions and an 1840 edition. Allom's name alone appears on a second 1840 edition and a third 1845 edition. Available online: https://bit.ly/2DkxmDl (accessed January 7, 2019).

12 Beginning in the nineteenth century, with an increase in the number of European women visiting Istanbul, the rise of a foreign language press in the city, the founding of magazines directed at Ottoman women, and the circulation of photographs, information about current fashions moved in a variety of ways between European and Ottoman women in Istanbul. Previously that information circulated in more limited ways, primarily through trade, reports of travelers, and the pre-photographic images discussed above. For more on conversations among Euro-American and Ottoman women, see Lewis and Micklewright, eds., *Gender, Modernity and Liberty: Middle Eastern and Western Feminisms, a Critical Sourcebook* (London: I.B. Tauris, 2006).

13 The following discussion of this fashion transformation is a summary of a complex and lengthy process. For more detailed accounts, see Lale Görünür, *Osmanlı İmparatorluğu'nun son Döneminden Kadın Giysileri, Sadberk Hanım Müzesi Koleksiyonu/Women's Costume of the late Ottoman Era from the Sadberk Hanım Museum* (Istanbul: Vehbi Koç Vakfı, 2010); Onur Inal, "Women's Fashions in Transition: Ottoman Borderlands and the Anglo-Ottoman Exchange of Costumes," *Journal of World History* 22, no. 2 (2011): 243–72; Selin İpek, "Fashion in Court Women's Attire of the Eighteenth and Nineteenth Centuries in the Light of Written and Visual Sources kept in the Topkapi Palace Museum [in Turkish]", unpublished PhD thesis (Mimar Sinan Fine Arts University, Istanbul, 2009); Nancy Micklewright, "Women's Dress in Nineteenth Century Istanbul: Mirror of a Changing Society," PhD diss., (University of Pennsylvania, Pennsylvania, 1986); and Nancy Micklewright, "Tracing the Transformation of Women's Dress in Nineteenth Century Istanbul," *Dress* 13 (1987): 33–42.

14 The complex transformations that took place in Ottoman society over the course of the nineteenth century are well outside the boundaries of this article, but for our purposes it is important to note the gradual emergence of what eventually became a middle class of bureaucrats, career military, merchants, educators, and others. The wives of these men, while not having the same financial resources as their more wealthy counterparts, would have had access to the same fashion periodicals and the new shops displaying current fashions and thus would have been able to experiment in more modest ways with these new modes. The garment discussed here is one surviving example of this experimentation.

15 The use of gathers or pleats to create the impression of a shaped garment, which are known as *çantalı entari*, can be seen in any number of examples. See Lale Görünür, *Women's Costume*, 52.

16 Women travel writers who visited Istanbul and had the opportunity to observe Ottoman women's dress were particularly astute commentators on such subtle aspects of their fashion choices. For this early period, Julia Pardoe is an important source. See Julia Pardoe, *The City of the Sultan and Domestic Manners of the Turks in 1836* (London: Henry Colburn, 1837).

17 Lale Görünür includes a very useful discussion of *bindallı* in *Women's Costume*, as well as numerous examples of *bindallı* garments in the catalog of the book.

18 It is outside the scope of this chapter, but nonetheless intriguing to note the resurgence of *bindallı* garments in contemporary Turkey—and elsewhere—worn by the bride on her *kına gecesi*, or henna night, an all-female event that takes place the evening before the wedding. Connected to tradition by their name, these garments bear little resemblance to the historic versions apart from gold embroidery and a preference for red fabric.

19 Please see the chapter by Afsaneh Najmabadi in this volume for an analysis of the similarly complex and fluid practices of wedding photography in the Iranian context, and the larger social changes such practices embody.

20 I thank Yasmine Nachabe Taan for noting this tradition, which bears further investigation both in terms of fashion practice and the complications it presents for dating garments by their appearances in wedding photographs.

21 The family is identified as military based on the uniform worn by one of the male figures in several of the snapshots.

22 For a full discussion of this aspect of the snapshots, see Nancy Micklewright, "Harem/House/Set: Domestic Interiors in Photography from the Late Ottoman World," in *Harem Histories. Envisioning Places and Living Spaces*, ed. Marilyn Booth (Durham: Duke University Press, 2010), 239–60.

23 Based on both the exterior views of the house in which this family lives, as well as the furnishings of the interior, this is a family which is well off, but not among the wealthiest members of Ottoman society. The house displays none of the interior features which would have been seen in the palaces and *yalıs* (waterside villas) of the court elite but does contain newly fashionable European style furniture and decorative accessories. Their status and ethnicity are discussed in more detail in Micklewright, "Harem/House/Set: Domestic Interiors in Photography from the Late Ottoman World".

24 Görünür, *Women's Costume*, 56.

25 For a discussion of one of these, see Selim İpek, "Festive Finery for the Harem: Seamstress Mademoiselle Kokona's Order Book," in *Topkapi Palace: The Imperial Harem, House of the Sultan* (Istanbul: Ministry of Culture and Tourism, 2012), 56–59.

26 Personal observation of the author, 1983.

27 Günsel Renda, ed., *Women in Anatolia: 9000 Years of the Anatolian Woman* (Istanbul: Ministry of Culture, 1993), 249.

28 The circumstances surrounding the events of his brief reign are confusing and contested, and outside of our concerns here.

29 Of online sources for Fehime Sultan's biography, the Wikipedia article is definitive and is repeated virtually unchanged on numerous English and Turkish sites: https://bit.ly/2E09BSM (accessed January 4, 2021).

30 For this period of Turkish history, see Carter Vaughn Findley, *Turkey, Islam, Nationalism and Modernity, A History, 1789–2007* (London: Yale University Press, 2010) and Erik J. Zürcher, *The Young Turk Legacy and Nation Building, From the Ottoman Empire to Ataturk's Legacy* (London: I.B.Tauris, 2010).

31 Nur Bilge Criss, *Istanbul Under Allied Occupation, 1918–1923* (Leiden: Brill, 1999), 120.

32 For a discussion of the engagement of royal women with portraiture and a selection of examples, see Bahattin Oztuncay, *Hanedan ve Kamera, Osmanlı Sarayından Portreler/Dynasty and Camera, Portraits from the Ottoman Court* (Istanbul: Aygaz, 2010).

33 For a recent work on the Worth fashion enterprise in this period, see Amy De la Haye and Valerie D. Mendes, *The House of Worth 1890–1914: Portrait of an Archive* (London: V&A Publishing, 2014).

CHAPTER 3

TRAINING SLAVES FOR THE CAMERA: RACE AND MEMORY IN REPRESENTATIONS OF SLAVES, CAIRO, AND KHARTOUM, 1882–92

Eve M. Troutt Powell

Soon after the introduction of photography in the second quarter of the nineteenth century, the eyes of photographers in Europe, the United States, the Ottoman capital and its Arab provinces were drawn to the bodies of slaves, particularly African slaves from Sudan and Ethiopia. Their ways of viewing these people were influenced by their intellectual backgrounds, their artistic training, their cultural, and social upbringing.[1] Their gaze could be deeply affected by current events in a rapidly changing Middle East, and how much money was paid by patrons commissioning particular representations for very specific exhibitions, scientific enquiries, or newspapers. Whether the camera became a kind of social microscope focusing on racialized types when applied to the bodies of slaves or whether it mimicked and mirrored highly stylized Orientalist painting, those using this instrument were in constant dialogue with current discussions of race, inferiority, and colonialism—vibrantly so. Often the viewing of slaves crossed from literature to the camera, and back, through literary salons and the international art market in which images from, of, or about the Middle East were extremely important. The landscape and politics of Egypt and Sudan in particular fascinated European governments as much as the people of the region inspired topics for European art markets.

This chapter explores how a dramatic series of armed occupation and political rebellion in the regions of the Nile Valley challenged the narrational talents of two very different men—one a writer, the other a diplomat and photographer. In 1882, Egypt's nationalist political movement, known as the `Urabi rebellion, had been put down by British forces, who then occupied the country. This occupation would last for seventy years. In that same year, about 1,400 miles south in the city of Khartoum, Egyptian and British administrators and military figures were beginning to reckon with the rising force of the Mahdiyya, an Islamic rebellion against the Egyptian administration of Sudan. Louis Vossion was a French diplomat who was sent to Khartoum in 1882 because of his talent for photography. Jurji Zaydan was a Lebanese immigrant to Egypt, gifted with languages, who worked in Khartoum in 1884 as an interpreter for the British and who would return to Egypt to become a literary giant. All of Zaydan's work, and much of Vossion's, are still in print today; so well regarded were both for their abilities to chronicle the politics of the times. Both Zaydan and Vossion blended their sense of racial identities and differences in their work on late nineteenth-century Sudanese society.

Seeing Black

…up float his misshapen and bloated images of the Negro, like the fetid bodies of the drowned.[2]

There were many translators in Cairo and Khartoum, for example, who could linguistically move with ease between the racial vocabularies of Paris, London, and Istanbul, in Arabic, Turkish, French, and English. Jurji Zaydan was one of these cultural shape shifters. Here are some of his words about race and slaves in Cairo:

Transliteration in this chapter is based on the system recommended by the *International Journal of Middle East Studies*.

Figure 3.1 "Fadl-el-Anaza, négresse du Sennar, 28 ans, femme d'un juge du tribunal" (Fadl-el-Anaza, negress of Sennar, 28 years old, wife of a tribunal judge), published in *Types du Soudan*, Louis Vossion, 1884. Collection anthropologique du prince Roland Bonaparte. Source: gallica.bnf.fr (Bibliothèque nationale de France).

If you were to enter the park in the evening, and came to the platform surrounded by the gas lights and the whistling music, you would see people gathering around from all different races, inclinations, incomes, languages and colors, from the Caucasian of pure whiteness to the Negro of pitch-black darkness ...[3]

As he stood there [in the smoking room of the Cairo Opera House] a eunuch appeared, tall in size, frail in build, stout of body, no hair on his face, wearing black foreign clothing and on his head a red tarbush, who then presented him with a polite greeting.[4]

As shown in these two brief excerpts from his 1892 historical novel, *Asir al-Mutamahdi*, Jurji Zaydan outlined demographic details by emphasizing the social structures of race; the racial mixtures and differences found on the parks and streets of Cairo and the presence of Sudanese eunuchs in the public leisure spaces and private homes of the Egyptian elite. Zaydan, a towering literary figure in Egypt by the time this novel was published, was personally caught in the four years—1881 to 1885—when Egypt lost its colony in the Sudan to the rebellion of the Mahdi and almost simultaneously was itself colonized by the British. He worked in Khartoum as a translator for British intelligence in 1884 and was skilled in interpreting British officials' racial observations in both Egypt and Sudan.[5] Zaydan's time in Khartoum occurred at the same time as two series of acclaimed photographs about the races of Sudan were published in Paris by a French photographer named Louis Vossion.

The constructions of racial identity framed in *Types du Soudan* (1884) and *Souvenirs de Khartoum et du Soudan égyptien* (1881–82) closely echo themes in Jurji Zaydan's novel; both men paid very close attention to the vocabularies of race then current in Sudan.[6] In 1881, Vossion, a member of the French consular corps, was commissioned by Prince Roland Bonaparte to travel to the part of Africa then known as the Egyptian Sudan and capture by camera the images of the residents of its capital city. Bonaparte—a nephew of the former emperor—played a huge role in the establishment of French scientific institutions, most notably the Société Géographie in Paris, and this commission was one of many whose fruit—photographs—filled exhibition halls with images of diverse people newly available to French art, photography, and the budding field of anthropology.[7]

Vossion applied great energy to his job and took 108 images for the volume *Types du Soudan* which appeared in 1884. This is an authoritative volume, in which the most important European, Egyptian, and Sudanese officials were presented, many of whom would later be known as major architects of Sudanese colonial history.[8] But *Types du Soudan* is not only a who's who of colonial officials. Most notably for this essay, the photographer paid close attention to slaves. Vossion chronicled the relationships between Sudanese women and their European or Arab husbands, registered surprise at the word "marriage" when interracial couples produced children, and regularly photographed enslaved people from different parts of the Sudan. The photographer left copious captions, as can be seen in Figure 3.2, some with the photos and some left in his notes, which show how fascinated he was with the varying levels in which black people participated in Khartoum society.

Vossion's *Souvenirs de Khartoum et du Soudan égyptien* was published a few years earlier, with a more informal and personal collection of photographs. This volume visually documents his own relationships with Sudanese and European leaders, and his own servants and slaves. There is a quiet peace in this volume, a calm Khartoum in which the photographer is shown to be completely at ease with daily life. But brewing behind the pastoral scenes was a huge rebellion in Egypt, in which Egyptian soldiers demanded "Egypt for the Egyptians!" and an Islamic revival and rebellion that was on its way to conquering much of the Sudan. The year after Vossion completed his collections, the Mahdist rebellion had besieged Khartoum. By 1885, many of the officials photographed by Vossion were either dead, imprisoned, or sold to the Mahdist armies. Some of these same figures worked with Zaydan, and are also featured in *Asir al-Mutamahdi*.

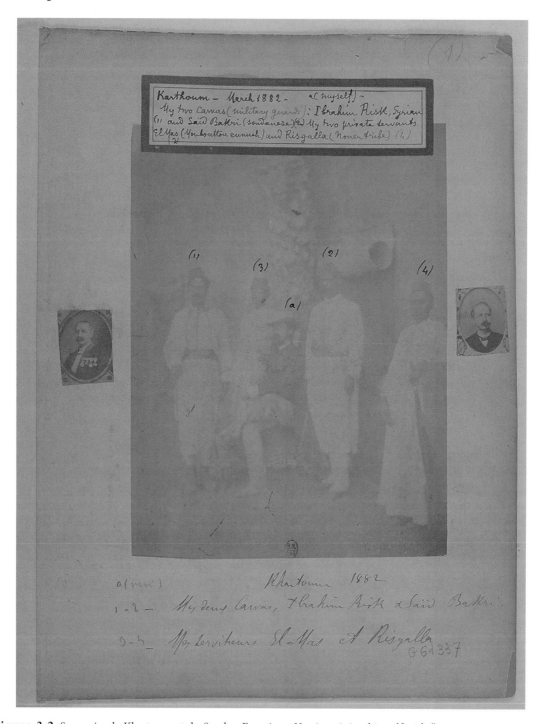

Figure 3.2 Souvenirs de Khartoum et du Soudan Egyptien—Vossion sitting himself with "my two private servants El Mas (Moubouttou eunuch) and Rizgallah (Nouer tribe)," Louis Vossion, 1881–82. Source: gallica.bnf.fr (Bibliothèque nationale de France).

Drawing on the two photographic collections, Vossion's notes, and Jurji Zaydan's *Asir al-Mutamahdi*, this essay explores how the networks of slavery figured so prominently in both men's work and how the bodies of enslaved men, women, and children were staged and configured. As certain as both the photographer and the novelist were about where to place black bodies in their social and cultural hierarchies, both often expressed confusion when presented with or imagining racial mixing or racial passing. Damage was done to Vossion's sense of race when he tried to represent what seemed to him the strange intimacies taken with the bodies of enslaved mothers, particularly those treated with respect (see Figures 3.8 and 3.9 on pages 59 and 61). Zaydan knew that in the Khartoum of the early 1880s, there was more than skin color that could identify blackness. Both men felt keenly the power of the Mahdiyya; Khartoum would change forever. By the time Vossion's photographs were published, in 1884, the Mahdi's armies had almost completely besieged the city. The relationships that Vossion photographed were devastated by 1885, making it even more significant that these pictures became prominent displays in a European museum and that the characters involved were purposefully rescued from oblivion by the novelist in 1892.

The Photographer as Consul and Consult

Against the backdrop of this brutality the Rive Gauche *penseur* poses in an immaculate white designer shirt. It is not simply the paradox of this elegantly dressed man in contrast to the setting that strikes me, it is the assumption that the photograph is meaningless to his audience without his presence. He lends gravity to the situation.[9]

In Figure 3.2, Louis Vossion is the center of the photograph, taken in 1882 at his residence in Khartoum. The residence is the French consulate, where Vossion had performed the role of vice-consul for two years. On either side of him stand two sergeants (*cawass*), and his "private servants": El Mas and Rizgallah. El Mas he names as a eunuch and Rizgallah as being from the Nuer tribe. Both descriptions would imply at that time that they were enslaved or manumitted members of the consulate. This is the first photograph presented in *Souvenirs de Khartoum*, and it immediately introduces Vossion as the authority with the experiential authenticity. This is both technologically and culturally important. Vossion's *Types du Soudan* was only the second volume to be published in France that had photographic images embedded within their pages—a huge technical achievement that only became available in 1880.[10] Culturally it fortified a particular kind of faith in the veracity of the camera: "This authenticity of the gaze, reinforced by the transparency registered by the camera (supposé de l'enrégistrement photographique), is also the justification of the pact made between the author-photographer and the reader: 'I went there and I saw it for you.'"[11] Vossion was both author/photographer and a political leader for the French government and his dual authority is echoed throughout his volumes.

Vossion had joined the French consular corps in 1877, and Khartoum was his first major posting. He arrived at a time of increasing economic and political turbulence. The Sudan was administered by the Egyptian government; in Khartoum this meant Turco-Circassian army officers, Egyptian soldiers like Ahmed `Urabi—whose discontent with the Egyptian government was fueled partly by his service in Sudan—Coptic traders and translators, merchants from the Levant and from Europe, traders in Arabic gum, ivory, and slaves from Sudanese provinces. For years, the Egyptian *Khedive* (Viceroy) Isma'il had also hired British officials to regulate the slave trade, and in 1877, the most famous of these, General Charles Gordon, outlawed the sale of slaves from the Equatorial province of Sudan—what is now South Sudan. The threat of income loss was keenly felt in Khartoum's business networks and the new law was interpreted as a provocation by the Mahdi and his followers—that it was issued by a Christian British military officer did not increase its popularity.

As Vossion's photos show, the anti-slave trade law was not very effective; there are slaves in over half of his pictures. But its fitful implementation threatened a vibrant commercial tradition in which Northern Sudanese tribes were deeply invested, like the Dongolawi, the Mahdi's own tribe. Gordon and other officials of the Egyptian government became the targets of the Mahdi's pronouncements, viewed as obstructionists to the establishment of a purer, simpler Islamic state along the Nile. In Egypt, concurrent protests against corruption, financial misuse, and increased European political influence took on a more secular, but no less demonstrative, tone. Isma'il, the same khedive who had hired General Gordon, had become bankrupted by the loans British and French banks gave to his treasury. In 1878 he was deposed in favor of his son Tawfiq, and British and French advisors took over the treasury, under an office known as the Public Debt Commission. This commission demobilized, without pay, thousands of Egyptian soldiers and officers, leaving them destitute in Egypt's biggest cities, and prompting `Urabi's movement to reinstate their pay.[12] This means that all of those photographed by Vossion found themselves, in 1882, between two significant and growing movements, `Urabi's and the Mahdi's, that meant to restructure the political and economic infrastructure of all major locations along the Nile Valley. Through his pictures, Vossion attempted to articulate the social status quo of these intimately connected regions of the Nile Valley. As in the introductory picture of *Souvenirs du Khartoum*, the ladders of hierarchy are carefully resurrected.

The Writer Sets the Scene

Jurji Zaydan used a different lens—narrative description—to transcribe the physical presence and the voices of slaves caught between their experience in Sudan and their lives in Egypt. Through the figure of Bakhit, a fictional eunuch serving an elite Egyptian family in Cairo in 1881–84, Zaydan created a wise, sometimes passionate character with a unique understanding of the social hierarchies of the day.[13] In one instance, Bakhit uses this awareness to protect Fadwa, the beautiful, young, and sequestered daughter of his master, who is confused about the entire `Urabi rebellion and why the British are so interested in Egypt. Her questions come after a notably dishonest suitor has tried to see her as she and Bakhit ride in her veiled carriage. The primary work of an urban elite eunuch in late nineteenth-century Cairo was to protect the honor of his charges, especially unmarried daughters. But one of her suitors, `Aziz, is more concerned with penetrating her privacy. He is in serious competition for her with his more brilliant and courteous friend, Shafiq, and is bristling with pride that he is now a uniformed soldier in `Urabi's army. Catching up to Fadwa's curtained carriage on horseback, `Aziz blocks the way forward and tries to speak to Fadwa. Bakhit cannot tolerate this attempt at intrusion. Recognizing `Aziz as the rude interlocutor, Bakhit intervenes:

> "What do you want, Effendi?", asked Bakhit.
> `Aziz answered, "I want to greet the young mistress."
> "Custom does not work like that," responded Bakhit. "It is more appropriate for you to preserve her honor."
> "Watch your manners yourself! Know that you are speaking to a respected army officer." `Aziz said this in a loud voice, thinking that when Fadwa heard of his new position she would lift the curtain.
> But Bakhit said "Your attire revealed your position, but men of war don't pomade their hair nor perfume themselves. And they don't treat a woman like this. There can be no respect for your uniform now if you have not been respectable your entire life."
> `Aziz rose up in anger and embarrassment and screamed, "In my position I do not have to speak to a slave. Therefore, I will speak to your mistress."
> "Then protect your position. I worry about you – this is not like you" answered Bakhit.
> "Tell your mistress that Shafiq is still a student in school and not an officer in the army," yelled `Aziz.

Bakhit's anger rose, and he shouted, "Begone, you scoundrel before I beat you!"

With that, he ordered the carriage to turn around and return home. `Aziz remained there, stunned by the failure of his mission to speak to Fadwa.[14]

This encounter speaks to many points of social and cultural power in late nineteenth-century Egyptian society. The eunuchs of elite Egyptian households held the reins of much power over the education and social lives of the women in these households, a power bestowed to them by the most senior man in the house—often the original buyer of the same eunuch. Other examples can be found of eunuchs being the revered and sometimes resented punishers of the family, as noted in the memoirs of some of their charges, like Huda Sha'arawi.[15] Yet the tumult of Egyptian society in the early 1880s shook even the structures of household custom. Both Bakhit and Fadwa are upset by this encounter with `Aziz. Fadwa admonishes Bakhit for letting it go on for so long, and Bakhit remains upset by `Aziz's audacity. It leads them to discuss the sensitive position of the Egyptian military at a time when soldiers are in rebellion against the Egyptian throne and the menace of British colonialism. With his unique position vis-à-vis power, it is again Bakhit's role, in the novel, to explain colonialism to Fadwa while protecting her interests—by not telling her father that her privacy and honor were almost breached while under his care.

At first, Bakhit praises `Urabi's ability to unite the tribal chiefs of rural and Upper Egypt. The unified support for `Urabi, he explains to Fadwa, made the British and French governments wary. "I learned that they both sent to the khedive notification of their readiness to help in any way to support the power of His Excellency," Bakhit tells Fadwa. And when Fadwa asks why the two governments feel obligated to enter Egyptian affairs, he responds that Egypt owes them huge debts, and the French and British are protecting their debts as their rights. Meanwhile, the fuming `Aziz also considers that Fadwa rightfully belongs to him, is in fact owed to him. He looks for ways to revenge himself against Bakhit, so that the eunuch servant will not be a stumbling block to `Aziz getting closer to Fadwa.[16] Bakhit's body, then, serves many functions. With his intelligence he can protect Fadwa, he can educate her, and he can learn. His body is the gate to her and around her. His situation makes him uniquely sensitive to the political upheaval in Egypt, and the reality of impending European colonialism. But even with the heroism granted to him by Jurji Zaydan, he is also an obstacle to be overcome.

No camera caught the image of Bakhit; in Jurji Zaydan's novel there is no illustration of this character either. But Zaydan invested in his descriptions of Bakhit the collective imagery of eunuchs held in the minds of his readers, an audience increasingly at home with photography. As Stephen Sheehi writes of this period, *al-Nahda* era—when artistic and literary culture thrived in the Middle East—a perspective that was reproduced "through the photographic image, a perspective and *verum factum* that is narrated in an abundance of textual, poetic, epistolary, and literary forms – from the romanticism of Jubran and the 'realist' language of `Isa al-`Ubayd to the historical novels of Jurji Zaydan…"[17] Zaydan was arguably the most preeminent writer in Arabic of his time, and as Sheehi has shown, deeply literate in the language of photography as well.

Sheehi explores photography during this period from "the prism of Ottoman modernity and *al-nahda al-`Arabiya*." As he describes, his book has thus

resisted looking through a derivative lens of European photography by instead examining images produced by indigenous photographers, through their photographic practice and the social practice of the image's circulation, and through their voices in primary Arabic sources. The project of 'provincializing' European photography and centering marginalized histories such as that of the Ottoman Arab world entails parsing out the European master narrative from the "nature of photography," from its templates and genetic patterns, from the practices and representations that accompanied it.[18]

This divorce from the "European master narrative" of photography is harder to enforce when looking at the images of slaves in the Sudan in the late nineteenth century, although I agree with Sheehi about its significance. As mentioned earlier, Louis Vossion was a government official fully vested in photographing racial and social hierarchies in Khartoum society. His pictures were dedicated to, and perhaps diminished by, their exploration of "types" instead of lives. Nor was Vossion an artist. There is no investment in the aesthetic of the slaves' bodies in his photographs; none of the pathos we see in abolitionist photography of Sudanese or other African slaves, nor the beauty of Orientalist constructions of Africans' skin color that can be found in photos taken of Ottoman eunuchs by artists who studied in Paris with the likes of Jean-Léon Gérôme.[19]

The eunuchs in Figure 3.3 bear Bakhit's dignity but remain silent on the page—they are also tall in size, no hair on their faces, wearing foreign clothing, and on their heads tarbushes. Their dignified bodies serve as a protective gate, just as Zaydan's Bakhit served his ward Fadwa, particularly for the vice-consul/photographer himself. Any security granted to Vossion, a French citizen, would have to have come either from the British or the Egyptian army—there would have been no French soldiers in Khartoum in 1882 unless they had been hired by the khedive. Rizgallah and El Mas are never shown in any other role than that of guard. And in the more formal *Types du Soudan*, they are not even named. As in Figure 3.4, the reader has to use Vossion's notes and compare the faces to know who these "servants" are.

There is one picture, however, in *Types du Soudan* that bears testimony to the unique relationship that Sudanese eunuchs had to local politics, wealth, and power. In Figure 3.5 (top right image on this page from his album) seven eunuchs posed for Vossion's camera. The short caption describes them as the principal eunuchs of the harems of Khartoum, but the longer description identifies them as "groupe d'eunuques noirs appartenant aux principaux musulmans de Khartoum" (a group of black eunuchs belonging to the leading Muslims of Khartoum). They embody the power of prominent Muslims—in Sudan and in Egypt—so worrisome and illegal in the eyes of French and British colonial officials—the power to continue buying and selling slaves. These eunuchs played a very different, much more intimate role than those guarding Louis Vossion himself.

This menacing power is also embodied in the photograph of Shaykh Soliman, whose portrait is the first that Vossion racially characterizes. The caption in *Types du Soudan* reads "Cheikh Soliman, pure race du Soudan, prévot des marchands du Khartoum" (pure Soudanese race, provost of the Khartoum merchants). The note to race is important; through Shaykh Soliman, Vossion introduces his readers to the construction of religion and race in Sudan. The same photograph of the Shaykh (Figure 3.6) first appeared in print in *Souvenirs de Khartoum*, with the merchant in the same pose—heavy, opulent, and jauntily holding a cigar—but the caption is quite different. Here, Vossion represents him as a classic "Musulman de Khartoum" (Khartoum Muslim). The caption then reads "provost of the merchants of Khartoum. Dealer in ostrich feathers and more or less in slaves. Has, afterwards, joined the Mahdi – a pure scoundrel." This could reflect Vossion's investment in the ostensible Anglo-Egyptian mission of General Charles Gordon which had set to extirpate the slave trade from the Sudan. It could also be an angry memorial to the majority of his photographic subjects who were either imprisoned or killed by the Mahdi's armies. But never in either volume is slavery repudiated. The photographer's mission is completely buffeted by the slaves around him.

In *Asir al-Mutamahdi*, there is little mention of slaves once the protagonist reaches Khartoum, a society in tumult where the racial lines feel dangerously fluid. As the *Mahdi* (the Rightly Guided) and his armies approach the besieged Khartoum where Gordon leads the defense, Shafiq reemerges. After British forces bombarded Alexandria and effectively shut down the ʿUrabi rebellion, Shafiq joined the British army, thinking that his fluency in English would help the cause of Egyptian sovereignty. He was sent to the Sudan to serve British intelligence and was assigned to serve General Hicks, the leader of forces sent to release Gordon from Khartoum. The Mahdi's forces cut that expedition down to the last man, seized tons of ammunition, and became an even deadlier force.[20] Many in Egypt assumed that Shafiq was dead, but he had predicted Hicks'

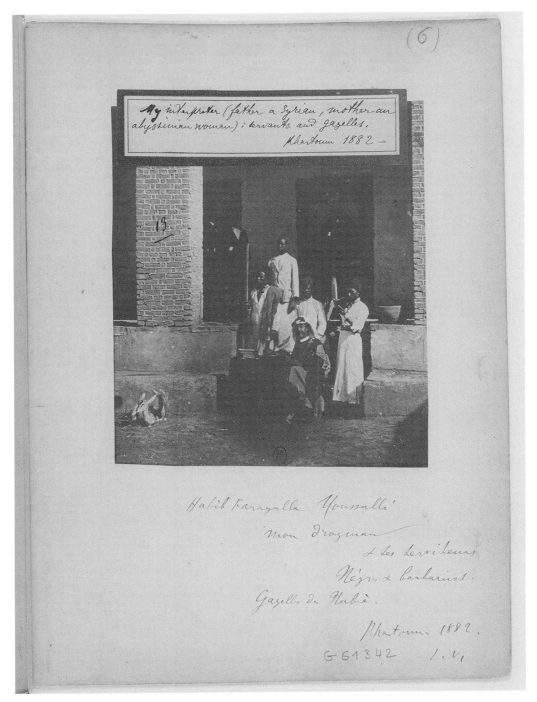

Figure 3.3 Souvenirs de Khartoum—"My interpreter (father a Syrian, mother an Abyssinian woman); servants and gazelles, Khartoum, 1882," Louis Vossion, 1882. Source: gallica.bnf.fr (Bibliothèque nationale de France).

Figure 3.4 Photograph of anonymous sitters, published in *Types du Soudan*, Louis Vossion, 1884. Collection anthropologique du prince Roland Bonaparte. Source: gallica.bnf.fr (Bibliothèque nationale de France).

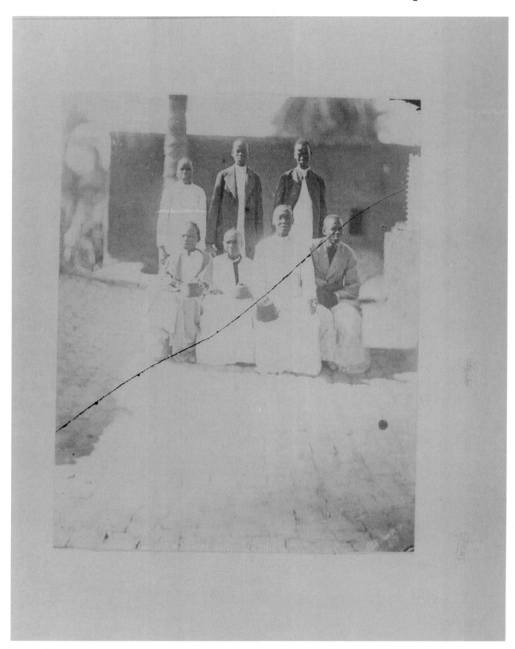

Figure 3.5 "Les principaux eunuques des harems de Khartoum" (the chief eunuchs of Khartoum's harems), published in *Types du Soudan,* Louis Vossion, 1884. Collection anthropologique du prince Roland Bonaparte. Source: gallica.bnf.fr (Bibliothèque nationale de France).

Figure 3.6 Souvenirs de Khartoum—"Cheikh Soliman, provost of the merchants of Khartoum. Dealer in ostrich feathers and more or less in slaves. Has, afterwards, joined the Mahdi – a pure scoundrel," Louis Vossion, February 1882. Source: gallica.bnf.fr (Bibliothèque nationale de France).

defeat and hid from the Mahdi's army. His light skin and English abilities gave him a cultural alias in the British forces, but long days on the run change him. Shafiq slips into blackness because of the harshness of the Sudanese sun.[21] Wearing his darker skin and the *jubba*—the patchworked tunics of the Mahdist *Ansar*—as camouflage, Shafiq finally reaches the British headquarters in Khartoum, in January of 1885. His racial disguise enables him almost miraculously to break through the siege, and he enters the palace where Gordon and his inner entourage bravely but anxiously wait to see who will come first: rescue from the British or the Mahdi.

When Shafiq finally reaches Gordon's inner sanctum, he is introduced to a circle of famous Egyptians, Europeans, and Sudanese who meet with him. These officials, including Gordon, are confused by his *jubba*, his perfect English, his command of Egyptian and Sudanese Arabic, and his brown face, and spend the beginning of the encounter trying to figure out his race.[22] This is in fact Shafiq's secret weapon and his blessing—he is a racial shape-shifter at a time of concretizing racial difference and origin—both the slave trade and the colonial administration are built on these premises. He is as sensitive to this as Bakhit is when explaining colonialism to Fadwa. Perhaps this is why Bakhit constantly defends the memory of Shafiq and is the faithful protector of his memory and reputation.

Vossion's camera captures this historical moment differently from the fictional novel. Two of the men who encircle Shafiq in the book when he reaches Gordon in Asir are actually present in Vossion's photographs, and one of them has also, through his Khartoum family, thrown the photographer's "types du Soudan" into confusion. The Greek consul Nicola Liontedes is mentioned in the novel and shown in Vossion's photographs (Figure 3.7).[23]

Also represented in both volumes is the Syrian trader Fathallah Djehami. He was notable to Zaydan for being an intimate of Gordon's until the last minute, but in Vossion's pictures, he is more notable for his family. Fathallah Djehami married an Abyssinian woman, with whom he had several children. In several photographs, he is proudly surrounded by them, even holding his mixed-race children, who are dressed just like him, tenderly (Figure 3.8).

Sartorial Protection, Slavery, and Marriage

An important group of Vossion's subjects were notable for their own abilities to shift between racial identities, or certainly able to confuse the photographer himself. In some instances, French words like *nègre*, *négresse*, *noir*, *arabe* and his translations of them into "nigger," "black," "arab" cannot do justice (as if these words should be expected to) to the situation he observed. In both *Types du Soudan* and *Souvenirs de Khartoum*, no one is Sudanese, as all black people are in *Asir al-Mutamahdi*. For Vossion, "black," "nègre," "nigger," and sometimes "arab" are used irrespective of the ethnic or racial origin of the slaves he has posed. They tend to be naked or half-naked, unless they are eunuchs (see Figure 3.5). So the nudity of servants, slaves, dancers— and these women are described as Arab—is a signifier of lives lived at the very bottom of Khartoum's social hierarchies. For those who visually look to be people of color but who are not enslaved and hold positions of power, Vossion places them more in terms of geographical or ethnic origin.[24] Merchants and soldiers, consuls and doctors are "égyptien," "syrien," "pur race du Soudan," and "de race turque et de race négroïde." Europeans are "anglais," "grecs," and "allemands." No European women are depicted in these photographs. All of the wives shown are married to Egyptians and Syrians and are themselves identified as "abyssiniennes" or "darfouriennes"—such as indicated in the captions of Figures 3.8 and 3.9. This is a far cry from the rigid protection of women's privacy noted repeatedly in Jurji Zaydan's *Asir al-Mutamahdi*.

Vossion shows us Faragallah Adjouri, "Syrian of Khartoum, with his wife" (Figure 3.9), a mustachioed official with a tall and elegant Abyssinian woman by his side.

Figure 3.7 The Greek consul Nicola Liontedes, published in *Types du Soudan*, Louis Vossion, 1884. Collection anthropologique du prince Roland Bonaparte. Source: gallica.bnf.fr (Bibliothèque nationale de France).

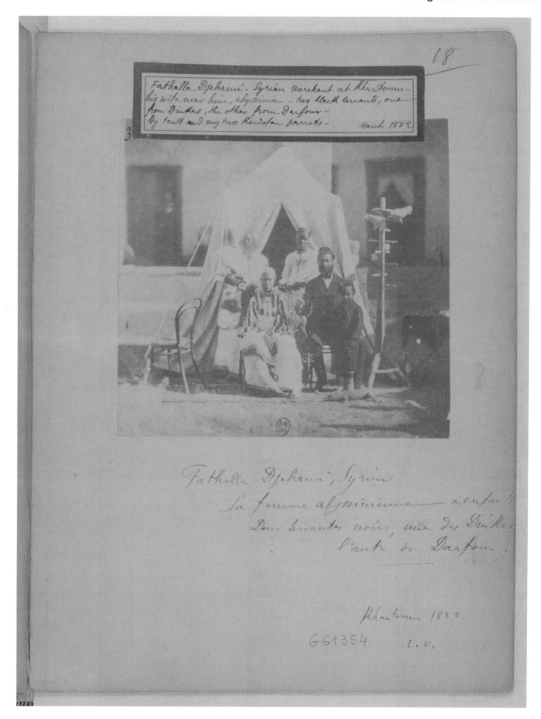

Figure 3.8 Souvenirs de Khartoum — "Fathalla Djehami, Syrien, et sa femme Abyssinienne" (Fathalla Djehami, Syrian, and his Abyssinian wife), published in *Types du Soudan,* Louis Vossion, 1884. Collection anthropologique du prince Roland Bonaparte. Source: gallica.bnf.fr (Bibliothèque nationale de France).

We see Ibrahim Effendi Khalil, "head of the Coptic colony of Khartoum, and his sons, born of an Abyssinian woman," as a well-dressed man in a *tarboush* and a suit, holding his mixed-race sons closely and tenderly in his lap while he laughs (Figure 3.10).

There is another picture, this time of Habib Houry, of which Vossion noted "Syrian and his family—in the center, the negress wet nurse—to the left, a Dinka servant—to the right, an Abyssinian servant" (Figure 3.11). The wet nurse holds the eye of the viewer. She is bare-breasted, and on each side of her is one of Houry's children. Houry himself has his arm around her; this, and her direct gaze at the camera, are the clues to her centrality in the household. She actually seems to be the household, as they sit and stand posed before one of Vossion's white tents.[25]

In Figure 3.12, Onorato Moussi, "Maltese established in Khartoum," poses with his family: "a negress servant, and Maltese-Abyssinian children." In this volume there are two photographs of Fathallah Djehami, as mentioned, with his Abyssinian wife, and his two "negress servants, one from Darfur, the other from Dongolah." The next batch of photographs in *Types du Soudan* shifts to only slave women and dancers, as if in contrast to these families.

In Figure 3.13, Vossion displays "Slave women of diverse races, belonging to the chief of the Coptic colony of Khartoum." Like the Sudanese merchant Soliman Bey who was discussed earlier, there emerges from this photo an insinuation about the nature of this slaveholder's power, this other business in which Ibrahim Effendi Khalil should be named. And finally, in Figure 3.14, Vossion photographed three little girls, all dressed up and their hair in curls, whom he noted as "little girls, born out of the marriage between a Syrian Catholic and an Abyssinian woman" then the father himself.

These are the "types" that defy, just by their presence in the photographs, the pure races that Vossion was hoping to find. One senses from Vossion a great curiosity about the society of Khartoum, and yet a deep and judgmental commitment to hierarchical racial orders that conflicted with what he hoped to chronicle from the lens of his camera. He came from a society in which social mobility depended on the public adherence to this structure—in 1900 when he was the French consul in Sydney, Australia, he had shamed a consul general he assumed was illegitimate by publicly questioning his name in a derisory manner.[26] The captions Vossion wrote for his photographs of miscegenation bear an air of the same derision, and mockery of the African women's elevated positions. He made this even clearer when looking back at his volume several years later, in his notes. He described certain African servants as the "concubines," explaining that for the Syrian men, "polygamy was widely practiced, not officially but very much present." He went on that the picture of Habib Houry and his family "gives an idea of the incredible mixing of races that operates in Khartoum, and that makes it so difficult to conduct ethnographic research."[27]

Vossion's derision of many of the Syrian, Egyptian, and Sudanese men in the photographs—Muslim or Coptic—suggests his own racial condescension to these non-white men, and this attitude adds to the sense of hierarchies in which the photographer and his European subjects sit on top. And how would non-European audiences view these pictures? The wives of these men even posing for Vossion's camera is a blurring of hierarchies; Muslim wives—whether Syrian, Egyptian, or Sudanese—would never have been allowed to pose or be exhibited in such a public and open way. As Mary Roberts has shown with harem paintings, women like these, who fit more into Vossion's definition of wife and not concubine, women like Jurji Zaydan's Fadwa, would themselves have protested:

Respectable Muslim women would not pose for European male painters; thus European women were commissioned to undertake their portraits … A major priority for the harem women was that these portraits were not to be seen by men. This requirement necessitated that the paintings were entirely executed within the harem, including the varnishing and framing, and that they be covered at all times.[28]

Figure 3.9 Faragallah Adjouri, "Syrian of Khartoum, with his wife," published in *Types du Soudan*, Louis Vossion, 1884. Collection anthropologique du prince Roland Bonaparte. Source: gallica.bnf.fr (Bibliothèque nationale de France).

Figure 3.10 Effendi Khalil, "head of the Coptic colony of Khartoum, and his sons, born of an Abyssinian woman," published in *Types du Soudan*, Louis Vossion, 1884. Collection anthropologique du prince Roland Bonaparte. Source: gallica.bnf.fr (Bibliothèque nationale de France).

Figure 3.11 Habib Houry, "Syrian and his family—in the center, the negress wet nurse—to the left, a Dinka servant—to the right, an Abyssinian servant," published in *Types du Soudan*, Louis Vossion, 1884. Collection anthropologique du prince Roland Bonaparte. Source: gallica.bnf.fr (Bibliothèque nationale de France).

Figure 3.12 Onorato Moussi, "Maltese established in Khartoum," "a negress servant, and Maltese-Abyssinian children," published in *Types du Soudan,* Louis Vossion, 1884. Collection anthropologique du prince Roland Bonaparte. Source: gallica.bnf.fr (Bibliothèque nationale de France).

Figure 3.13 "Slave women of diverse races, belonging to the chief of the Coptic colony of Khartoum," published in *Types du Soudan,* Louis Vossion, 1884. Collection anthropologique du prince Roland Bonaparte. Source: gallica.bnf.fr (Bibliothèque nationale de France).

Figure 3.14 "Little girls, born out of the marriage between a Syrian Catholic and an Abyssinian woman" and their father, published in *Types du Soudan*, Louis Vossion, 1884. Collection anthropologique du prince Roland Bonaparte. Source: gallica.bnf.fr (Bibliothèque nationale de France).

The visibility of the slaves and the concubines here is, paradoxically, a cloak of invisibility to the cultural norms of public behavior and exhibition.

The Photographic and Literary Conclusion of these Black Bodies

By the end of the novel *Asir al-Mutamahdi*, Zaydan's character Bakhit loses his definition and succumbs to the fever of stereotype. For example, he and another Sudanese guardian are injured in a fight with local bandits in Lebanon, and their exertions have made the family notice their bodies in a new way: "the smell of the Sudanese that all humans curse."[29] When the families learn that Shafiq is fine and on his way out of Sudan, he starts to dance "like he is crazy." Bakhit and another slave Ahmed dance uncontrollably when Shafiq does return to his loved ones.[30] And finally, when Aziz tries to apologize to Shafiq and to Fadwa for his dangerous and malicious behavior, Bakhit begs for the permission to kill him but Shafiq orders him not to. Bakhit retreats into subservience.[31]

In Vossion's society of Khartoum, many of the protagonists we see in the photographs are dead by the time his pictures were exhibited. The photographer continued to keep a close eye on Sudan, noting that the eunuch Rizgallah was sold to Gessi Pasha, and that El Mas was sold to Yusuf Pasha, governor of Shaka.[32] These notes were sent also to King Leopold of Belgium, a monarch deeply interested in the racial hierarchies of other territories in Central Africa. Vossion shared no record of what happened to the Abyssinian wives and the mixed children of the officials shown in his photographs. They live on, unclaimed, in his pictures.

Even though missing a photographic gravesite, the black people in his photographs found ways in which to make their own light shine. They used ornaments or hairstyles or touched each other, details in which their humanity defies being "bloated images of the Negro" as loathed by Ralph Ellison. In Figure 3.1 on page 46, we can see a woman who has owned so much of the pose that even Vossion comments. Her caption reads "Fadl el-Anazi, négresse du Sennaar; 28 ans; femme d'une juge du tribunal" (Fadl el-Anazi, négresse du Sennaar; 28 years old; wife of a court judge). In his notes, however, Vossion describes her more carefully: "A beauty of the country, wife of a tribunal judge: her hairstyle shows the universal style adopted by the women of Khartoum province, ribbons and fine braids framing the face."[33] With his hint at her stylishness, the reader can see this beautiful self-fashioning in many of the wives posing with their husbands, in the dresses in which they present themselves and the quiet stillness of their poise. We can see among these women a will to be seen, and seen correctly. This article hopefully serves as a remembrance of their selfhood, and their lives, untypified by racial categorizations.

Notes

1 Stephen Sheehi, *The Arab Imago: A Social History of Portrait Photography, 1860–1910* (New Jersey: Princeton University Press, 2016), xix.

2 Jill Lepore, "Ahab at Home," quoting Ralph Ellison, *The New Yorker*, (July 29, 2019), 50.

3 Jurji Zaydan, *Asir al-Mutamahdi* (Prisoner of the False Mahdi) (Cairo: Dar al-Hilal, n.d. This historical novel was first published in Arabic in 1892. This translation is mine), 6.

4 Ibid., 30.

5 Eve M. Troutt Powell, *A Different Shade of Colonialism: Egypt, Great Britain and the Master of the Sudan* (California: California University Press, 2003), 115. See also Richard L. Hill, *Biographical Dictionary of the Anglo-Egyptian Sudan* (UK: Clarendon Press, 1951), 388, and Thomas Philipp, *Jurji Zaydan and the Foundations of Arab Nationalism* (Syracuse: Syracuse University Press, 2010), 31.

6 These two volumes are available for viewing on the Bibliothèque Nationale de France's (BNF) website: gallica.bnf. fr. The pictures in *Types du Soudan* were published four to a page, sometimes three. The BNF has also curated them

as larger single images. I have alternated between the grouped photographs and the singles in this chapter. The photographs in Souvenirs de Khartoum are all presented as one to a page. Where necessary I have added Vossion's own captions. In *Types du Soudan* these are in French; in Souvenirs de Khartoum these are in English and French.

7 G. Grandidier, "Obituary of Roland Bonaparte," *Nature*, no. 2847 (May 24 1924), vol. 113, 755. Grandidier notes that the prince "had gathered together a magnificent botanical collection and he died, pen in hand, just when he was writing the last word of his sixteenth pteridological paper …."

8 Hill, *Biographical Dictionary*, 374.

9 Mahjoub, *A Line in the River* (London: Bloomsbury, 2018), 86–87.

10 Thomas Cazentre, "Entre l'album et le livre: Images du bout du monde dans les collections Imbault-Huart et Vossion," *Revue de la Bibliothèque Nationale de France*, no. 2 (2013), 25–35.

11 Ibid.

12 Troutt Powell, *A Different Shade of Colonialism*, chapter 1.

13 Orit Bashkin has rightly stated that more scholarship is needed on Zaydan's novels offering an "important medium for channeling social and political ideas." Orit Bashkin, "Harems, Women and Political Tyranny in the Works of Jurji Zaydan," in *Harem Histories: Envisioning Places and Living Spaces*, ed. Marilyn Booth (North Carolina: Duke University Press, 2010), 292.

14 Zaydan, *Asir al-Mutamahdi*, 89–90. The translation is mine.

15 For example, my discussion of Huda Sha'arawi and her Ottoman peer Halide Edib Adivar in *Tell This in my Memory: Stories of Enslavement from Egypt, Sudan and the late Ottoman Empire* (Stanford, CA: Stanford University Press, 2012), chapter 4.

16 Zaydan, *Asir al-Mutamahdi*, 92.

17 Sheehi, *The Arab Imago*, 196.

18 Ibid., 196.

19 Many of these can be found in the British Anti-Slavery Society archive, Oxford University, special collections, or in the Jean-Léon Gérôme archive in the Ecole des Beaux-Arts, Paris.

20 Mahjoub, *A Line in the River: Khartoum, City of Memory*, (London: Bloomsbury, 2011), 44–45.

21 Zaydan, *Asir al-Mutamahdi*, 236.

22 Ibid., 240.

23 Hill, *Biographical Dictionary*, 211.

24 In the current exhibit at the Musée D'Orsay—Le Modèle Noir à Paris—the curators make an interesting point about racial terms used by painters of the nineteenth century: "The titles of the works of art are part of a historical heritage. Many old titles use dated ethnic classifications such as 'negro,' 'mulatto,' 'capresse,' which were current in the 19th and 20th centuries but are no longer used today. Most titles do not reveal anything about the identity of the models. Thanks to research carried out for this exhibition, we succeeded in identifying some of the models hence our suggesting, within the framework of this show, new titles mentioning the name of the model where it is known. Some works will therefore be exhibited with both this new title and the original one which recalls the historical statement."

25 In his notes written in 1883 from his second posting, in Burma, Vossion describes the situation of this photograph. The wet nurse is in the center, holding her own baby and "fixing her eyes to the camera" while Houri's children, whose Abyssinian mother had died "three months before." "Notices inscrites au bas de 91 éprouves photographiques fournissant la collection de Types du Soudan et de l'Égypte offerte à Sa Majésté Leopold II et à Son Altesse le Prince Roland Bonaparte, de Rangoon, 1883. Archives nationales de la France, Richelieu—Société de Géographie, SC WE-311.

26 Ivan Barko, "Georges Biard d'Aunet: the Life and Career of a Consul General," *Australian Journal of French Studies* 39, no. 2 (2002): 277.

27 Louis Vossion, "Notices inscrites au bas des 91 épreuves photographiques fournissant la collection de types du Soudan et de l'égypte offerte à Sa Majésté le Roi Léopold II et à Son Altesse le Prince Roland Bonaparte," from Rangoon, 1883—Vossion's next posting after Khartoum. Archives Nationales de la France, Richelieu – Société de Géographie, Cote SG – WE-311.

28 Mary Roberts, "Contested Terrains: Women Orientalists and the Colonial Harem," in *Orientalism's Interlocutors*, eds. Jill Beaulieu and Mary Roberts (North Carolina: Duke University Press, 2002), 193.

29 Zaydan, *Asir al-Mutamahdi*, 250.
30 Ibid., 292.
31 Ibid., 303.
32 Archives Nationales de France, Richelieu – Société de Géographie – SG WE-311.
33 Vossion, "Notes Inscrites."

CHAPTER 4

PATRONAGE, TASTE, AND POWER: SLAVE, MANUMITTED, AND FREE SUBJECTS IN THE FASHIONING OF MIDDLE EASTERN MODERNITY

Reina Lewis

Introduction

To analyze dress and embodiment in the making of modern identities in the Middle East from the 1850s to the early twentieth century I apply models from contemporary cultural studies and critical fashion studies; the circuit of culture from du Gay et al.[1] and of style-fashion-dress developed by Susan Kaiser.[2] To augment attention to royal and elite clothing—often the only garments surviving—I marshal literary and visual sources, including harem literature and memoirs, to demonstrate how elite, non-elite, enslaved, and manumitted subjects contributed to the formation of modern bodies through fashion. Engaging with reconceptualizations of historical and contemporary fashion as transnational and global,[3] I track the agentive role of differently placed social subjects in the transmission of style. This connects gender segregated royal and elite harems with the spaces and populations of the streets and the markets from whence came fashion commodities and services, focusing particularly on the Ottoman and Egyptian metropolitan consumptionscape.

My early sections explain the circuit models: focusing on Ottoman sumptuary regulation first, then identity formation and subjection in the context of slavery in Islamicate societies—i.e. those where Islam was culturally dominant for Muslims and non-Muslims alike.[4] I explore how moral panics about women's participation in changing distribution modes, from pedlars to new department stores, differentially affected majority and minority religious and ethnic populations. The 1869 visit of Empress Eugénie to Istanbul as a moment of transnational style transmission is connected to existing regional fusion fashion. I use concepts of fashion mediation and embodied aesthetic labor[5] to reveal the determining impact of slaves, eunuchs, ex-slaves, and free women and men in the formation of styles[6] and the consecration of taste.[7] In conclusion, I consider regional conventions of gifting fashion commodities onto others' bodies as a gendered exercise of power; bringing into visibility the embodied histories of gender, race, and sexuality in the modernizing Middle East.[8]

Circuits of Culture: Consumption, Regulation, Representation

The circuit of culture model (Figure 4.1) developed by du Gay et al. in 1997 to explain late twentieth-century developments in consumer culture displaced the primacy previously accorded to production to emphasize equally the role of consumption. Focusing on the phenomenon of the Sony Walkman, they explored the linked

I'd like to thank Yasmine Nachabe Taan and Nancy Micklewright for generous responses to chapter drafts, and Serkan Delice and Anna-Mari Almila for invaluable specialist advice.
Transliteration in this chapter is based on the system recommended by the *International Journal of Middle East Studies*, except for quoted material which is given in the original format.

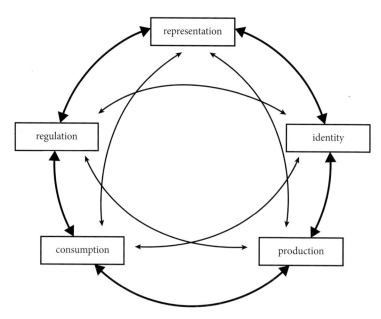

Figure 4.1 "The Circuit of Culture," in Paul du Gay, Stuart Hall, Linda Janes, Anders Koed Madsen, Hugh Mackay, and Keith Negus, *Doing Cultural Studies: The Story of the Sony Walkman*, 2nd edn (1997; Milton Keynes: Open University, 2013).

processes by which commodities are brought to fruition and gain meaning in consumers' lives. Their circuit situates production and consumption as nodal points alongside representation, regulation, and identity within a set of reciprocal relationships. In conceptualizing the consumer as active not passive, the authors do not valorize agency as unrestricted. The perceived "choices" of consumption operate in the context of formal and informal modes of regulation—often overtly moralized—which limit what can be produced and how it might be consumed. I transpose this focus on the necessarily constrained activity of the consumer to the historical context of the Middle East, where formal and informal sumptuary regulation were central components of fashion experiences and played a constitutive role in social control.

For the Ottoman domains, Madeline Zilfi emphasizes, "sartorial law [as] uniform, disguise, fashion, street wear, underwear, gift, robe of honor, corporal covering, and symbolic coverture [was] the principal delineator of social place and relationships of power."[9] Dress and appearance were to be transparent indicators of community—religious, ethnic, "national"—occupation—guild, military, *ulema* [Muslim religious scholars]—and rank—within occupation, community, and especially relationship to the sultan and imperial family. The status and wealth of all Ottoman subjects—free, manumitted, unfree—was subject to changes in the sultan's will or favor. Sumptuary measures were sometimes welcomed; as state fiscal management, regulation might protect traders from the impact of rapid fashion innovation; minority populations might find benefits for community self-regulation in being visually distinctive. Sumptuary laws were also constantly flouted and punishments could be harsh for consumers, craftspeople, and traders.[10] Infractions by women and non-Muslims, "society's preferred others," were especially concerning; regarded as "a danger rather than just an annoyance."[11] Into the early Turkish republic—as with other post-Ottoman, post-colonial states—centralized control over appearance and the consumption of clothing goods remained a priority.

For any fashion history where material objects may be rarely preserved beyond elite or ceremonial clothing the category of representation is invaluable; it underscores that "meaning does not arise directly from an object, 'the thing in itself', but from the way in which an object is *represented* in language, both oral and visual."[12] For Ottoman dress before 1900 very few items beyond the clothes of the imperial family are extant.[13] Accordingly, historians harvest data about Middle Eastern clothing from accounts by Middle Eastern and Western subjects. The visual repertoire includes Western and Ottoman paintings, drawings, costume books, and illustrated print media. The later period incorporates photographs; staged for Western and touristic consumption and produced by local take-up of amateur and professional photography.[14]

For foreign observers in the nineteenth century, as earlier, details of Ottoman women's dress were hard to find since prevailing codes of gender seclusion meant that women of the middle and upper classes—from Muslim and non-Muslim, or minority populations—were swathed in protective outerwear when they left the household. Non-Muslim women might sometimes veil their faces less rigorously, but a wardrobe of covers such as *çarşafs* or *feraces* commonly signified that the family was of sufficient status to "protect" its female members from external gaze.

These circumstances mean that written accounts by women travelers who could claim—and were presumed—to have visited women's domestic spaces were relied upon by their contemporaries; just as they remain central to researchers today.[15] This premium applied to women from outside the region and women grown up in Middle Eastern society who published at home and abroad. Written in European languages, harem literature centers on the cross-cultural contact zone of the harem visit.[16] Premised initially on the privilege of a female view "behind the veil" of segregating Islamicate society, harem literature was a popular middlebrow genre by the last quarter of the nineteenth century.

Often illustrated, with literary descriptions of dress a feature of women's ethnography,[17] representations of the body, dress, fashion, and consumption played a key role in the depiction of the modern self. With polygyny already in decline, the genre continued into the first decades of the twentieth century. This span encompasses the shift away from a sequestered world into the companionate nucleated, conjugalized,[18] family emblematic of personal modernity for many Ottoman and regional progressive elites[19]—with a residuum of social ties and patronage networks originating in slave relations.

Circuits of Fashion: Identity and Subjection

For my study of slave-owning societies, Susan Kaiser's repurposing of the du Gay circuit of culture into a circuit of style-fashion-dress in 2012 provides an indispensable focus on processes of subjectification. Kaiser recalibrates du Gay et al.'s "identity" into an ongoing process of "subject formation" (Figure 4.2). Always relational, subject formation inevitably includes experiences of subjection; the formation of self in ways "structured by others."[20] Most individuals have limited power over how prevailing social relations determine daily subject formation processes; more so in a society where dressed bodies include the enslaved and manumitted as well as those never enslaved.

The diverse forms of Middle East modernity emerged from societies in which the organization of genders included subjects such as eunuchs[21]—themselves objects of desire in Orientalist paintings.[22] Unable to accede to the position of full patriarchal male privilege—whether seen as neither male or female, or as failed "non-men"[23]—eunuchs had become central to the functioning of female seclusion and remained socially present through the modernizing period. To talk of the dressed body as a facet of Middle Eastern modernity, and to regard the processes by which the body became dressed as constitutive components of modernization for states and for individuals, is to talk of bodies whose sexual, gender, and social subjectification incorporated categories not routinely included in Western social frameworks in the same period. As Eve Troutt Powell establishes,[24] and I discuss below, it was a social norm that regional elite households contained enslaved and

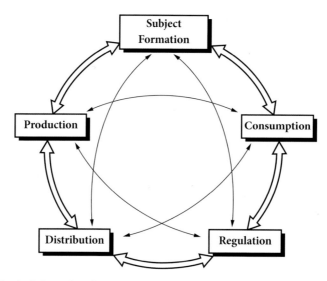

Figure 4.2 "Circuit of style-fashion-dress," in Susan Kaiser, *Fashion and Cultural Studies* (London: Bloomsbury, 2012).

manumitted individuals. This included the progressive and nationalist elite in Egypt and the Ottoman Empire. The once, or still, enslaved retainers who played an intimate role in the raising and socialization of royal and elite children included eunuchs as well as women of European, Central Asian, and African backgrounds. Elite feminists in Cairo or Istanbul may have had mothers and female relatives of slave origin; the mother of Egyptian nationalist Huda Shaarawi (1879–1947) was possibly a concubine and maybe of slave origin.[25] Others, like Ottoman Turk Halide Edib (c. 1883–1964),[26] would have grown up with slaves their own age as an intimate part of their childhood.[27]

Across the empire, slavery was understood as a potentially transitional status that did not preclude the enslaved having power over the free: "[b]eing someone's slave did not mean being everyone's slave."[28] The sultan's officials, whether slave or free, were "deputy sovereigns" on his behalf; and slaves and servants of non-royals could be endowed with "something of their own class and status."[29] Within the imperial and royal palaces an organizational hierarchy remunerated servants enslaved and manumitted with "wages, rations and clothing in proportion to their rank."[30] Cloth was currency: gifts of clothing at festivals or celebrations— marriages, births—dispersed imperial largesse, overseen in the palaces by the chief eunuchs. As with palace women who might be "given" in marriage to political allies when their manumission time arrived, women slaves in private homes also could presume on gifts to build a "manumission trousseau" for marriage or life outside the household.[31]

In Islamicate Middle Eastern modernities, where society was conventionally divided by gender within and outside households, women's spaces were recognized as a parallel public with their own conventions of patronage and power. Participation in the slave trade was central to the extension of women's and household influence. Young palace women "given" in marriage to men within the upper bureaucracy exported palace "protocols, educational principles and tastes" across the empire.[32] Outside the palace, elite women sometimes of slave origin themselves purchased enslaved girls to educate as consorts for family contacts and male relatives[33] or earned income by reselling them.[34]

Women slaves themselves functioned as public currency, maintaining the honor and status of the families they served—including that of women whose arrival in the household may have been through concubinage and slavery.[35] Unable to "own" their own honor, the "display of slaves as attendants with their mistresses was significant, both as allowing honorable mobility to the women they accompanied and as signifiers of wealth and power, the slaves themselves being richly attired."[36] Despite that social order regulated Middle Eastern women's movements outside the household, women were routinely present in a variety of mixed gender public spaces from the early modern period onward.[37] Outside the highest social orders, women worked within households and externally as *hamam* (bath) attendants, launderers, seamstresses, peddlers, and traders. Women from households able to afford seclusion visited mosques, hamams, pleasure gardens, popular theaters, royal pageants, and promenaded in carriages or on foot. Shopping brought women of all classes into mixed gender publics, as sellers, buyers, as overt political actors in commodity boycotts and street protests over prices.[38]

Across the Middle East in the nineteenth and twentieth centuries all shades of political opinion regarded changes in women's dress and visibility in mixed gender public spaces as indicators of broader social change; whether moral crisis or welcome social emancipation. Hardly surprising that clothes, the processes of acquiring them, and the experience of being seen and depicted in them, feature prominently in accounts by those few women whose lives entered the public record. Western harem literature and memoirs by Middle Eastern women[39] provide essential "intel" on how textiles and garments percolated through the modernizing cycle of fashion.

My chapter connects elite women's use of dress to articulate emancipatory femininity with the role of non-elite subjects of all genders in selecting, crafting, and exchanging commodities into style. Merchants, peddlers, palace guards, harem supervisors, and eunuchs, I delineate as agents of fashion. For Huda Shaarawi as a young married woman living in her parents' house, consent for a foray to Chalon—one of the Western-style department stores that characterized internationalized modernity in Alexandria—depended on the accompaniment of eunuch Said Agha.[40] Protecting the family's honor, he engineered a temporary "harem department" in the gender-mixed retail space.[41]

Distribution: The Spatialized Relations that Make Fashion

My desire to track the social relations that underwrite or impede modernizing practices of dress acquisition and display is enabled by a second key shift made by Kaiser: she expands du Gay's original node of "representation" into "distribution." This combines the "connotations of both material and representational elements."[42] Material elements include the physical distribution of commodities and the human and non-human actors involved. This brings into view the changing but relational spaces of distribution—bazaars and street markets continue alongside new department stores—and the human agents fulfilling conventional and new roles—from roving peddlers to store clerks. All bring access to commodities and services, adapting gender segregation conventions for new types of proximity. Kaiser places distribution "strategically between production and consumption" where it "ties together economy and culture."[43]

Du Gay et al. likewise emphasize the spatial and temporal locatedness of commodity usage in the "ongoing process"[44] of identity construction. They demonstrate the determining role of perceived boundaries between public and private in apparently disparate moral panics about the social impact of new commodities and related behaviors such as young people having private conversations in public on mobile phones. Applied to fashion controversies in the modernizing Middle East, this illuminates how and where to "see" the fashioning of the modern body and the moral concerns that accompanied it.

Middle Eastern distribution routes included the covered bazaar, weekly open street markets, traveling merchants and peddlers, plus specialist shops providing Western fashion commodities and tailoring in the Frankish or "foreign" quarters of major cities. Whether run by Muslims or minority communities, these operations were structured by gendered codes of public and private space. However, what "constituted public space, and the place of women within it [differed] greatly region to region where what set the acceptability of female conduct was the norms imposed by local society itself rather than any state directed social standard."[45] This includes the liminal space of the neighborhood or *mahalle*, in which proximate streets and alleys—subject to surveillance by neighbors—constituted a "semiprivate domain."[46]

The accommodations demanded in-store for the young Huda Shaarawi highlight the spatialized reputational risk of modern Frankish retail for respectable Muslim women; though it did not stop expeditions for foreign produced lifestyle items.[47] Back to the sixteenth century, commercial venues were the loci of worries about public gender mixing and interconfessional sociality.[48] By the eighteenth and nineteenth centuries, the rapid increase in the fashion cycle focused attention on fashion retail sites, with bans on women entering shops proof of women's constant consumption presence.[49] Unable to control women's "highly visible presence in the Ottoman market place," it was incumbent on the state to keep consumption spaces safe for women since "a state unable to ensure the safety of its female population was a failing one."[50]

In contrast to Halide and Huda's formative shopping experiences, for Musbah Haidar (1908–77) nearly two decades younger and socially elevated as member of the royal sheriffs of Mecca, trips to "the few English or French shops" in Pera were customary childhood excursions with her British-born mother.[51] Unusual for her, was a visit to the covered bazaar. Accompanied on the boat from Scutari by "a eunuch" they sat in the ferry "cabin reserved for the imperial family" further secluding themselves at the Albanian pudding shop where they "disappeared quickly to the back where there was a room reserved for Muslim ladies."[52] Within the mixed economy of gendered and classed spatial relations, her mother selectively utilized status-protecting seclusion.

Although women of all sorts were routinely present in the department stores of Pera and weekly markets by the turn of the twentieth century,[53] the persistent reputational risk of retail spaces explains the shock a little later of Demetra Vaka Brown on discovering young Muslim women shop clerks in the final years of the empire. As photographed by the now émigré Ottoman Greek on her return visit in 1921 (Figure 4.3), this young woman worker emblematizes the complicated transition into public labor for—in this instance—the now impoverished daughter of the Ottoman bureaucracy.[54] Given that distribution includes the embodied aesthetic labor of those who sell,[55] the unease relayed by Vaka Brown indicates the longevity and particularity of regional concerns about the moral risks of female public labor—as also women's public work in banks or offices. As with Euro-American panics about moral laxity of shopgirls—and their female customers—accompanying the development of the department store,[56] the transition into what were to become global distribution norms of fashion retail and lifestyle consumption brought generic and specific concerns to the modernizing Middle East.[57]

Elite Ottoman women rarely trained in a profession or trade, so fashion and lifestyle accomplishment skills were essential routes into respectable income generation in the hard years of the First World War and after. The location of labor and distribution networks mattered: in Istanbul in 1916 for the young widowed mother of Irfan Orga as with "many of the new poor [to] work in the privacy of their own homes was one thing, but to expose themselves in a Government [sewing] factory, quite another."[58] After the horrors of wartime factory work, his mother started taking her embroidery into the "bigger shops in Beyoğlu" where her own designs "gave a touch of uniqueness to her work, and individuality, which was liked by the discriminating foreign customers."[59] Visits to the European quarter aroused local attention and when she discarded her face veil—having "noticed that none of the foreign women wore them and that even a few of the more daring Turkish [Muslim] women from good families had ceased the practice"—his grandmother and local elders condemned her for behaving "like a fast woman or like a prostitute."[60] Neighborhood surveillance proved punitive and protective: after community men protected her—hence their—honor from a foreigner's unwelcome advances her "bare" face was countenanced.[61]

GIRL SERVING IN THE TURKISH
SHOP

Figure 4.3 *"Girl Serving in the Turkish Shop."* Published in *The Unveiled Ladies of Stamboul,* Demetra Vaka (Mrs. Kenneth Brown) (Boston: Houghton Mifflin Co., 1923).

"Western" Fashions and Modernity: Empress Eugénie and Cross-cultural Transmission

Despite that garments are produced by team input, hagiographic trends in fashion history and today's fashion media continue to subscribe to the unique creative imprint of the designer's singular vision. Taking hold in late-nineteenth-century Paris, this elevated role is often associated with the British designer Charles Worth who was integral to the development of the couture system.[62] Worth understood the advantages of having prominent women publicly wear his designs; for Empress Eugénie, this mutually beneficial relationship established her as a tastemaker in both Europe and the Ottoman Empire.

Eugénie's visit to Istanbul in 1869 with Napoleon III is now a well-known moment in the transnational transmission of fashion taste (Figure 4.4). Writing in 1907, while living in Europe, Zeynep Hanoum reminded readers that the empress's visit galvanized local styling for her grandmother's generation and was understood as significant beyond matters of fashion:

> The Empress of the French was incontestably beautiful – but *she was a woman*, and the first impression which engraved itself on the understanding of these poor Turkish captives, was, that their master, Abdülaziz, was paying homage *to a woman*…
>
> [After the visit] the women of the palace and the wives of the high functionaries copied as nearly as they could the appearance of the beautiful Empress… High-heeled shoes replaced the coloured *babouches*; they even adopted the hideous crinolines, and abandoned forever those charming Oriental garments the *chalvar* and *enturi,* which they considered symbols of servitude, but which no other fashion has been able to equal in beauty.[63]

Adapting French styles of dress and presentation, the imperial and social elite aligned themselves with an exceptional and aspirational model of femininity. Empress Eugénie's prominence in popularizing new styles of dress and body management[64]—learning to walk in high heels—is presented by Zeyneb Hanoum as

Figure 4.4 Empress Eugénie reviewing Ottoman troops. *Le Monde illustré,* November 6, 1869, p. 296. Source: gallica.bnf. fr (Bibliothèque nationale de France).

inseparable from her prominence socially. Visiting as a French empress, she is accorded masculinized spatial privileges unavailable to royal and elite Ottoman women, including the honorific function of reviewing the troops in a gender-mixed domain. Visual reports in the European press show Eugénie receiving the diplomatic corps in bustled[65] gown with long train characteristic of Worth's amendment to the previously fuller-fronted crinoline; echoed by the assembled diplomatic wives, this style was soon to become the Ottoman norm: "As might be supposed, the middle class soon followed the example of the palace ladies and adopted Western costume. Then there was a craze for everything French [which] lasted until our generation."[66]

Eugénie's 1869 visit continued rather than commenced processes by which the staging of Western fashion came to be a defining mode of modern dress for the Ottoman female elite and therefore of modernity for society as a whole. Knowledge of European fashion had long circulated through imported print media and was evaluated in the expanding Ottoman and Egyptian women's and feminist press of the late nineteenth century.[67] The press also "bombarded" Ottoman women throughout the empire with advertisements for imported fashion and household commodities, "which further 'globalized' female spending."[68]

Muslim Ottoman women were already acquiring and selectively adapting European styles.[69] So too minority population women, especially Greeks and Armenians whose community access to Western goods and foreign visitors may have accelerated commodity acquisition and style adaptation.[70] The celebration of Eugénie's Istanbul visit in the European illustrated press places her and her spectators in a communications medium through which European visuality was inserted into Ottoman life and vice versa.[71]

Zeyneb Hanoum's presumption that style would transmit from the palace elite to the middle classes accentuates that the Ottoman city had established mechanisms for the "trickle-down" of fashion styles so often regarded as a Western facet of modernity.[72] Imperial elite seclusion did not prevent wardrobe innovations being shared. The royal seasonal calendar might produce "a spurt of fashion excitement,"[73] as when the royal *khedival* family transferred from Egypt to their Bosporus *yalıs* (summer homes). Across the empire, the Turko-Circassion elite held tremendous cultural capital as tastemakers, influencer we might say today, in the creation of modes of modernity that encompassed the clothing, training, and daily activities of the modern body.

The Ottoman elite were imbricated in the early success of couture whose business model lent itself to adaptation for regional proprieties. Worth sent designs for approval and adjustment, and women from Ottoman and Egyptian court society shopped at European couturiers when they later traveled.[74] Fashion plates with fabric swatches in the Topkapı palace archives reveal material engagement from the 1870s.[75]

Fusion Fashion: Individuated and Collective Identification in the Expression of National Modernity

Two years prior to Empress Eugénie's visit, Sultan Abdülaziz himself toured the capitals of Europe. His triumphant return is described by Leyla Hanımefendi (1852–1936) in her account of life in the imperial palaces under seven sultans, compiled in the early 1920s.[76] Daughter of the royal surgeon, Hekim (doctor) Ismail Paşa, she was placed at four years old in Çırağan Palace as a lady-in-waiting to Munire Sultan, daughter of Sultan Abdülmecid.

Writing retrospectively, Leyla Hanımefendi describes how in 1867, then herself "a grand young lady" living with her parents, she was invited back to the Dolmabahçe palace to celebrate the arrival of Sultan Abdülaziz:

That day, all the princesses and the ladies of the Palace were wearing dresses in green … I knew very well that green was considered to be the colour of satisfied hopes and wishes [but] it had not occurred to me that I should wear this colour to the Serail on the occasion of His Majesty's return. By a happy circumstance, my dress was also green and I was rather relieved.

The *sultanes* wore green dresses, quite light, and trimmed with beautiful white lace. They had long trains and they wore big diadems along with rather simple necklaces. The older *kalfas* [their senior attendants] also wore green dresses, some plain, some striped and some even polka dots. The youngest girls wore light green dresses mixed with white … all the young ladies and young girls had completely abandoned the old dresses with three tails or trains and the baggy pants underneath; fashion now demanded skirts with a single train which was caught up and attached to the belt – there were now petticoats instead of *şalvars* or the baggy pants previously worn.[77]

The abandoned dresses were of a conventional *entari* design with side seam splits below the waist creating three trains.[78] The new garment with a single train to the rear was part of ongoing alterations to Middle Eastern garment construction. Unlike European-style tailoring that fitted clothes closer to the body, conventional Ottoman apparel for women and men achieved style by layering color and pattern in loose fitting garments. Standardized fabric lengths accommodated slower paced changes in cut, style, or color preference.

The fortunately green dress had been made that very day by Leyla Hanımefendi herself because her father, who "bought me everything necessary for my toilet" was "inflexible" that he "would not permit me to have my dresses made up by a dressmaker." Having learned to sew, she also had to teach the family's Circassian slaves "in those days quite a few."[79] Her gown was an exercise in multiple forms of transcultural fashion:

Among the materials which my father had bought for my future trousseau, there were three pieces of ancient watered silk especially woven in Lyon for *feraces*. This material was one meter twenty centimetres in width and had flowers along the two edges. By those days, *feraces* were no longer in style and the materials used for them were generally made up into dresses.[80]

European cloth manufactured for outmoded Ottoman garments is repurposed into contemporary Ottoman fusion dress. As a proactive consumer who also creates,[81] Leyla Hanımefendi melded past and present to transform transnational textile commodities into the latest local fashion, extending the value of her cache of high-status European fabrics.[82]

Fashion changes approved by tastemakers in the imperial harem were displayed in their own ensembles and on the enslaved, or manumitted, bodies of favorites, concubines, and kalfas. Adaptive practices in cut and fit combine with regional conventions of collective dressing to reaffirm color symbolism and group distinction. This communal mode of modernizing subject formation contrasts Western-centric views of fashion as central to the construction of the individuated choosing subject, the entrepreneurial self, of Western liberalism.[83] Methodologically, collective practices allow me to conceptualize how production and distribution play a role in the network of multiple fashion systems that were and are the reality of global fashion.[84] The expanded research base on Ottoman slavery enriches analysis of the role of style-fashion-dress in the formation of identity. Like many high-level Ottoman bureaucrats, Leyla Hanımefendi's own father, who was of Greek Christian origin, had been sold into slavery as a boy before converting to Islam and rising to senior roles.[85]

Free and Unfree Genders in the Construction of Taste and the Demonstration of Distinction

Huda Shaarawi reports on how women peddlers brought fashion goods to her elite family's home in Cairo:

These women, Coptic, Jewish and Armenian [displayed] their goods to the members of the household, they urged them to buy … claiming that the wife of a certain pasha or bey had purchased a particular article. If anyone inquired about the health of these ladies the peddlers disclosed bits of gossip and were quick to elaborate … although some were quite witty [they] often damaged prominent families through their indiscretion and lies. They also charged exorbitant prices. As a young girl I was cautioned about the peddlers and told of the trouble they could cause. With the unfolding of the years I saw this borne out.[86]

Leyla Hanımefendi details socially and ethnically stratified participation in textile and fashion selling and shopping in 1860s Istanbul. My selections highlight power relationships within the hierarchized Ottoman consumptionscape, tracing social subjects whose role in commodity distribution and fashion mediation might otherwise remain obscured. Like Shaarawi, Leyla Hanımefendi confirms that interactions with "strolling merchants" brought moral risks: a class of vendor "never admitted" to the palace[87] and considered "entirely unsuitable for our household,"[88] they were more

> successful in insinuating themselves into the *konaks* [large households, sometimes official residences]. First of all, they would seek to gain the good graces of the *kalfas* or the slaves by their persuasiveness and by the very thrill of buying something … Often they would even reach the young ladies of the house themselves. They were terrible intriguers and were sometimes involved in the most despicable trades.[89]

"[A]lmost completely disappeared" by her time of writing in the early 1920s, the strolling merchants were part of a diversified distribution system that ran from the permanent retail space of the covered bazaar, through "temporary" weekly markets to the "wandering merchants … Jews for the most part" selling from boats on the Bosphorus to ladies in waterside summer homes.[90] At the most exclusive end of the shopping chain, the royal ladies would "from time to time" shop in the covered bazaar.[91] As it was "not considered suitable to stop [their carriage] in front of the shops, much less to enter them," the princesses would be accommodated in the imperial section of the mosque.[92] The shopkeepers "would bring their merchandise to them and, in turn, these would be presented to the princesses by the eunuchs. The princess would then make her choice, the material would be cut into the appropriate sizes … the eunuch would settle the accounts with the merchants."[93]

A similar process was used when the kalfas shopped for themselves and other non-royal harem inhabitants. These high ranking stewards "had the choice of going shopping in these boutiques, but generally they preferred to make up a small list of articles … which they would give to the eunuch who, in turn, could order a footman to bring it to the purveyors to the Serail in the Bazaar."[94] Note that the kalfas abrogated to themselves a status-enhancing seclusion by avoiding the bazaar when not sequestered with royals. Note also there were preferred suppliers; the "purveyors to the Serail." Royal warrants did not ensure a palace retail monopoly, but their enhanced status as royal supplier—often over many years[95]—did presumably make them preferable to the kalfas whose proxy social status was dependent on connection to their royal mistresses. Arrived at the palace, further spatial dispersal transformed cloth into clothes: after distributing the bulk-bought fabric among their peers "and the girls [a] part of the material just purchased was then immediately sent to the dressmakers who already had all the measurements and quickly made up the dresses and returned them to the Serail."[96]

Within this circuit, which emphasizes the constant—controlled—permeability of the imperial harem's spatial boundaries, individual fitting is not yet required for custom making. Several fashion systems operated simultaneously; while European-style tailoring adapted the Ottoman garments worn to welcome the sultan, standardized garment pieces were not yet redundant. Patronage networks could still be enacted by the gifting of garments from one body to another.

Outside the palace, the "ladies of the konaks" also sent "the eunuch or woman in charge of their household to the Bazaar to pick out samples of material so they could make their choice at home."[97] When they did visit, they eschewed the mosque to avoid "the impression of imitating the Imperial Harem."[98] Down the social scale, "ladies of the small bourgeoisie" shopped in local weekly markets; visited occasionally by rich women heavily veiled to "preserve the strictest incognito."[99]

Women routinely present in weekly markets were the "[m]any Turkish [Muslim] women [selling] their own handwork";[100] Leyla Hanımefendi doesn't say if these poorer Muslim women wore *yaşmaks* over their hair and mouth or/and face veils over their eyes. By the turn of the twentieth century, women of all social classes crowded into the weekly outside markets.[101] Yet, "higher visibility was not necessarily related to frequency of visibility … poor women in crowds formed an 'invisible' mass, but rich women [were] more visible for they represented power and wealth."[102] Secluded elite women sometimes communicated directly with "notes to their dressmakers," like the late eighteenth-century princess Behice Sultan, but mostly "harem servants would act as intermediaries when placing orders."[103]

The dangers and opportunities of being visible in public underwrite why textiles and fashion commodities passed through so many, and such particular, hands before they reached the ladies of the imperial harem or the secluded elite household. As well as imbrication in material distribution networks—literally transporting goods—I see here forms of fashion mediation creating meanings and values for commodities. The merchants, male and female, deciding which goods to push to which client, as also the eunuchs and slaves or kalfas, were all surely involved in arbitrating which commodities would fall before the eye of their various consumers. This would have included, increasingly, a familiarity on everyone's part with the imported fashion imagery seen by elite subscribers to the periodic press and cascading—as in Europe—through the rest of the household. Alert to these variables, the proxy shoppers became key agents in the circuit of style-fashion-dress; grasping individual women's aesthetic preferences, familiar enough with height, body shape, and complexion to know what would fit and flatter, and able to make judgments on price and quality. When in Alexandria, Shaarawi eventually shed her shopping retinue of eunuch and women slaves it was because her mother had experienced for herself the dual advantages of "shopping in person"; "a wide range of goods to choose from [and] money to be saved through wise spending."[104]

The merchant's power as gatekeeper of taste and commodities could work against the client over more than price. Describing an incident from when she was very young, Leyla Hanımefendi recounts how at the wedding of Abdülmecid's daughter, Princess Munire, her mother was furious when another guest was wearing a "costume in every way identical to hers";[105] despite the merchant's assurance of exclusivity. The issue, beyond the comprehension of the child reporter, was not simply about competitive dressing. A footnote inserted by Leyla Hanımefendi's son informs that wearing dresses of same fabric signaled too much of an attachment between wearers: "In those days an identical dress worn by two ladies was considered to be an external sign, an express manifestation of a reciprocal sympathy which went beyond the admissible limits of pure and innocent friendship."[106]

This single reference to non-heteronormative relations—written not by Leyla Hanımefendi but inserted as explanation for what the child did not understand and the adult woman did not relay—indicates the fine gauge of dress practices. Sharing a color, shades of green at Abdülaziz's reception, was an acceptable collective dress act. So too, the same design in different colors, as with the princesses Cemile Sultan and Munire Sultan's matching wedding trousseau outfits. But wearing exactly the same ensemble might give rise to presumptions of unsanctioned intimacy or attachment.

The Displayed Body: Gifts and Aesthetic Labor as Fashion Mediation

I turn to a final movement of fashion commodities; not between seller and buyer, or seamstress and wearer, but between owner and slave, patron and client, gifter and giftée. In classic anthropology literature the gifting of objects is frequently relational and inherently ambiguous, building obligations to reciprocate which can be—a competitive—opportunity for status enhancement or loss.[107] Articles circulated as gifts may be fully alienable and transfer entirely to the giftée, or fully or partly inalienable with some components remaining in perpetuity with the original owner to whom, in some cultures, the article eventually returns. My exploration of fashion gifting as an aspect of gendered power also considers whether regional conventions of displaying finery on the bodies of others—mostly, but not only slaves—instigate parallel relations of prestige and servitude, obligation and reciprocity.

Within the royal palaces routine gifting of cloth, clothing, and jewelry to family and retainers was an institutionalized form of power and obligation itemized in palace accounts and monitored by all concerned.[108] Leyla Hanımefendi recounts: "It was the custom at the Serail, upon the occasion of Bayram [festival] to give brand new clothes to all the kalfes and to all the girls according to their station [and the] first eunuchs and the chiefs of the masculine personnel of the household."[109] In the khedival court English governess Emmeline Lott emphasized that gifted jewels "constitute the sole private fortune of their possessors" on the death of their "lord."[110] Pensions given as clothing allowance maintained patronage connections to ex-members of the imperial harem, including royal relations and manumitted slaves; mirrored in non-royal elite and middle-ranking households. Among women, the fashion commodity especially functioned as an essential form of patronage, allowing royal and elite women to exercise cultural capital as tastemakers within a system of sartorial status maintenance.[111]

While items endowed as gifts might be ostensibly alienable—forming a woman's wealth—in the Ottoman context asset ownership was generically insecure. For slaves—including the most elevated *kul*, the sultan's own male slaves—property ownership was always uncertain: as "human property" themselves, any riches an unmanumitted slave acquired—including jewels, property, clothes, and slaves—could be seized at whim by the sultan, or their owner.[112] For the sultan's non-slave subjects asset ownership was also chronically uncertain, with many families endowing *vakıf* (charity foundations) to protect assets at risk of reappropriation if they fell out of favor.[113]

As a young girl in the palace, Leyla Hanımefendi was gifted predictably at celebrations and spontaneously—evening gloves and feraçe for an unexpected dinner engagement. In either context, the object's connection to the royal donor was paramount: "My Sultane [Munire Sultan] gave me a present at Bayram – one of her dresses chosen among the most beautiful of all …"[114] Previously worn garments shared the status of the wearer with the recipient: "clothes that were worn by a princess were considered to be far more precious than anything brand new."[115] The honor of proximity through cloth to the royal body was granted several times to Leyla Hanımefendi, including her sister upon marriage receiving matching gowns worn in their trousseaux by princesses Cemile and Munire Sultan.[116]

Varied forms of distinction were available to free, manumitted, and unfree subjects by porting the fashion commodities of others. The display of garments and jewels on people's bodies was a common practice in the Middle East, recruiting slave and manumitted women, eunuchs, and free subjects into the embodied expression of royal or household wealth and status. Julia Pardoe wrote in 1835 of her visit to the Istanbul household of Mustafa Effendi, the Egyptian chargé d'affaires, where as a foreign woman she was accorded the masculine privilege of meeting the minister and sitting by his side. He had "four attendants":

two fine boys of twelve or fourteen years of age, and two pretty little girls, one or two years younger, gorgeously dressed, and wearing magnificent brilliant diamonds on their heads and bosoms.

The rage for diamonds is excessive among both the Turks and the Greeks; but while the Greek ladies delight in heaping upon their persons every ornament for which they can find space, many of the fair Osmanlis trousseaux … content themselves with a clasp or two, a bracelet or some similar bagatelle; and decorate their slaves with their more costly and ponderous jewels.[117]

Lott recounts similar in 1865 on Viceroy Ismail's ceremonial bayram harem visit:

Then the Grand Eunuch and his corps, dressed in new richly-embroidered uniforms, threw open the doors of the stone Hall trousseaux … and there stood trousseaux … like files of infantry, the whole retinue of slaves trousseaux … two such dazzling and brilliant lines of sparking jewels, as perhaps it never fell to the lot of an European lady to behold. There stood upwards of two hundred women, with their persons decorated with the most resplendent precious stones which the mineral kingdom had produced trousseaux …[118]

The royal wives and young princesses also "were resplendently ornamented with precious jewels" as were the "ladies of the Harem, and the whole of the slaves, were dressed in the richest silks, and were adorned with jewels, almost as costly as those of their Highnesses."[119] Despising nearly all the women she encounters, Lott's vicious racism rains on the black slaves:

It seemed to me quite a monstrosity, and absolute sin, that such immense wealth should be expended on those brilliant gewgaws merely to sparkle on the tawny and ebony skins of slaves, many of whom were repulsive in their looks; and whose habits, manners, customs, and appearance in general were totally repugnant to European feelings.

It was bad enough in all conscience to behold the white *oustas*, 'slaves,' bedecked with gems of almost priceless value, many of whose *sarats*, 'trunks,' contained *parures* far more valuable than the jewel-cases of the noblest and wealthiest of the lovely beauties of the European Courts trousseaux …[120]

The display of jewels on slaves is not a gift: it is another form of appropriation of their body into service in which women slaves and eunuchs performed a mannequin function for palace audiences. In Euro-America, techniques of the body for the effective display of fashion commodities not of one's personal possession were also being developed—by the female mannequins who established the modern role of fashion model from the 1880s.[121] Here, the governance of the paid-for body on display entwined moral and commercial concerns into international modeling norms—the disdainful gaze, still with us today. So too did slaves of all genders in elite harems learn comportment. In both terrains, the embodied aesthetic labor of the mannequin might offer advantages through proximity to high status fashion commodities not of one's own. To port the patron's possessions could be status-enhancing for slave and free subjects alike. When an entire cohort of eunuchs or women slaves are dressed in new clothes the generalization reduces opportunities for distinction. But when selected subjects are given different outfits or jewels the individuation could show favor and advancement.

Note then, Leyla Hanımefendi's account of displaying the wealth of others: accustomed to seeing "such a profusion of beautiful jewelry around my mistress – often I would wear some of it myself," she attested that "precious stones and money [never provoked] envy or desire."[122] Having demonstrated aesthetic appreciation without covetousness, she itemizes Princess Munire's finest jewels, ending, "finally, there was a set of diamond knots [earrings] which the Princess let me wear when she took me on a walk."[123] The "let me wear" implies either and both a child's request or imperial benevolence. The bejeweled saunters of the favored girl were presumably within a palace garden, or pleasure garden, which screened royal women from public view; her patron's status and taste communicated to an audience of women residents, visitors, slaves, servants, and eunuchs. These incidents of clientage reveal her infantile role in advancing family social capital, with jewels lent also to her sister.[124] When jewels are paraded on the bodies of the free, the honor of wearing ornaments that carry the imprint of their royal owner—like the enhanced value of hand-me-down royal clothes—produces forms of status distinction not dependent on acquiring an inalienable right to the item.

Fashion gifting provided giftees with opportunities to express attachments traversing space and time. In the non-verbal communication of social relations paying attention to the history of garments and cloth—the social life of things[125]—was important. Returning from the festivities at Dolmabahçe palace, Leyla Hanımefendi was unexpectedly invited to the palace of Fatma Sultan. Changing quickly, she "[took] care to wear a fine dress; I had a pearl gray feraçe which I had made from one of the four pieces of silk the Sultane has sent me in Crete [where her father had been governor], and white gloves."[126] Consciousness of when and where to deploy the silk in the years after its bestowal maximized the gift value: Leyla Hanımefendi took "care" in crafting a toilet that included the Sultan's silk, reinforcing her association with and loyalty to her royal patron.

Conclusion

This chapter has applied contemporary circuit models of culture and style-fashion-dress to the modernizing Middle East to delineate the actors who bring fashion commodities onto bodies in processes of modern subject formation. Across social sectors I connect fashion activities of enslaved, manumitted, and free subjects. My focus on the nodal point of fashion distribution repositions women and eunuch slaves and servants as fashion mediators alongside peddlers and merchants. Brokering consumption for the wealthy and contributing to the formulation of taste, they are agentive in regional adaptations of emerging Westernized norms of fashion retail and consumption.

My focus on gendered spatiality within a socially stratified consumptionscape relates women's changing consumption opportunities to their uneasy entry into public fashion work in the First World War and after. I explore the regional convention of displaying finery on the bodies of slaves and clients as aesthetic labor; comparable to the coterminous professionalization of fashion modeling. The dispersal of fashion artifacts as payment and patronage I read through gift theory, detailing how cultural and social capital enables clients to recraft gifted fabrics into strategic displays of contemporary transnational fusion fashion.

Notes

1   Paul Du Gay, Stuart Hall, Linda Janes, Anders Koed Madsen, Hugh Mackay, and Keith Negus, *Doing Cultural Studies: The Story of the Sony Walkman*, 2nd edn (1997; Milton Keynes: Open University, 2013).

2   Susan Kaiser, *Fashion and Cultural Studies* (London: Bloomsbury, 2012).

3   See, for example, Leslie W. Rabine, *The Global Circulation of African Fashion* (Oxford: Berg, 2002); Jennifer Craick, *Fashion: Key Concepts* (London: Bloomsbury, 2009); Sandra Niessen, Ann Marie Leshkowich and Carla Jones, eds., *Re-orienting Fashion: The Globalization of Asian Dress* (Oxford and New York: Berg, 2003); Giorgio Riello and Peter McNeil, *The Fashion History Reader: Global Perspectives* (London: Routledge, 2010).

4   Marshal G. S Hodgson, *The Venture of Islam: Conscience and History in a World Civilization*, vol. 1 (Chicago: University of Chicago Press, 1974).

5   Chris Warhurst and Dennis Nickson, "Employee Experience of Aesthetic Labour in Retail and Hospitality," *Work, Employment and Society* 21, no. 1 (2007): 103–20; Joanne Entwistle, *The Aesthetic Economy of Fashion: Markets and Value in Clothing and Modelling* (Oxford: Berg, 2009).

6   Like Kaiser, I draw on Carol Tulloch, "Style—Fashion—Dress: From Black to Post-Black," *Fashion Theory* 14, no. 3 (2010): 273–303.

7   Joanne Entwistle and Agnès Rocamora, "The Field of Fashion Materialized: A Study of London Fashion Week," *Sociology* 40, no. 4 (2006): 735–51.

8   See also Afsaneh Najmabadi, *Women with Mustaches and Men without Beards: Gender and Sexual Anxieties of Iranian Modernity* (Berkeley: University of California Press, 2005); Joseph Boone, *The Homoerotics of Orientalism* (New York: Columbia University Press, 2014); Dror Zeʾevi, *Producing Desire: Changing Sexual Discourse in the Ottoman Middle East, 1500–1900* (Berkeley: University of California Press, 2006); Serkan Delice, "The Janissaries and their Bedfellows: Masculinity and Male Homosexuality in Early Modern Ottoman Istanbul, 1500–1826," PhD thesis (University of the Arts London, 2015).

9   Madeline C. Zilfi, *Women and Slavery in the Late Ottoman Empire* (Cambridge: Cambridge University Press, 2010), 46.

10 Ebru Boyar and Kate Fleet, *A Social History of Ottoman Istanbul* (Cambridge: Cambridge University Press, 2010), 180–81.

11 Zilfi, *Slavery,* 44.

12 du Gay et al., *Cultural Studies*, xxx–xxxi, original emphasis.

13 Suraiya Faroqhi, "Introduction, or Why and How One Might Want to Study Ottoman Clothes," in *Ottoman Costumes: From Textile to Identity*, eds. Suraiya Faroqhi and Christof K Neuman, 15–48 (Istanbul: Eren, 2004).

14 Sarah Graham-Brown, *Images of Women: The Portrayal of Women in Photography of the Middle East 1860–1950* (London: Quartet, 1988); Nancy Micklewright, "Personal, Public and Political (Re)Constructions: Photographs and Consumption," in *Consumption Studies and the History of the Ottoman Empire, 1550–1922*, 261–288 ed. Donald Quataert, 261–88 (New York: SUNY Press, 2000); Ali Behdad and Luke Gartlan, eds., *Photography's Orientalism: New Essays on Colonial Representation* (Los Angeles: Getty Research Institute, 2013).

15 Billie Melman, *Women's Orients: English Women and the Middle East, 1718–1918: Sexuality, Religion and Work* (London: Macmillan, 1992); Meyda Yeğenoğlu, *Colonial Fantasies: Towards a Feminist Reading of Orientalism* (Cambridge: Cambridge University Press, 1998); Teresa Heffernan, *Veiled Figures: Women, Modernity, and the Spectres of Orientalism* (Toronto: University of Toronto Press, 2016); Reina Lewis, *Gendering Orientalism: Race, Femininity and Representation* (London: Routledge, 1996); Reina Lewis, *Rethinking Orientalism: Women, Travel, and the Ottoman Harem* (London: IB Tauris, 2004); Ruth Bernard Yeazell, *Harems of the Mind: Passages of Western Art and Literature* (New Haven, CT: Yale University Press, 2000); Ruth Barzilai-Lumbroso, "Turkish Men and the History of Ottoman Women: Studying the History of the Ottoman Dynasty's Private Sphere through Women's Writing," *Journal of Middle East Women's Studies* 5, no. 2 Spring (2009): 53–82.

16 Mary Louise Pratt, *Imperial Eyes: Travel Writing and Transculturation* (London: Routledge, 1992).

17 Mary Roberts, *Intimate Outsiders: The Harem in Ottoman and Orientalist Art and Travel Literature* (Durham: Duke University Press, 2007).

18 Najmabadi, this volume.

19 Alan Duben and Cem Behar, *Istanbul Households: Marriage, Family and Fertility, 1880–1940* (Cambridge: Cambridge University Press, 1991). See also for Lebanon where nucleated was not the model of family modernity, Stephen Sheehi, "A Social History of Early Arab Photography or a Prolegomenon to an Archaeology of the Lebanese Imago," *International Journal of Middle East Studies* 39, no. 2 (May 2007): 175–206, 191 (original emphasis).

20 Kaiser, *Cultural Studies,* 21

21 Leslie Peirce, "Writing Histories of Sexuality in the Middle East," *American Historical Review* 114, no. 5 (December 2009): 1325–39.

22 James Smalls, "Menace at the Portal: Masculine Desire and the Homoerotics of Orientalism," in *Orientalism, Eroticism, and Modern Visuality in Global Cultures*, eds. Julie Codell and Joan Del Plato, 43–72 (London: Routledge, 2018); Jateen Lad, "Panoptic Bodies: Black Eunuchs as Guardians of the Topkapı Harem," in *Harem Histories: Envisioning Places and Living Spaces*, ed. Marilyn Booth, 136–76 (Durham: Duke University Press, 2010).

23 Scott Siraj al-Haqq Kugle, *Homosexuality In Islam* (London: Oneworld Publications, 2010).

24 Eve Troutt Powell, *Tell This in My Memory: Stories of Enslavement from Egypt, Sudan and the Ottoman Empire* (Stanford: Stanford University Press, 2012)

25 Ibid., 121–27. See also Margot Badran, *Feminists, Islam, and Nation: Gender and the Making of Modern Egypt* (Princeton: Princeton University Press, 1996).

26 Halide Adivar Edib, *Memoirs of Halidé Edib* (London: John Murray, 1926).

27 On nostalgic renditions of childhood relations with slaves in women's memoirs, see Troutt Powell, *Tell This*, 120.

28 Zilfi, *Slavery*, 15

29 Ibid.

30 Sevgi Ağca, "Organizational Structure of Topkapı Harem," in *Topkapı Palace: The Imperial Harem: House of the Sultan* (Istanbul: Topkapı Palace Museum, 2012), 14.

31 Topkapı Palace Museum, "Chest" plate 28, 142; Zilfi, *Slavery*, 124.

32 Ağca, *Organizational Structure,* 14.

33 Kate Fleet, "The Extremes of Visibility; Slave Women in Ottoman Public Space," in *Ottoman Women in Public Space*, eds. Ebru Boyar and Kate Fleet, 128–49 (Leiden: Brill, 2016). See also Melek Hanoum, *Thirty Years in the Harem: or the Autobiography of Melek-Hanoum, Wife of H.H. Kibrizli-Mehemet-Pasha* (London: Chapman and Hall, 1872); Mary Ann Fay, "From Concubines to Capitalists: Women, Property, and Power in Eighteenth-century Cairo," *Journal of Women's History* 10, no. 3 (1988): 118–41.

34 Zilfi, *Slavery.*

35 Fleet, *Extremes of Visibility.*

36 Ibid., 148–49. Also Fanny Davis *The Ottoman Lady: A Social History from 1718–1918* (New York: Greenwood Press, 1986).

37 Ebru Boyar, "An Imagined Moral Community: Ottoman Female Public Presence, Honour and Marginality," in *Ottoman Women in Public Space*, eds. Ebru Boyar and Kate Fleet (Leiden: Brill, 2016), 208.

38 Ibid.

39 And some by men.

40 Nancy Reynolds, *A City Consumed: Urban Commerce, the Cairo Fire, and the Politics of Decolonization in Egypt* (Stanford: Stanford University Press, 2012).

41 Named in Shaarawi's account, Said Agha became a personage of sufficient prominence to be caricatured alongside the reformer herself in the satirical press. Troutt Powell identifies him as al-Bash Aga in the cartoon shown in *Al-Kashkul*, January 21, 1926. See also Zilfi, *Slavery*, 117.

42 Kaiser, *Cultural Studies*, 19

43 Ibid.

44 du Gay et al., *Doing Cultural Studies*, 79–81

45 Edith Gülçin Ambros, Ebru Boyar, Palmira Brummett, Kate Fleet, Svetla Ianeva, "Ottoman Women in Public Space: an Introduction," in *Ottoman Women in Public Space*, eds. Ebru Boyar and Kate Fleet (Leiden: Brill, 2016), 3.

46 Janet L. Abu-Lughod, "The Islamic City – Historic Myth, Islamic Essence, and Contemporary Relevance," *International Journal of Middle East Studies* 19 (1987): 155–76, 168.

47 Kate Fleet, "The Powerful Public Presence of the Ottoman Female Consumer," in *Ottoman Women in Public Space*, eds. Ebru Boyar and Kate Fleet, 128–49 (Leiden: Brill, 2016).

48 Zilfi, *Slavery.*

49 Zilfi *Slavery* cites 1847 and 1861.

50 Fleet, *Public Presence*, 108

51 Musbah Haidar, *Arabesque* (London: Hutchinson, 1944), 49.

52 Ibid., 50

53 Fleet, *Public Presence*, 99.

54 Demetra Vaka (Mrs. Kenneth Brown), *The Unveiled Ladies of Stamboul* (Boston: Houghton Mifflin Co., 1923).

55 Lynne Pettinger, "Brand Culture and Branded Workers: Service Work and Aesthetic Labour in Fashion Retail," *Consumption, Markets and Culture* 7, no. 2 (June 2004): 165–84.

56 Susan Porter Benson, *Counter Cultures: Saleswomen, Managers, and Customers in American Department Stores 1890–1940* (Champaign: University of Illinois Press, 1988).

57 Reynolds, *City Consumed*, 67.

58 Irfan Orga, *Portrait of a Turkish Family* (London: Victor Gollancz, 1950), 157.

59 Ibid., 185.

60 Ibid., 186.

61 Ibid., 188.

62   And alert to the international market, Caroline Evans, *The Mechanical Smile: Modernism and the First Fashion Shows in France and America, 1900–1929* (New Haven: Yale University Press, 2013).

63   Zeyneb Hanoum, *A Turkish Woman's European Impressions*, edited and with an introduction by Grace Ellison (London: Seeley, Service and Co., 1913), 96–98, original emphasis.

64   Marcel Mauss, "Techniques of the Body," *Economy and Society* 2, no. 1 (1973): 70–88.

65   On the bustle as Ottoman influence, Charlotte Jirousek, "Ottoman Influences in Western Dress," in *Ottoman Costumes: From Textile to Identity*, eds. Suraiya Faroqhi and Christof K Neumann, 231–51 (Istanbul: Eren Publishing, 2005).

66   Hanoum, *European Impressions,* 98

67   Beth Baron, *The Women's Awakening in Egypt: Culture, Society and the Press* (New Haven: Yale University Press, 1994).

68   Fleet, *Public Presence*, 117.

69   Elizabeth B. Frierson, "Mirrors Out, Mirrors In: Domestication and Rejection of the Foreign in Late-Ottoman Women's Magazines," in *Women, Patronage, and Self-Representation in Islamic Societies*, ed. Dede Fairchild Ruggles, 177–204 (New York: State University of New York Press, 2000).

70   Onur İnal, "Women's Fashions in Transition: Ottoman Borderlands and the Anglo-Ottoman Exchange of Costumes," *Journal of World History* 22, no. 2 (June 2011): 243–272.

71   Roberts, this volume

72   From the eighteenth century, Fleet, *Public Presence*, 115.

73   Ibid., 119.

74   Alex Aubry, "Beyond Orientalism: A Journey Through Two Centuries of Muslim Patronage at the Paris Haute Couture," in *Contemporary Muslim Fashions*, eds. Jill D'Alessandro and Reina Lewis, 64–73 (San Francisco: Fine Arts Museums of San Francisco, 2018).

75   Selin İpek, "Festive Finery for The Harem: Seamstress Mademoiselle Kokona's Order Book," in *Topkapı Palace: The Imperial Harem: House of the Sultan*, ed. Gül İrepoğlu (Istanbul: Topkapı Palace Museum, 2012), 56–59; Semra Germaner and Zeynep İnankur, *Constantinople and the Orientalists* (Istanbul: İşbank, 2002).

76   Leyla Hanimeffendi's narrative appeared as interviews in the Turkish press in the early 1920s, and was then revised with her son for French publication in 1925—translated into English in 1994. Although her retrospective composition likely melds episodes and observations, her rare insight into the imperial court until the dissolution of the sultanate in 1922 is invaluable to researchers. She is unusually attentive to fine distinctions in consumption habits among the royal elite, other social classes, and slave communities. See also Reina Lewis and Nancy Micklewright, eds., *Gender, Modernity and Liberty: Middle Eastern and Western Women's Writings: A Critical Sourcebook* (London: I.B. Tauris, 2006).

77   Leyla Hanımefendi, *The Imperial Harem of the Sultans: Memoirs of Leyla (Saz) Hanımefendi* (1922; Istanbul: Peva Publications, 1994), 162.

78   Micklewright, this volume. See also Lale Görünür, ed., *Women's Costume of the Late Ottoman Era from the Sadberk Hanım Museum Collection* (Istanbul: Vehbi Koç Foundation, Sadberk Hanım Museum, 2010).

79   Leyla Hanımefendi, *Imperial Harem*, 160–61.

80   Ibid., 161.

81   Contemporary transnational fashion studies illuminate on diaspora infrastructure for designer/consumer. See Parminder Bhachu, *Dangerous Design: Asian Women Fashion the Diaspora Economics* (London: Routledge, 2004).

82   Fleet, *Public Presence*.

83   Nikolas Rose, ed., *Governing the Soul: The Shaping of the Private Self*, 2nd edn (1989; London: Free Association Books, 1999).

84   Parallels include contemporary *aso-ebi* (cloth of the family) as gifted and purchased uniform dress in Nigeria and beyond—I thank Tolu Omoyele.

85   Born on an Aegean island, Hekim Ismail Paşa was bought in the Izmir slave market as a trainee by a Jewish doctor. His senior positions in the Ottoman bureaucracy included serving as Governor General of Izmir, and later Crete.

86   Huda Shaarawi, *Harem Years: The Memoirs of an Egyptian Feminist (1879–1942)*, trans. and ed. Margo Badran (New York: The Feminist Press, [n.d.] 1987), in Lewis and Micklewright, *Gender, Modernity and Liberty*, 191

87   Leyla Hanımefendi, *Imperial Palace*, 117.

88   Ibid., 180.

89   Ibid., 117–18.

90   Ibid., 117.

91   Ibid., 115.

92   Ibid.

93   Ibid.

94   Ibid., 115–116.

95   Topkapı Palace Museum, "Order Book," caption 34, 125.

96   Leyla Hanımefendi, *Imperial Harem*, all 115–16.

97   Ibid., 116.

98   Ibid.

99   Ibid.

100   Ibid.

101   Fleet, *Public Presence*, 99.

102   Ambros et al., *Ottoman Women*, 6.

103   Ipek, *Festive Finery*, 56–58.

104   Shaarawi, *Harem Years*, 192.

105   Leyla Hanımefendi, *Imperial Harem*, 203.

106   Ibid., n 208.

107   For a summary regarding fashion, see Anna-Mari Almila and David Inglis, "On the Hijab-Gift: Theoretical Considerations on the Ambiguities of Islamic Veiling in a Diasporic Context," *Journal of Cultural Analysis of Social Change* 3, no. 1 (2018).

108   Ağca, *Organizational Structure*.

109   Leyla Hanımefendi, *Imperial Harem*, 144.

110   Lott, *Harem Life*, 129.

111   Zilfi, *Slavery*.

112   Ibid., 101

113   Foundations also protected assets of manumitted slaves. Boyar and Fleet, *A Social History of Ottoman Istanbul* (Cambridge: Cambridge University Press, 2010), 144–49.

114   Ibid., 144.

115   Ibid., 185. On receipt of a dress belonging to Refia Sultane, Leyla Hanımefendi discovered that the princess "had had it adjusted to my size," ibid., 178.

116   Ibid., 190.

117   Julia Pardoe, "The City of the Sultan, and the Domestic Manners of the Turks, in 1836" (London: Henry Colburn, 1837), in *Gender, Modernity and Liberty*, ed. Lewis and Micklewright, 113.

118   Lott, *Harem Life*, 162.

119   Ibid., 160.

120   Ibid., 128–29. The trunks were likely their manumission "trousseaux."

121   Evans, *Mechanical Smile*.

122   Leyla Hanımefendi, *Imperial Harem*, 183.

123   Ibid., 189.

124   Ibid., 188–89.

125   Arjun Appadurai, ed., *The Social Life of Things: Commodities in Cultural Perspective* (Cambridge: Cambridge university Press, 1988).

126   Leyla Hanımefendi, *Imperial Harem*, 166–67.

CHAPTER 5

CONSTANTIN GUYS AND THE PAINTERS OF GLOBAL MODERNITY

Mary Roberts

Until recently, art historians have considered Paris the capital of nineteenth-century modernity, with the most radical avant-garde developments in picture-making emerging in the context of this modern city that was systematically transformed by Georges-Eugène Haussmann's vast public works program. In 1863, Charles Baudelaire famously essayed these profound changes to life and art, championing the work of Constantin Guys as the exemplary painter of Parisian modern life.[1] Contemporary fashion and the modern body were brought to center stage in Baudelaire's essay, and made radically prominent in the realm of high art. For Baudelaire, Guys' sketches of modern bodies in Paris are significant because they visualize the contingencies of modernity. In the same period, cities of the Near East, by contrast, so the art historical story goes, were rendered in an indeterminate time of the "orient," sealed out of modernity, in the hands of European artists, even on the canvases of aesthetic radicals such as Eugène Delacroix.[2] The terms of such art historical verities, its eurocentrism, are now being called into question as art historians address the intersecting visual cultures of global modernity. This essay is concerned with a range of images by Ottoman patrons and European artists that trouble such accounts of nineteenth-century modernism and Orientalism. They exemplify a little-studied impulse in European art: the Orientalism of modern life.

What is the Orientalism of modern life? We find it in the midst of French modernism, in Baudelaire's iconic essay that includes Guys' sketches of Istanbul during the Crimean War. Guys' Orientalism was an aesthetics of alliance, attuned to the sartorial modernity of the city's Ottoman elites and the contingencies of cross-cultural encounter between Ottoman, British, and French allies in Istanbul at this pivotal moment in modern military history. Comparing these sketches to prints derived from them for the *Illustrated London News* provides rare insight as to procedures of visual mediation through print journalism. From sketch to print, Ottoman culture is rendered more exotic, less engaged in defining its modernity. Like Guys, two decades later Walter Charles Horsley rendered the Ottoman imperial capital for the British illustrated press. Horsley's Orientalism inscribed the contingencies of seeing and looking for passengers within Istanbul's novel urban infrastructure, the new underground railway, the second in the world. Horsley crossed the divide between popular culture and high art when he brought his Orientalism of modern life to the Royal Academy in London. The imperial messaging of his painting is evident through its sartorial iconography and their global circulation through colonial networks of collecting. Such Orientalist impulses were selectively embraced and contested by local elites. Throughout this essay, I analyze this Orientalism of modern life contrapuntally, within a more expansive cultural geography that encompasses contemporaneous art and patronage of Ottoman elites. Such a conjunction reveals that elite Ottoman women's engagement with visual culture shares some of the experimental approach to aesthetics that Baudelaire recognized in the work of Constantin Guys.

Sincere thanks to Reina Lewis, Yasmine Nachabe Taan, and Catherine Blake.
All words are in contemporary Turkish unless they are in the quotations in which case I have kept them as rendered in these sources.

The Orientalism of Modern Life

The anecdotal humor of Walter Charles Horsley's painting, *Great Britain in Egypt, 1886* (Figure 5.1) is premised upon the contingencies of a casual encounter between strangers in a Cairo street café. The joke is encoded through sartorial contrasts and varied dispositions of bodies. Two military men, off-duty avatars of British Empire, are served by a young woman in a splendid yellow silk dress dexterously pouring coffee into the small *fincan* and *zarf* poised on her tray. There is a frisson to this proximity of bodies. The sensuous East is teasingly close to these restrained soldiers of Empire. In response the kilted Scotsman's eyes are studiously engaged at head height, while his English companion stares straight ahead, body rigid, avoiding eye contact with the woman whose cleavage is within inches of his face. Uniforms of Empire constrain and discipline these British bodies in counterpoint to the more climatically appropriate clothing and casual dispositions evident across the arc of local men who scrutinize these foreigners. The glowing white clothing of the man on the right registers the extreme heat and bleached light on this Cairo day in 1886. This man's effort to shield his eyes from full sun in order to see what is transpiring under the canvas awning underscores the locals' curiosity about these foreign soldiers.

Figure 5.1 *Great Britain in Egypt, 1886*, 1887, by Walter Charles Horsley. Oil on Canvas, 122.5 x 154.9 cm. Art Gallery of New South Wales, Sydney.

Although the humor is at the expense of these discomfited British soldiers, it stands on the firm ground of an unassailable fact of modern British imperial might. In this painting of commercial sociability, Great Britain in Egypt is incongruous but ultimately benign. The British occupying forces are welcomed with a cup of coffee, attended to by a woman who is overdressed for a Cairo street café but whose sartorial opulence serves a British audience's expectations of a luxurious Orient. In 1887 the critic for the *Athenaeum* read her as a young Jewish woman, implying a level of insight that the city's respectable Muslim women would not work in such a capacity nor unveil in this public space.[3] But the sensuous charge of the encounter recalls the Orientalist trope of the odalisque.[4] It is this sensuality that allows our artist to stage his wry humor about cultural difference for an art audience in the British imperial capital in 1887, when it was shown at the Royal Academy.

Horsley's painting journeyed to another far-flung site of British Empire in 1888 for the Centennial International Exhibition in Melbourne, Australia, where it struck a chord with the trustees in the colony of New South Wales. They were moved to purchase it in 1889 for their fledgling collection in Sydney.[5] In this context British Orientalism promised to bolster the cultural capital of the aspiring young settler colony. This painting's perambulations, implicated in the global reach of British Empire in the southern hemisphere, cues us to the international mutability and local particularity of Orientalism's cultural geography. This is an imperial painting, an artifact of colonial collecting but, perhaps most radically, this Orientalism is a painting of modern life.[6]

An Aesthetics of Alliance

The Ottoman capital Istanbul has been occluded from histories of nineteenth-century French modernism in our own time, yet that most renowned avatar of the French avant-garde, Baudelaire, connected the city to an aesthetic discourse of modernity through Constantin Guys' sketches produced on the "operatic" shores of the Bosporus. While in the employ of the *Illustrated London News*, Guys' visits to the theater of modern warfare in the Crimea between 1853 and 1856 were punctuated by extended spells in Istanbul.[7] Like Horsley's *Great Britain in Egypt, 1886*, Guys represented a British military presence in the Near East. In Istanbul Guys observed public ceremonies and incidents of daily life at a moment when the allied British, French, and Ottoman troops were ubiquitous in the public spaces of this cosmopolitan capital.[8] For Baudelaire, Guys' genius resided in his swift renditions of contingent encounters between East and West.

The French critic discovered within Guys' carefully observed and passionately rendered crowd scenes at a ceremony in Sultanahmet, not a timeless Orient but a quintessentially modern spectacle:

> Monsieur G. excels in treating the pageantry of official functions, national pomps and circumstances, but never coldly and didactically, like those painters who see in work of this kind no more than a piece of lucrative drudgery. He works with all the ardour of a man in love with space, with perspective, with light lying in pools or exploding in bursts, drops or diamonds of it sticking to the rough surfaces of uniforms and court toilettes.[9]

Baudelaire's Istanbul was one of the cities in which this man of the world, "an 'I' with an insatiable appetite for the 'non-I,'" immerses himself in the crowd, "at every instant rendering and explaining it in pictures more living than life itself."[10] In this city, according to the critic, compelling art is born through Guys' passionate encounter with cultural difference; Baudelaire's aesthetic privileges the disjunctive signifiers of cultural contact.

In Guys' sketch of the Kurban Bayramı[11] ceremony in the Topkapı palace courtyard (Figure 5.2), his fascination with the crowd emerges in his rendering of the military band with a remarkable economy of

Figure 5.2 *The Ceremony of Kurban Bayramı* (reference sketch for illustration published in the *Illustrated London News*), 1856, by Constantin Guys. Photographer: Jenni Carter.

lively ink marks. Italian composer Donizetti is at the helm, conducting the Ottoman Palace band, but his presence is diminutive compared with the lively rendition of his musicians whose bodies are fused with their instruments.[12] Look, for example, at our clarinetist, third from the right, whose rigid body channels all effort into marshaling breath to create sound through his reed instrument. So too, the syncopated bells of the brass instruments are rhythmically disposed across the grouping. Guys draws music.

We can situate Guys' sketch within an Ottoman lineage of visualizing such ritualistic performances of loyalty to the Ottoman sovereign at the Gate of Felicity in the Second Courtyard of the Topkapı Palace. An earlier work, destined for the palace collection, was painted by the Ottoman-Greek artist Konstantin Kapıdağlı in 1789 for Sultan Selim III and a later one, a preliminary oil sketch honoring Sultan Abdülaziz, was rendered by his Polish court painter Stanisław Chlebowski.[13] In all three works the ceremonial massing of bodies in this courtyard forms art's visual rhythm. But in the two paintings, the Empire's continuity, order, and renewal are rendered through costume, ceremonial objects, and the paintings' visual logic. Disciplined bodies are massed in clear social groupings whose place in the Empire's administrative, religious, and military sectors are legible through their distinctive costume. All render obeisance to the Sultan.

This crowded ceremonial courtyard is organized in strict hierarchical relation to the Empire's hereditary ruler and each representation, like the ceremony itself, invokes prior iterations and anticipates the next.[14] Sultan Murad III's 1585 ceremonial throne placed at the threshold of the Gate of Felicity is the most prominent material signifier of continuity, while renewal takes distinct forms that are appropriate to each painting's respective historic moment. In 1789, Kapıdağlı meticulously rendered the recently refurbished ceremonial gate with its lavish gilded arabesque architectural ornament and innovative landscape murals in all of its modern Ottoman Baroque magnificence.[15] In Chlebowski's oil sketch renewal is most conspicuously marked by Tanzimat costume reform in the dress uniforms of the military and administrative elites and the modern attire of the Sultan himself. These commemorative paintings are produced for very different contexts than Guys' sketch. His work traveled to London with instructions for how it was to be transformed for publication in the *Illustrated London News* (Figure 5.3).

Guys' sketch anticipates its transformation, indeed is directed toward it. Both sides of his page are encased with visual shorthand and extensive textual explanation and instruction to his printmaker that foreshadows the future work of this working drawing. The outcome is a collaboratively authored engraving published nineteen days after the ceremony. Across this spatio-temporal interval, Guys' panoramic survey of the courtyard ceremony and its audience has been cropped into a print that frames only its main actors, giving a new visual prominence to the *ulema*, the Empire's senior religious figures.

On the back of his sketch Guys writes:

> I showed the procession of the Ulémas in preference to the high dignitaries, not only as their costume is the only one that has [not] yet lost its oriental majesty and splendour, but as they are the only ones that prosterned themselves so low, and performed this old turkish farce in its original style.[16]

THE BAIRAM.—THE SULTAN'S LEVEE, IN THE GARDEN OF THE SERAGLIO.

Figure 5.3 *The Bairam – The Sultan's Levee, in the Garden of the Seraglio*, 1856, unknown engraver. Published in the *Illustrated London News*, August 30, 1856, p. 218.

In fact, contrary to this claim, Guys has barely rendered the ulema. A few quick lines register one among this group kissing the hem of the Sultan's cloak, but he has even less prominence than the figures of the European observers in their hats and parasols on the left behind the railing (see Figure 5.2). This sole representative of the religious fraternity is easily overlooked in favor of the noisy crowd and the band's musical exuberance. Giving them greater prominence will become the work of his collaborator in London. The rows of dignitaries on either side of Sultan Abdülmecid, who will be rendered in such detail in the print, exist only as indicative text in Guys' sketch. A vivid description of the costume of the ulema resides on the verso of this page, where Guys writes:

> The Ulémas here (body of) are the priests that belong to all the mosquées of Constantinople – Every one of them wears a peculiar colour, and more or less Embroidery according to the importance of their Parish! – the Turbans are more or less modernized that is the smaller the more approaching the European importations – some have green, some white ones – only there is a flat extremity with a gold fringe falling on the left, there are young and fine fellows, with Elegant faces, and a very distingué – air, some are nearly negroes some with white beard and bronze faces – && so that there is an immense field for displaying variety of, the only uniformity that exist[s] in their costume is in the shape of their gowns – the upper part of it, I mean the collar and body, being made like a common coat and embroidered like an European court dress – so, but sleeves are loose, and yellow babouches! Look again for the rest of Explanations.[17]

To compensate for his cursory treatment of the ulema in his larger drawing at some point Guys turned his page over and rotated it to add the full-length figure of a bearded religious man in profile (Figure 5.4). The engraver in London evidently seized upon this parenthetical figure and multiplies him center stage across the foreground of the *ILN* print (Figure 5.3). These figures in darkest shades prominently inhabit the foreground of the print pushing to the margins our military and administrative elites in their modern uniforms. The age and racial diversity of the ulema that Guys writes about is absent, so too the most conspicuous sartorial detail of modernization in their dress. The prominent jaunty collar, an *au courant* modification in ceremonial dress, is absent in the *ILN* print (Figure 5.3). It's a change that renders a sharp divide between the Empire's religious men as bearers of tradition and the modernizing military and administrative elites, whereas in Guys' drawing modernity is inscribed through a whole range of sartorial hybridities across the social spectrum.[18]

In Baudelaire's prose Sultan Abdülmecid and his administrative elite—the energetic avatars of the Empire's Tanzimat modernization—exhibit aristocratic torpor. Speaking of one of Guys' many images of Istanbul's regal dynastic pageants, Baudelaire asserts that the sultan displays "endless *ennui*" and the "Turkish functionaries" are described by him as "real caricatures of decadence, quite overwhelming their magnificent steeds with the weight of their fantastic bulk."[19] The trope of the sick man of Europe is read onto the body of the Sultan and his corpulent, feeble elite.[20] According to Baudelaire, this remnant, modern aristocratic spectacle is the catalyst for the genius of Guys, who transforms into art this quintessentially modern encounter of East and West.

David Wilkie's account of his portrait sittings to Sultan Abdülmecid conveys an altogether different image of this leader. During sittings for the British artist in 1840, Sultan Abdülmecid occasionally commandeered the painter's brush in order to communicate his aesthetic preferences while undertaking a lively discussion of matters of contemporary public interest with the artist's interpreter.[21] These interventions by Sultan Abdülmecid indicate the patron's agency in image production that was even more pronounced in the account of his daughter Fatma Sultan's art patronage.

On the lower left of his Topkapı Palace courtyard drawing (Figure 5.2), Guys underscored one instruction: "Not a single Turkish woman is to be seen in the Seraglio." It's an insistence indicating a crucial absence for veracity of reportage. This is a departure from the ubiquity of veiled Ottoman women in Guys' Istanbul street

Figure 5.4 Detail of verso of the sketch *The Ceremony of Kurban Bayramı*, undated, by Constantin Guys. Photographer: Jenni Carter.

scenes across which they become an index of the city's cultural difference. As, for example, his sketch of the recently completed neo-Renaissance British Embassy in Pera, designed by William James Smith, its gated entrance is dramatically staged in relation to the street life below (Figure 5.5).[22] Here two veiled women wait while a street vendor weighs their purchase, a *hamal* (porter) passes by with his heavy load and the ever-present Istanbul street dogs leap into action in response. These veiled women take their place among an Orientalist catalog of Istanbul types.

In another sketch, of Kağıthane—known to Europeans as the Sweet Waters of Europe—(Figure 5.6), Guys foregrounds cultural encounter by positioning a Muslim family as spectators. A staging of seeing and being seen at this popular leisure site is a familiar Orientalist trope, but here the veiled women with their backs to us watch nearby European men on horseback. Foremost among them is our roving reporter Guys, whose curved narrow-brimmed hat is familiar from numerous Cairo and Istanbul street scenes.[23] This polite proximity of anonymous veiled Ottoman women and European men—in a scene where, to invoke and invert Baudelaire's

Figure 5.5 *Entrance of the British Embassy, Constantinople*, undated, by Constantin Guys. Ink, ink wash and watercolor, 17.1 x 20.2 cm. Location unknown. Photographer: Jenni Carter.

terms, the 'non-I' scrutinizes the 'I'—has a more socially ambiguous counterpoint in Guys' sketch of a *Garden Near Constantinople* (c. 1854–56). Here a frisson is created by the proximity of Ottoman men to bourgeois European women.

This cross-cultural gendered seeing and being seen is characteristic of modern life in Guys' Istanbul. Another important feminine marker of modernity in his drawings of the city's street life is women's hybrid fashion, which he observed in the dress of women of differing social classes. For Baudelaire, it was Guys' representation of the city's sex workers, who were the indices of modernity—as they had been for him in Paris. But in the Ottoman capital, the mark of this modernity was the mix of Eastern and Western dress. Istanbul's *femmes galantes* (courtesans) are, Baudelaire declares, women from the Empire's minority communities in southeastern Europe:

> some have kept their national costume, embroidered jackets with short sleeves, flowing sashes, enormous trousers, turned-up slippers, striped or spangled muslins, and all the tinsel of their native land; others, and these the more numerous, have adopted the principal badge of civilization, which for a woman is invariably the crinoline, but in some small detail of their attire they always preserve a tiny characteristic souvenir of the East, so that they look like Parisian women who have attempted a fancy-dress.[24]

Figure 5.6 *Excursion to the Sweet Waters of Europe*, undated, by Constantin Guys. Pencil, ink, ink wash, and watercolor, 28.4 x 46.8 cm. Location unknown. Photographer: Jenni Carter.

A world away from Baudelaire's feminine masquerade of the demimonde, another hybrid fashion revolution was taking place inside the harems of the city's Ottoman elites. Signs that some elite women were adopting the crinoline and combining them with their veils and *feraces*—the cloaks they wore in public—could be seen on the city streets. In a remarkably powerful image Guys renders one such modern Ottoman lady charging out of the page toward us (Figure 5.7). Buttressed either side by her attendants, this woman's imposing scale defies the small size of the drawing. The Ottoman mosque dome and minarets combine with her modish crescent moon parasol to locate us in the Ottoman capital, while her voluminous ferace-covered crinoline mark her modernity and elite status.

It's a remarkable drawing because it distills the city's modernity into a shorthand of stage-managed visual prohibition and access. In the mid-nineteenth century, entry to Istanbul's mosques such as the one in the background here were highly regulated for non-Muslim foreigners like Guys. This limited access is staged in another of Guys' drawings where he renders himself and fellow Europeans at the threshold of the Yeni Cami (the New Mosque), on a Ramadan evening. While a *ferman* (official permit) enabled foreign men like Guys access to the city's major mosques at times when they were not in use for religious ritual, the private sphere of the city's elite harems was *verboten*. It was only foreign women who were invited to cross this threshold, and their visits were controlled carefully by the senior women of these households. Guys' drawing of one of these elite Ottoman ladies traversing the streets of Istanbul (Figure 5.7) is remarkable because she is both modern and veiled, visible and covered. He has created a work in which the agent who orchestrates this seeing and being seen is an unknown woman.

Figure 5.7 *Femmes Turque en Promenade*, undated, by Constantin Guys. 27 x 19.5 cm. Musée Carnavalet, Histoire de Paris (D.1292). © Musée Carnavalet/Roger-Viollet.

Guys' drawings of Istanbul are compelling because he's consistently staging the limitations of his own levels of access, rather than magicking them away through illusions of a perfect vantage point. The differences between his drawings and the *ILN* prints (e.g. Figure 5.3) illuminate this crucial dynamic. Guys' works are drawings from the vantage of the reporter wandering the street, among the city's crowds with all of its dance of proximity and distance, visibility, and invisibility. As a result, his work gauges the contingent visuality of meetings between Ottomans and Europeans during this moment when the Ottoman State was endeavoring to carefully orchestrate the political alliance with their British and French allies on the streets of their capital.

In this context Guys' drawing (Figure 5.8) that combines this stage-managed visibility of elite Ottoman women with state ceremony is thus particularly fascinating. It's a drawing of the ceremonial procession on day two of the marriage of Sultan Abdülmecid's daughter, Fatma Sultan, when Fatma was escorted by carriage up the Bosporus from Abdülmecid's Çırağan palace to her new home. She would live in the waterside mansion in Baltalimanı that had recently been purchased by the Imperial Treasury from her groom's family and assigned to Fatma Sultan. The marriage was a political alliance securing bonds of allegiance between the Sultan and one of his most powerful Tanzimat bureaucrats, Mustafa Reşid Paşa, whose son, Ali Galib Paşa—himself an important Ottoman bureaucrat—was marrying Fatma Sultan. Within this domestic arrangement it was Fatma Sultan, the Sultan's esteemed daughter, who by all accounts had the upper hand in this unhappy marriage during the Sultan's lifetime.[25]

On the second day of her marriage ceremony, Fatma Sultan traveled up the shore of the Bosporus in a long procession cheered on by crowds lining the circuitous carriage road. With an eye to finding a vantage where this long procession could be animated across a page, Guys' drawing (Figure 5.8) is located at a bend in the

Figure 5.8 *The Marriage of the Sultan's Daughter, the procession,* 1854, by Constantin Guys. Ink and watercolor on paper, 32 x 49 cm. Private Collection. Photographer: Jenni Carter.

road, where the procession begins its descent to the seaside mansion. The ceremony is in motion toward us from the top left, turning in the foreground in prelude to entering a precipitous descent on the lower right of this page. Guys renders the melee of this long procession of state, which the *ILN* printmaker distills into legibility (Figure 5.9). The Şeyhülislam—who had officiated the marriage—the only figure wearing white, has already turned in front of Guys, and behind him the palace eunuchs are in various stages of negotiating the corner, the most senior among them with his prominent epaulets and splendidly caparisoned steed is on the cusp of the bend. Behind them and receding into the most cursory of notations is the long line of carriages among which is the one carrying Fatma Sultan, drawn by six black horses. It is impossible to discern which one is hers from Guys' sketch, and the distinction between the places occupied by the procession's spectators and its participants is only discernible because of the lines marking their boundaries. The *ILN* engraving (Figure 5.9) and its accompanying text transformed Guys sketch, drawing the viewer closer to the procession, rendering the eunuchs in familiar Orientalist caricature, and delineating one prominent carriage occupied by the princess that is shrouded by curtains.

This legibility in print contrasts with the sketch's ambiguous marks, which render the limits of visibility through their patches of opacity. Our journalist has chosen a spot at a bend in the road that offers a considerable line of sight, and he picks out key figures and animates his foreground through the agitation of the horses closest to us. Nonetheless, his marks register the difficulty of spectating such an event. He renders the partial view of the roving reporter, a crowd's eye view of a ceremonial event that, at this moment during the Crimean War, the Ottoman State orchestrated for visiting foreigners such as himself as much as for the Empire's local inhabitants.

Figure 5.9 *Marriage Procession of the Sultan's Daughter at Constantinople*, 1854, unknown engraver. Published in the *Illustrated London News*, September 9, 1854, p. 228.

Fatma Sultan and the Minefield of Modern Visual Culture

Although Fatma Sultan is represented in the *ILN* print (Figure 5.9) as an absent presence in her shrouded carriage, and is even less discernible in Guys' processional annotations (Figure 5.8), she is by no means a passive object in this visual history. She too was negotiating her way through the minefield of modern visual culture. Although her life was governed by the protocols of gendered segregation that were strictly observed by senior members of the Sultan's family, she kept abreast of local and foreign political news and the latest French fashions. Fatma Sultan was an avid reader of daily newspapers and illustrated fashion magazines, and commissioned her own portraits. One of the city's British expatriate artists, Mary Adelaide Walker, worked under commission to Fatma in her Baltalimanı mansion.

The painting itself is no longer available to view, but Walker's account of these sittings reveal that Fatma wanted a modern portrait appropriate to her elevated status within the imperial family. She adorned herself with a miniature portrait of her father, the Sultan set in brilliants[26] and an Ottoman order in the shape of a large diamond star. The hierarchical system of orders was a relatively recent innovation in Ottoman statecraft, bestowed by the Sultan and worn on the body of his subjects at national ceremony, thus intimately incorporating them as subjects of the Empire. What Fatma wore for her portrait may have been the rare Order of Distinction, the Nişân-ı İmtiyâz, created during Sultan Abdülmecid's reign and bestowed upon women of the dynasty.[27] Fatma also wore a "diamond necklace of immense value," large diamond earrings and an "enormous stone on the little finger."[28] But the standout among this exquisite jewelry was her girdle, "a broad band composed entirely of diamonds" that was, we are told, probably the one given to Fatma by the Sultan at the time of her wedding. The large double clasp of this belt had formerly fastened Sultan Abdülmecid's cloak of ceremony and thus, like her other jeweled adornments, signals her familial bonds with the Empire's hereditary ruler.

Fatma Sultan had clear ideas about how her portrait should look that did not conform to Mary Walker's understanding of what constituted an aesthetically pleasing honorific portrait. Fatma was a lively and demanding interlocutor, and a strident aesthetic debate took place between them during the sittings. The Ottoman princess asserted her modernity through fashion and pose. According to Walker, despite the splendor of her jewels, their "effect was utterly destroyed" because Fatma insisted upon wearing "a dress of the poorest French silk," in a "dead unlovely white," because it was "'moda' 'à la frança'".[29] The jewels, Walker complained, did not stand out against this white fabric. The upper part of her attire was made "like a European lady's ball-dress, while from the waist downwards it was fashioned into the orthodox antary [entari (dress)] and schalwars [şalvar (voluminous pants)]." The stiff bodice formed her body into an upright pose that Walker found jarring.

In the preliminary stages of this full-length portrait, the Ottoman princess took hold of the artist's charcoal to mark up the canvas indicating that she required Walker to render her taller. She also asserted that the figure shading should be reduced, resulting in a radical flattening and she was to be rendered as "'full face' as possible." Walker laments what might have been had she been able to represent the princess in her other "robes stiff with gems, draperies of fairy tissue."[30] Evidently her objections are shadowed by Western pictorial ideals of odalisques and fairy princesses.

What she describes is a portrait in which a seamless picture surface of pictorial illusionism is riven with disjunction and angularity, flatness where roundness and color contrasts should prevail. This portrait has striking resonances with what would emerge as avant-garde visual strategies in France and Britain a decade later—Whistler's *Woman in White* that was rejected by both the British Royal Academy and the French Salon springs to mind. My willful, anachronistic comparison is motivated by desire for aesthetic reappraisal of this Ottoman outsider artist–patron in order to make a case for her inclusion in our global

Figure 5.10 *Fatma Sultan, or daughter of the Sultan,* 1857, unknown artist. Published in *Catalogue of the Oriental Museum* (London: Leicester Square, 1857), p. 20.

histories of nineteenth-century modern art. Walker's diary registers two very different aesthetic judgments in confrontation, and it is Fatma Sultan's choices that land closer to the kind of aesthetic experimentation that Baudelaire applauded in Guys' work. For Baudelaire, Guys' capacity to articulate a new aesthetic language was at least in part enabled by the fact that he was not trained within the French Academy. So too, we find engagement with art by Ottoman elites in this same period less encumbered by some of the familiar aesthetic languages and functions for art that held sway in the European metropoles.

In Walker's eyes, Fatma's modern aesthetic revolution was not art, and certainly not good portraiture. She protested, "I objected … to such unintelligent dictation; tried to reason." Fatma's rejoinder that "the portrait must be done according to her wishes, or – not at all" is a reminder of the cultural hierarchy that pertained in Fatma's harem on the Bosporus.[31] At this moment, Fatma becomes the portrait's author and Walker its staunch critic as she disavows her own compromised work. The British artist consoled herself with a comment that underscores the Ottoman context of reception for this modern art:

> the picture when finished would rarely, if ever, be seen by persons competent to judge the merits of a painting. As the features of women are veiled, so also, according to orthodox custom, must a female portrait be hidden from the gaze even of the men who perform the rough work of the house. The ultimate fate of the picture is either to lie hidden away in some dark closet, or, if too large, and destined to remain in one of the sitting-rooms, curtains are fastened on to the frames. This portrait ... was eventually honoured with a large curtain of rich white silk.[32]

Ottoman women of Fatma Sultan's generation who commissioned such portraits circumscribed their audience through measures that ensured they conformed to social codes of restricted visibility. The scant evidence we have of these portraits and their conditions of circulation indicates that these young Ottoman women engaged with modern visual culture, but this era of increased mechanical reproducibility of images carried risks. Fatma Sultan commissioned photographic portraits that did not circulate widely in her lifetime, yet an earlier portrait by Rupen Manas was reproduced in Paris in 1854, and her representation in the *Catalogue of the Oriental Museum* (Figure 5.10), published in London in 1857, is loosely derived from the same portrait. The circulation of these images demonstrates that her efforts to circumscribe her representation were not entirely successful.[33]

But these contraventions—if she was even aware of them—did not deter her engagement with self-representation. Like Oscar Wilde's portrait of Dorian Gray, Fatma's harem portrait changed over time. Walker writes two accounts of painting inside Fatma Sultan's harem, the first in 1859, the second sometime after the Sultan's death in 1861, likely in the late 1860s or early 1870s. At this stage Fatma's status has fallen as a result of the death of her father, underscoring her derivative power. During this later visit, the princess required Walker to repaint her earlier portrait. But it was not an aging countenance that would transform on this canvas, instead sartorial changes were required by this modern Ottoman woman to ensure her portrait was up to date. Again, sartorial change is the marker of modernity for a painting that, like a modern fashion illustration, becomes out of date within a short temporal interval. This was a form of portraiture for modern times, one subject to revision. Like Guys' illustrations, the ontology of this portrait is marked by its status as a provisional rendering.

Whose Modernity?

Walker prefaces her harem memoirs with an equivocal nostalgia for old Constantinople–"let us look back thirty years." Her opening paragraph poses a series of questions asking if such visualization is even possible given the dramatic transformations in an urbanscape that had been her home since the close of the Crimean War. Modernity threatens to eclipse her Istanbul memories. It's a compelling prompt to read further as Walker's tentative hold on a recent past lends her testimony a melancholy urgency to conjure these memories. She asks: "Can we at the present time fully realise the different conditions of men and things as they existed here at the long-past date?"[34]

This characteristically modern urban *tristesse* is soon leavened by a city resident's pragmatism. Walker's opening gambit lays bare an internal struggle between artist and resident. And this conflict finds its way into many of her subsequent word pictures of the city's domestic and public spaces when Walker's narrative voice shifts between an ethnographic tone of descriptive neutrality and the artist's often harsh aesthetic judgments of the effects of modernity on the ancient city.[35] In her account of modern Istanbul, the Orientalist picturesque finds itself at odds with a rhetoric of urban improvement. I find a similar negotiation in Guys' drawings, but the stakes are higher in Walker's text because she has lived more of her own history in this place.

With all the precision of an urban geographer, Walker asks her readers to recall an embodied memory of regularly moving up and down the long, steep "Step Street" when this was the main means of traversing between the elevated suburb of Pera, home to the European embassies and many expatriates, and Galata, the commercial district below. For a middle-class Istanbullu, both foreign and local, this arduous journey which could be taken on foot or by sedan chair, had been replaced by the convenience of the new subterranean funicular that opened to great fanfare in January 1875.[36] Plenty of the lower classes among the city's residents still walked this arduous hill, but the new infrastructure provided an alternative for those who had 2 kuruş for first class or 1 kuruş for second class travel.[37]

Walter Charles Horsley visualized this funicular as a harbinger of Istanbul's entry into urban modernity for his series on the city published in *The Graphic* between April and July of 1876 (Figure 5.11). The accompanying text offers the paper's readers a short history of this speculative commercial venture designed by French engineer Eugène-Henri Gavand who had been granted the necessary concessions from the Ottoman government to build the line, an enterprise financed by a British firm. Here is international capital in action, economic imperialism delivering one of the "conveniences of civilization" to Pera, the district of the city that *The Graphic* declared was now the "Frank capital" (European capital).[38] But *The Graphic*'s neat division of Pera and Galata as the "capital of the Franks" belies a more complex history of the role of these city districts during its modernization in the nineteenth century. The Pera prefecture was a zone of urban experimentation for the Ottoman government.[39] A photograph of the Tünel station, taken on the occasion of the 1884 anniversary of Sultan Abdülhamid II's accession to the throne (Figure 5.12), is a visual riposte to such appropriations of Pera as exclusively a site of European modernity. The Ottoman insignia of star and crescent crowns the entrance to the station, under which is a declaration of loyalty to the Sultan in Ottoman and French.[40] Across these varied renditions in photographs and press illustrations, Pera emerges as a social space where multiple claims were staked by the city's diverse inhabitants.

As with his Cairo café scene, *Great Britain in Egypt, 1886* (Figure 5.1), Horsley's illustration of Pera for *The Graphic* (Figure 5.11), invokes modernity through an unexpected cross-cultural encounter. But in Horsley's print it is contemporary urban infrastructure that spatially orchestrates the intimacies of this quintessentially modern experience. The spectator "In the Underground Railway" occupies the place of a modern fellow traveler within the first class carriage that opens in cross section.[41] It is a compositional strategy also used in contemporaneous paintings of modern rail travel in Britain and France. For instance, Augustus Egg's *The Travelling Companions* (1862), Abraham Solomon's *First Class: The Meeting* (1854), and Honoré Daumier's *First-Class Carriage* (1864).[42] But it's the veiled women in Horsley's carriage (Figure 5.11) that marks this as modern transport in the Islamic world.

This short interval of track, the second underground line in the world, inaugurated that unique experience of subterranean travel that erases the epidermal street view whereby the traveler can continually take stock of their own movement through the city's geography. Instead the distance between places is phenomenologically erased and replaced with a temporal interval inside the mobile carriage. This new experience of city time-space is inscribed in the structure of Horsley's image (Figure 5.11) because we are unable to discern if the carriage is at the beginning, middle, or end of its journey, or indeed if it is traveling up or down the tunnel.

A curtain at the top right of Horsley's carriage in Figure 5.11 is drawn back revealing our travelers. Respectable gender boundaries appear to prevail despite the random physical proximity of these strangers in transit. The central woman angles her left shoulder creating a slight physical barrier between the European

IN THE UNDERGROUND RAILWAY

Figure 5.11 *In the Underground Railway*, 1876, by Walter Charles Horsley. Published in *The Graphic*, April 15, 1876, p. 364.

Figure 5.12 *(110) Station du Tunnel à Péra Constantinople,* 1884, by Vassilaki Kargopoulo, albumen print. Getty Research Institute, Los Angeles (96.R.14).

gentleman nearby as her voluminous ferace cascades instead over her female companion. Like the other men in this carriage, he comports himself in preoccupied isolation, clasping his walking cane with steadying determination, perhaps contemplating the gravitas of his day's business. The Ottoman boy near him has a look of blank self-absorption, while our third gentleman precariously steadies himself with one arm on the carriage bar in order to read *La Turquie,* a local French-language newspaper.

It is the veiled women who look with the most curious interest at what is transpiring inside this carriage. Readers of *The Graphic* find themselves to now be the object of Ottoman women's curiosity which is abstracted from context through the medium of print journalism—these readers are simultaneously inside this Istanbul railway carriage and somewhere else reading *The Graphic*—(Figure 5.11). For them, the veiled women are bearers of a look that represents a distant localized curiosity, whereas our standing gentleman is part of their community of readers. Here is Hegel's newspaper reader, engaging in "the realist's morning prayer," orienting himself "toward the world," secure that he knows where he stands.[43]

Like the reader of *The Graphic,* *La Turquie*'s reader is consuming a patchwork of local reports and foreign stories extracted from a range of international papers by local and traveling journalists. As Benedict Anderson alerts us, they may not be reading the same stories but from it they conjure a modern abstracted notion of the world and through it an imagined community of the nation.[44] In this polyglot Istanbul neighborhood that was home to all of the foreign European embassies, surely any imagined community of the nation was never far from a simultaneous imagined alliance of select European nations—a notion of the Concert of Europe from which the Ottomans were becoming increasingly isolated by the late 1870s.[45] The date mark on *La Turquie*'s masthead is illegible in *The Graphic* (Figure 5.11); it's a perspicacious abstraction eliding the time lag between Horsley's drawing and the print's appearance on the pages of the British illustrated paper. As such, *The Graphic*'s *La Turquie* renders the abstracted simultaneity of time that is fundamental to this modern imagined community of newspaper readers wherever they are across the globe.

Unlike Guys' drawings for the *Illustrated London News* (Figures 5.2 and 5.8), Horsley's drawings have not survived. We have no measure whether there was a difference between his preliminary study made in Istanbul and its transformation into print. As a consequence we don't know who created the illustration's fundamental error. Despite all of its convincing anecdotal detail, this is a visual fiction inscribing a gendered integration that doesn't reflect the ways these carriages were utilized in these early years. From the time the railways and tramways were introduced into the Ottoman capital until the early years of the Turkish republic, curtains demarcated the section of the car that was for the exclusive use of women.[46] The gendered mixing of Ottoman women that we see here was proscribed. Local travelers in the Istanbul funicular would have been well aware of this error.

What would Mary Walker have made of this? Might she have looked upon the error as evidence of artistic license or inaccurate reportage? She wrote with disdain about naïve travelers who were underdressed on the Grand Rue de Pera because they had miscalculated the sophistication of her local Istanbul high street. They wore, she writes, "the most impossible costumes, well suited, perhaps, to tent life and the ruins of Baalbec, but of startling eccentricity in the very modern and up-to-date High Street of our suburb."[47] Horsley may have been seen as yet another casual visitor who was taking liberties with local protocols pertaining to her Istanbul neighborhood.

And Fatma Sultan—what would have been her response? Was *The Graphic* among the foreign papers she read inside her harem in Baltalimanı? What was her imagined community of readers given that she was reading Ottoman and foreign language papers? It's hard to say, but we know by the time she invited Walker to update her portrait she was now intervening stridently in an effort to modify not just her own portrait but also the harem images she knew Walker was likely to create once she left her home. Walker conjures a vivid word picture of Fatma's censorship:

> Upon one occasion the ousta [*usta*: mistress] charged with my well-being showed herself unusually anxious to ascertain the contents of my little hand-bag. 'What a pretty little bag you have, madama; let me take it upstairs for you. What do you bring in it? A book? No? What have you in that roll? The brushes? Ah! Yes – but, madama, is there not a little book somewhere? a lead-pencil book?' I now understand the drift of the questioning. I have been reported to the Sultana as having made some drawings in a pocket sketch-book. I produce the offender, which is borne off immediately to the 'Effendimiz' (our lady).

> There are sounds of distant laughter, and some time passes. At length the ousta reappears, returning the little book with, alas! one of the most cherished sketches of the 'classical draperies' scored all over with pencil marks and nearly torn away, and a polite message from the Sultana, who begs that I will not do any more pictures of her women in their morning dresses, 'with their robes all twisted about them; it is ugly, and the Franks will think her harem very ill-dressed.' I may, if I please, draw them in their best clothes – meaning plenty of starch and crinoline. The proposal does not tempt me to further efforts.[48]

Distant laughter, passing time, and Fatma's scoring and tearing of a sketchbook page. Her derision and fury still burns bright. In the pages of the British expatriate's diary, Fatma asserts the modernity of her harem against Walker's Orientalist classicizing picturing impulses. It's an affective investment in rendering modernity that calls to mind Guys, Baudelaire's "man of the world," who is uniquely driven by "an insatiable passion – for seeing and feeling."[49] They differ, but here too are the stakes of radically modern picture-making in the nineteenth century.

Notes

1   Charles Baudelaire, "The Painter of Modern Life," in *The Painter of Modern Life and Other Essays*, trans. and ed. Jonathan Mayne (New York: Da Capo Press, 1986), 1–40.

2   When Linda Nochlin first transposed Edward Said's *Orientalism* (1978) into art history she set in place what has become a conventional understanding of academic Orientalism. She asserted that the authority of academic Orientalism was premised on the absent Westerner whose controlling gaze is the organizing force in a hermetic world of the exotic east. This cultural politics has its inverse in the radical pictorial fragmentation of French avant-garde paintings of Parisian modernity for which Manet's *Masked Ball at the Opera* of 1873–4 is Nochlin's exemplar. Linda Nochlin, "The Imaginary Orient," in *The Politics of Vision. Essays on Nineteenth-Century Art and Society*, Linda Nochlin (New York: Harper and Row, 1989), 36 and 45. For a more complex appraisal of Delacroix's Orientalism, see Darcy Grigsby, "'Whose colour was no black nor white nor grey, But an extraneous mixture, which no pen Can trace, although perhaps the pencil may': Aspasie and Delacroix's Massacres of Chios," *Art History* 22, no. 5, December (1999): 676–704.

3   *The Athenaeum*, no. 3109, May 28 (1887), 710. The painting is reproduced in the "The Royal Academy Exhibition," *Art Journal*, August (1887): 247.

4   The literature on this Western stereotype of the female occupant of the Islamic harem, or segregated home is extensive. See, for example, Billie Melman, *Women's Orients: English Women and the Middle East, 1718–1918: Sexuality, Religion and Work* (London: Palgrave Macmillan, 1992); Reina Lewis, *Gendering Orientalism: Race, Femininity and Representation* (London and New York: Routledge, 1996); Joan Del Plato, *Multiple Wives. Multiple Pleasures: Representing the Harem, 1800–1875* (Madison: Fairleigh Dickinson University Press, 2002); Reina Lewis, *Rethinking Orientalism: Women, Travel and the Ottoman Harem* (London and New York: I.B. Tauris, 2004); Mary Roberts, *Intimate Outsiders. The Harem in Ottoman and Orientalist Art and Travel Literature* (Durham: Duke University Press, 2007); and Leslie Peirce, "AHR Forum: Writing Histories of Sexuality in the Middle East," *American Historical Review* 114, no. 5 (December 2009): 1325–39.

5   The *Sydney Morning Herald* cites the acquisition of this painting from the British Loan Collection as part of a good year "in the realm of art" in the colony. This "cultural progress" was recognized by the Queen herself with the prefix of "Royal" added to the Anglo-Australian Society of Artists by her Majesty's consent. See *Sydney Morning Herald*, Tuesday December 31, 1889, 9. See also *National Art Gallery of NSW Illustrated Catalogue*, Sydney (1917), Horsley's painting is catalogue no. 172.

6   *Great Britain in Egypt, 1886* is among a group of works Horsley exhibited at the Royal Academy between 1877 and 1900 where quotidian experiences of the British presence in Cairo since occupation in 1882 and the prior French occupation under Napoleon are all grist for Horsley's modern Orientalist narrative painting. This includes *Theological Students in the University Mosque, El Azhar, Cairo, and The French in Cairo*.

7   For a survey of Guys' Crimean War drawings, see Karen W. Smith, *Constantin Guys. Crimean War Drawings 1854–1856* (Ohio: Cleveland Museum of Art, 1978) and Pierre Duflo, *Constantin Guys: Fou de Dessin, Grand Reporter, 1802–1892* (Paris: Éditions Arnaud Seydoux, 1988).

8   For analysis of the impact of the Crimean War on Ottoman Istanbul, see Sinan Kuneralp, "The Thorny Road to Modernization: The Ottoman Empire and the Crimean War," in *Kırım Savaşı'nın 150nci Yılı (150th Anniversary of the Crimean War)*, ed. Bahattin Öztuncay (Istanbul: Sadberk Hanım Müzesi, 2006), 60–65. For an analysis of the conflicted views of the Crimean War alliance within the Ottoman Empire and Britain and the war's impact on the Ottomans' place in the international political landscape, see David Barchard, "'The Imperial Rescript' Bringing Turkey into the Family of European Nations," in Öztuncay, Bahattin, ed. *Kırım Savaşı'nın 150nci Yılı (150th Anniversary of the Crimean War)* (Istanbul: Sadberk Hanım Museum Publications, 2006), 70–73

9   Charles Baudelaire, *The Painter of Modern Life*, 22.

10 Ibid., 9.

11 The Kurban Bayramı is also known as the Feast of the Sacrifice.

12 On European music at the Ottoman Court, see Emre Aracı, "Giuseppe Donizetti Pasha and the Polyphonic Court Music of the Ottoman Empire," *Court Historian*, no. 7: 2 (2002): 135–43 and Emre Aracı, *Osmanlı Sarayı'ndan Avrupa Müziği/European Music at the Ottoman Court*, London Academy of Ottoman Court Music (Istanbul: Kalan, 2000). On photography and Ottoman military bands, see Michael Talbot, "Sparks of Happenstance: Photographs, Public Celebrations, and the Ottoman Military Band of Jerusalem," *Journal of the Ottoman and Turkish Studies Association* 5, no. 1 (Spring 2018), 33–66.

13 This is likely to be a study for a painting for Sultan Abdülaziz although the finished work has not been located. The Polish artist worked closely with the Sultan between 1865 and 1872. For an analysis of these commissions, see Mary Roberts, "The Battlefield of Ottoman History," in *Istanbul Exchanges: Ottomans, Orientalists and Nineteenth-Century Visual Culture*, (Berkeley: University of California Press, 2015), 37–74.

14 For a history of this ceremonial courtyard in the early modern period see Gülru Necipoğlu, *Architecture, Ceremonial, and Power: The Topkapı Palace in the Fifteenth and Sixteenth Centuries* (Cambridge: MIT Press, 1991).

15 This gate was rebuilt in the Ottoman Baroque style soon after the accession of Sultan Abdülhamid I. See Ünver Rüstem, *Ottoman Baroque: The Architectural Refashioning of Eighteenth-Century Istanbul* (Princeton: Princeton University Press, 2019), 242.

16 The text on the recto and verso of this drawing is reproduced and transcribed in Smith, *Constantin Guys,* Catalogue entry no. 35, 77–78.

17 Ibid., 78.

18 This detail bears out what Baudelaire says about Guys, "If a fashion or the cut of a garment has been slightly modified … be very sure that his eagle eye will already have spotted it from however great a distance." Charles Baudelaire, "The Painter of Modern Life," 11.

19 Charles Baudelaire, *The Painter of Modern Life*, 21–22.

20 On January 9, 1853, Russian Tsar Nicholas I characterized the Ottoman Empire as the "Sick man of Europe". It was a turn of phrase that would gain broad currency in later years. See Şükrü Hanioğlu, *A Brief History of the Late Ottoman Empire* (New Jersey: Princeton University Press, 2008), 79.

21 Wilkie wrote: "His Highness was most particular about the likeness, which, in the course of sitting, I had to alter variously, the Sultan taking sometimes the brush with colours, and indicating the alteration he wished made … His Majesty conversed with Mr. Pisani with great familiarity, and upon subjects, from the names mentioned, relating to public affairs. He seemed at times greatly amused, showed complete relaxation, and displayed that expression most favourable to a portrait." Allan Cunningham, *The Life of Sir David Wilkie; With his Journals, Tours, and Critical Remarks on Works of Art and a Selection from His Correspondence* (London: John Murray, 1843), vol. 3, 351.

22 Esma İgüs, "A British touch on Tanzimat: Architect William James Smith, Tanzimat'a İngiliz Dokunuşu: Mimar William James Smith," *Journal of Ottoman Legacy Studies (JOLS)/Osmanlı Mirası Araştırmaları Dergisi (OMAD)* 2, no. 3 (July 2015), 66–87.

23 Guys draws himself among the crowd on the shoreline at Scutari (Üsküdar) when the body of an officer lost at sea was being carried from a boat, speaking with nurses at the hospital in Scutari, during Ramadan at the entrance of the Yeni Cami, among Croatian workers at Balaclava, among a crowd on a busy Istanbul street, and on a donkey entering Alexandria with Captain Ponsonby. See Duflo, *Constantin Guys*, 179, 190, 303, 322, 327, and 329.

24 Baudelaire, *The Painter of Modern Life*, 22.

25 Necdet Sakaoğlu and Nuri Akbayar, *Sultan Abdülmecid: A Milestone on Turkey's Path to Westernization* (Istanbul: DenizBank Publications, 2002), no. 8, 215–21.

26 This is a somewhat unusual choice given that the medal portraits that had been initiated by Sultan Mahmud were not continued during the reign of Sultan Abdülmecid. For an account of the Tasvir-i Hümâyûn and the reasons it was discontinued, see Edhem Eldem, *Pride and Privilege: A History of Ottoman Orders, Medals and Decorations* (Istanbul: Ottoman Bank Archives and Research Centre, 2004), 132–33.

27 Eldem, *Pride and Privilege,* 135.

28 Mary Walker, *Eastern Life and Scenery: With Excursions in Asia Minor, Mytilene, Crete, and Roumania* (London: Chapman and Hall, 1886), vol. 1, 15–18.

29 Ibid., 15.

30 Ibid., 15–17.

31 Ibid., 17.

32 Ibid., 17–18.

33 *Catalogue of the Oriental Museum, Great Globe Leicester Square* (London: W.J. Golbourn, 1857). Ünver Rüstem has analyzed this museum in "Dressing the Part: Ottoman Self-Representation in the Age of Orientalism," paper presented at Objects of Orientalism, Clark Art Institute, Williamstown MA., April 29–30, 2016.

34 Mary Walker, *Eastern Life and Scenery*, vol. 1, xi.

35 Mary Walker and her brother Charles Curtis, chaplain of the Crimean Memorial Church in Pera wrote about the impact of these modern Ottoman transport initiatives on the historic peninsula. Again modernization was wrought by making the fragment visible, but this time it was fragments of the city's Byzantine past that were revealed and in some

cases destroyed as a result of the railway works in 1871 around the circumference of Sarayburnu. Here the Ottomans are construed as thoughtless modernizers. See Charles George Curtis, *Broken Bits of Byzantium, lithographed with some additions by Mary A. Walker* (Constantinople: Lorentz and Keil, 1887).

36 For an account of its development in the context of changes to the urban fabric of Istanbul across the nineteenth century, see Zeynep Çelik, *The Remaking of Istanbul. Portrait of an Ottoman City in the Nineteenth Century* (Berkeley: University of California Press, 1993), 96–99.

37 The laborious work of the hamal is inscribed in the centre of Horsley's illustration of Yüksek Kaldırım for *The Graphic*, May 13, 1876.

38 "The Eastern Question – Sketches at Constantinople," *The Graphic*, April 1, 1876, 315 and *The Graphic*, April 15, 1876, 363. Gavand himself writes. Gavand himself writes a more fine-grained account of his struggles to negotiate the concessions, expropriate the land, and build the tunnel. See Eugène-Henri Gavand, *Chemin de Fer Métropolitain de Constantinople ou Chemin de Fer Souterrain de Galata a Péra Dit Tunnel de Constantinople* (Paris: Typographie Lahure, 1876). See also P. Oberling, "The Istanbul Tünel," *Archivum Ottomanicum* 4, (1972), 217–63.

39 It was not just Pera and Galata that were undergoing modernizing urban reform in this period. The historic peninsula was being transformed as transport networks expanded across the Ottoman capital and around the Empire. See Zeynep Çelik, *The Remaking of Istanbul* and Peter H. Christensen, *Germany and the Ottoman Railways. Art, Empire, and Infrastructure* (New Haven: Yale University Press, 2017). The Ottoman photographic record of modernity within the Empire is extensive, see Zeynep Çelik and Edhem Eldem, *Camera Ottomana: Photography and Modernity in the Ottoman Empire, 1840–1914* (Istanbul: Koç University Press, 2015).

40 For an account of this and the other buildings across the city that were illuminated on this ceremonial occasion, see Bahattin Öztuncay, *Vassilaki Kargopoulo: Photographer to his Majesty the Sultan (Istanbul*: Birleşik Oksijen Sanayi, A Ş, 2000*), 76.*

41 In fact there were two classes within this carriage and another car was designed to carry animals, goods, and could even accommodate a horse-drawn carriage.

42 *The Travelling Companions*, 1862, by Augustus Leopold Egg, Birmingham Museum and Art Gallery; *First Class – The Meeting. "And at first meeting loved."*, 1855, by Abraham Solomon, Yale Center for British Art; *First-Class Carriage*, 1864, by Honoré Daumier, Walters Art Museum.

43 Georg Wilhelm Friedrich Hegel, *Miscellaneous Writings of G.W.F. Hegel*, ed. Jon Stewart (Evanston: Northwestern University Press, 2002), 247.

44 Benedict Anderson, *Imagined Communities: Reflections on the Origin and Spread of Nationalism*, rev. edn (London and New York: Verso, 2006), 33–36.

45 For a succinct account of these shifting Ottoman political alliances across the nineteenth century, see, M. Şükrü Hanioğlu, *A Brief History of the Late Ottoman Empire* (New Jersey: Princeton University Press, 2008).

46 Gavand writes that each compartment has a movable curtain which can be used for gender segregation as necessary and illustrates these carriages: Gavand, *Chemin de Fer Métropolitain de Constantinople*, 28 and Plate 23.

47 Mary Adelaide Walker, *Old Tracks and New Landmarks: Wayside Sketches in Crete, Macedonia, Mitylene, etc.* (London: Richard Bentley and Son, 1897), 331.

48 Walker, *Eastern Life and Scenery*, vol. 1, 312. The rank of usta is that of a leading administrative supervisor within the royal Ottoman harems. For more on these imperial harem ranks, see Leslie Peirce, *The Imperial Harem: Women and Sovereignty in the Ottoman Empire* (Oxford: Oxford University Press, 1993), 142.

49 "the dandy aspires to insensitivity, and it is in this that Monsieur G. dominated as he is by an insatiable passion – for seeing and feeling – parts company decisively with dandyism" Baudelaire, *The Painter of Modern Life*, 9.

CHAPTER 6

LOOKING AT/AS NUDES: A STUDY OF A SPACE OF IMAGINATION
Kirsten Scheid

For its adherents in 1930s Beirut, nudism countered physical debilitation, political corruption, and all forms of social falsity. The movement apparently launched with Fouad Hobeiche's loose translation of a French "educational novel" that he published in 1930 as *Rasul al-'Uri* (The Prophet of the Nude). In 1934 Hobeiche founded *al-Makshuf* newspaper which provocatively combined "pornographic" imagery and literature. It was also an important forum for visual and literary art coverage and criticism, for trenchant political critique of nationalist elites and French colonial authorities, and for attacks on social problems related by their authors to "cultural backwardness," "oppression of women," and "ignorance." Nudism's journalistic, political, and artistic facets converge on a space of imagination that has gone unmapped in our histories of modernism. Painted nudes and practicing nudists were clearly part of modernist renewal projects, but why? This chapter explores the intertwining of two ways of learning to look: the one at nudes and the other as nudes. I analyze these ways of learning to look as emergent emotional practices—from Monique Scheer—that were deliberately introduced into the changing urban context to cultivate new sensibilities by naming, mobilizing, communicating, and regulating mental-physical experiences. Thus, in his autobiography, artist Moustapha Farrouk (1901–57) recounts that to become a professional artist meant seeking out an encounter with a naked female model, developing an "overwhelming" physical reaction to the encounter, and controlling it through breathing practices, sketching, reading the Qur'an, showering in cold water, and sketching again. His subsequent compositions enfolded such complex experiences of looking at and being looked at as a viewer of nudes, as did the work of several Beirut-based peers, including Omar Onsi (1901–69), and Cesar Gemayel (1898–1958), and others whose memory has not lasted. Art had a special role for Lebanon's nudists because it combined space in otherwise unmappable ways and modeled, like figures on a catwalk, what nudism could entail and endow, to those who live as nudes. Nudists and nude paintings help us remap the commonly relied upon boundaries of society, politics, and possibility, and lay out a space of imagination to which we otherwise have little access today.

Nudes, Nudism, and the Champions of the Nude in Beirut, 1920s–1930s

Carrie, a standing nude seen from the back, painted by Khalil Saleeby (Khalil al-Salibi, 1870–1928), inhabited downtown Beirut's public space for a few weeks in 1921 at the Beirut Industrial Fair, as can be seen from a postcard produced at the time (Figure 6.1).

A press report blandly enjoined audiences not to miss the painter's "persons and views."[1] The fair aimed to develop local commerce and showcase territory newly mandated by the League of Nations to French "advisory" administration as implementing post-Ottoman modernity.[2] The apparently casual inclusion of Saleeby's *nu au dos*, included even in official documentary postcards of the event, counters a dense regional

My transliteration of Arabic names in the body of this text follows the public figures' preferred signatures but initially cites the *International Journal of Middle East Studies* transliteration of each name to connect them to Arabic sources. In the footnotes from Arabic sources and in all phrases cited in the body of the text, I adhere to the *International Journal of Middle East Studies* transliteration rules to enable locating sources.

Figure 6.1 Alfred Tarazi's stand at the Beirut Industrial Fair, Sarrafian, May 1921. *Carrie* appears in the lower left corner. Fouad Debbas Collection, Album Sarrafian #4 – 8304. Nicholas Sursock Museum, Beirut. Postcard printed June 5, 1923. Courtesy of the Fouad Debbas Collection, Sursock Museum, Beirut.

art historiography denying the presence of such images, and prompts the question: What was the role of the undressed body in the formation, staging, and interrogation of the modern Middle East?

Before the end of the decade, public nudity walked off canvases and into Beirut's streets. Locally born and recently arrived intellectuals, journalists, and artists contributed their thoughts and bodies to a blossoming nudist movement. According to an op-ed in the Francophone, pro-Mandate daily *L'Orient* in 1934, a whole class of impecunious male nudists had recently overtaken the Corniche where they daily sunned *au naturel* without "even attempt[ing] to recreate the pudic gesture lent to the Venus of Milo."[3] Newspaper cartoons from the period also suggest young women had their own practice (Figure 6.2).[4]

Beirut's nudist movement congealed around a loose translation by Fouad Hobeiche (Fu'ad Hubaysh, 1904–73) of a French "educational novel" that he published in 1930 as *Rasul al-'Uri* (*The Prophet of the Nude*). Michel Zakkur's politically independent journal, *al-Ma'rid*—active 1921–35—provided a forum for discussing the benefits of nudism. Hubert Schonger's *La Marche au Soleil* (1932), portraying life in a German nudist colony, played at Beirut's Olympia cinema in 1934.[5] The following year Hobeiche founded *al-Makshuf* newspaper which was rife with pornographic imagery and literature.[6] Art criticism also abounded here, not least of nude paintings and of a new genre of writing called "Nudist literature." Proponents of the latter defined it as innovative, audacious writing to overcome social and political stagnation. In one 1935 sample, esteemed critic Amin Rihani commended the writing style to "all who yearn for complete and total independence."[7]

The nudist movement, the nude genre, and nudist-writing all share the Arabic term *'uri*,[8] which references nakedness more as a state of being than an object. I treat these projects as emergent *emotional practices*— "doings and sayings" undertaken to achieve desired emotions and modify undesired ones.[9] I analyze the early twentieth-century Beirut fashion for nudism as an investment in undressing that intertwined emotional

Figure 6.2 *"Bayrut fi al-Bahr, Afkar wa Mushahidat `Ariya"* (Beirut at Sea, Nudist Thoughts and Scenes), Ra`fat Buhairy, *al-Ma`rid* 11, no. 959, July 19, 1931, 9.

practices of looking; one *at* nudes and the other *as* nudes. Beirutis deliberately introduced these ways of looking into their changing urban context to cultivate new sensibilities. I focus on painted compositions that enfold experiences of looking at and being looked at as a viewer of nudes, specifically in the work of the Beirut-based artists Moustapha Farrouk (Mustafa Farrukh, 1901–57), Omar Onsi (`Umar al-`Unsi, 1901–69), and Cesar Gemayel (Qaysar al-Jumayyil, 1898–1958).[10] Often visual art dangles on the edges of sociopolitical analyses of change, leaving the impression that art is not integral to the shaping of new, active civic imaginations. This chapter contributes to a broader project of understanding how visual art integrated with other art forms—such as avant-garde literature—as well as political movements, including anti-colonialism, pan-Islamism, and feminism, that centered on the Levant but extended far beyond.

Nudity, in art and life, had a special role in Mandate Lebanon because it combined space in otherwise unmappable ways. It merged Beirut's urbanizing environment with other sites for the practice of nudism—primarily France, Germany, and the United States—with representations of denuding in literature and fine art rendered in other times and languages—from Renaissance Italy to contemporary French and Ancient Greek—and ultimately with the bodies, real and represented, of genders, ethnicities, and colonial subjects that were otherwise carved up into myriad divisions. For example, an article praised painter Omar Onsi "*fi `urihi*" (in his nudity), meaning in the painting of nudes but also, for adopting a nudist perspective—more on this review below.[11] In short, for self-proclaimed "partisans of the nude" (*ansar al-`uri*), as the movement called itself, nudity was a style of both art and life that challenged current conventional and otherwise concretizing boundaries.

Looking at Nudes: Developing an Emotional Practice

Returning to the 1921 fair at which *Carrie* greeted visitors, we must ask what the inclusion of this painting meant to audiences who got themselves to the fair, and how that might differ from its meaning for those who left the fair? The social setting of Mandate Beirut was *and was not* post-colonial: one ("Ottoman") lord declared an occupier, the ("French") liberator transformed rapidly into another occupier. Concurrently, population growth, wealth upheavals, and shifting access to resources all provided new roles for government and contact with a bureaucracy that had not earned people's trust or respect. Projects to become new people abounded and abutted, among them: Communism, Arab nationalism, anti-materialism, *revanchisme*, and forms of Islamism.[12] Among those projects, nudism is striking for its simultaneous transnationalism—accompanied by print, filmic, and painted media announcing its association with other places and peoples—and localism—relying only on a practitioner's body and glorifying it. Similarly, locally produced nude genre paintings allowed viewers to experience, in their own mind-bodies, a "universal" phenomenon, that was very old—attributed by supporters to the ancient Greeks[13]—and new at once. The model for Saleeby's canvas was the painter's American wife, Carrie Aude, who had joined him from Philadelphia upon his return to Beirut in 1900 and appeared in numerous compositions in his studio, clothed and unclothed. Aude herself was both "foreign" and locally present. So, how were audiences invited to meet her transformation into *Carrie*, and what can we know about their experience of the encounter?[14]

Many contemporary press reports detail how people, particularly government officials or nobility, responded to the Beirut Fair's fine art. Remarkably, while Arabic poetry provided an extensive vocabulary for discussing nakedness and sensual response, writing about the nudes displayed at the 1921 Beirut Fair did not draw on it. In the long-established *Lisan al-Hal* run by independent entrepreneur Ramiz Sarkis, the Jesuit mouthpiece *al-Bashir,* the "Eastern Catholic" encyclopedic observer, *al-Mashriq*, and the newly launched *al-Ma`rid* newspaper, run by political hopeful Michel Zakkur, writers quite straightforwardly praised the artwork contributed by Daoud Corm [Daud Qurm], Yusuf al-Huwayyik, Habib Srur, Jean Dibs, Alfred Sursuq, Khalil Ghurayyib, Khalil Saleeby, and many others.[15] All had produced nudes in a classicizing, *beaux-arts* tradition, some sculpted and some painted. The press reports emphasized the capacities invested in the works—repeatedly invoking words for "innovation," "craft," and "skill"—which assured readers the results were "beautiful" and indicated the makers' "superiority" and "taste."[16] Their descriptions of audience appreciation read like a primer for the anatomy of affect: "His eyes were turned by the beautiful drawings."[17] "[Jean Dibs'] scenes blinded the eyes of all who saw them."[18] "The beholder cannot but stare at the beauties and taste (*dhawq*) and be affected (*atta'athur*) by the meaning of truth shown in them."[19] To be so affected, however, audiences had to get to the fair, as a special site for conducting emotional practices, and they were regularly admonished to get themselves there. Delight, amazement, admiration, and comfort would ensue.

At no point do any of the newspapers define the style of the craft or describe what viewers saw, let alone address the issue of some subjects' nakedness.[20] The focus is, rather, on *who* responded and how. In this, a nude was like any other instance of fine art, and like any other instance of solid craft, including cured tobacco or carved furniture for that matter. One report discussing the visit of High Commissioner General Gouraud and British Representative Herbert Samuel singles out Saleeby's "picture of his wife," as the report obliquely refers to *Carrie,* for "its good drawing, which indicates skill and superiority."[21] An earlier review had focused on Saleeby to present the main "opportunity" of the fair: "to let Europeans see there is someone like that here, to see the innovation and ingenuity of the son of this country."[22] The reviewer had predicted that Saleeby's "paintings of persons and views will catch attention of the European foreigner among us and show there is someone who expends his life force for the sake of fine art, one who sacrificed his life and spent long years in Europe for the sake of succeeding in this art."[23] As if clinching that argument, this second review closes, "What is great about this fair is how it shows the Lebanese keeping up with the son of the West (*ibn al-maghrib*) in the craft of his own two hands."[24] Eschewing any language of indigeneity or authenticity, the press unanimously adopts a language of shared corporal sensuality. *Carrie* and nudes generally were part of the project of establishing peership.

Historian Monique Scheer urges us to consider how emotions are named, mobilized, communicated, and managed. We should not assume that being transfixed by, admiring, or appreciating art is a natural human practice, but rather ask how people come to be transfixable before nudes, capable of admiring them, and needing to announce their or others' appreciation to thousands of readers? As Scheer argues, "conceiving emotions as practices means understanding them as emerging bodily dispositions conditioned by a social context, which always has cultural and historical specificity."[25] The vocabulary and viewing practices developing in this period to address nudes focused not on the pictures as objects unto themselves but on their capacity for inducing audience self-awareness amidst practitioners of looking at nudes.

Collapsing Space and Establishing Peership

A controversy surrounding another set of paintings shown at the fair further substantiates that audiences sought peership from nudes. *Lisan al-Hal* reported later that month, that "apparently" according to *Al-Ahwal* newspaper, "unnamed viewers" demanded the removal of Khalil Ghurayyib's painting of women with bared chests.[26] One image showed a hollow-eyed woman seated against the side of a building, her uncovered legs sprawling into the street, an infant on her lap, so scrawny that its ribs protrude, clearly unable to nurse from the pendulous breasts exposed to it. By no means adopting the denunciation of the protesting viewers as its own, the report expounds that the images copy documentary photographs taken during the time of the 1915–18 famine, which it calls a painful memory for many attendees. Its care to locate a photographic source suggests that it attributed the viewers' objections specifically to the female subjects' emaciation and not their nakedness per se—the latter receives no apology. In other words, what disturbed viewers was not the application of the genre of the nude to local bodies but the inferiority of the genre's fulfillment when applied to local bodies: they fretted that local bodies filling it should be fitting ones. Ghurayyib's nudes, in this instance, were a little too local, and smacked of a local history from which viewers still smarted.

In relation to the artistic ideal of the nude, Saleeby's *Carrie* crystallized a new view of the native son as peer, whereas Ghurayyib's wasted bodies revealed too much difference from the ideal and pitifully little self-cultivation. Anthropologist Michael Jackson points to the "creative value of dissociation in managing unbearable experiences by shifting one's focus to something outside oneself, something that can be regarded as objective rather than subjective, not-me rather than me."[27] It is not hard to imagine that the First World War, with conscription that drastically reduced the male population, a famine that decimated those remaining at home, and the complete change of political leadership, shattered people's sense of reality and control. The use that local artists and audiences made of the Beirut Fair opportunity to look at nudes and look at themselves being looked at suggests they did adopt an inverted perspective, through borrowed genres of "fine art" and hard acquired "foreign" skills, on the self. By discussing the type of work—"fine art" (a term deliberately distinguishing their work from a long, rich tradition of local aesthetic production) and training involved (emphasizing years "in Europe")—the textual response to the 1921 Beirut Fair's artworks condensed the distance between peoples of East and West, bringing them side by side while demarcating boundaries between

Figure 6.3 *Al-Sajinan* (The Two Prisoners), Moustapha Farrouk, 1929. Oil on canvas, 38 x 47 cm. Reproduced from "*Tabi`a wa Turath*" (Nature and Patrimony), *M. Farrouk Series,* Portfolio 7, Beirut, Lebanon, 1995. Courtesy of Hani Farrukh.

them and enabling glances across that put them each in new perspective. Affects feature in this discussion, but as something that can be displayed and communicated to audiences of audiences. The communicative power of these affects, from delight to admiration, promised to impact interpersonal, social, and even international relations.

Looking at Oneself Looking at Nudes

The dissociating effect of art nudes could transport viewers yet further, prompting intimate experience of ways of being that, while not yet locally present, could become so. Take by way of example, *The Two Prisoners* (Figure 6.3), a nude that Moustapha Farrouk produced in 1929, with the stated goal of creating "modern society" among his fellow "sons of Lebanon."[28]

I have previously discussed Farrouk's style as a mechanism of dislocation that opened an existential gap in local society to usher in an awareness of alternatives elsewhere.[29] We know that Farrouk deliberately drew on a genre he had learned in art school in Rome, and on the body of a "foreign friend's wife," to construct an image of "the Eastern woman" that could charge viewers with the plan and will to change "Eastern society." We also know that Farrouk considered himself to be both a "son of the country" and fundamentally different from all other native sons. The difference lay in his learning to look at nudes to assess one's own reaction. In his posthumously published memoirs, the artist explains how he prepared to take the Roman Royal Academy of Art entrance exam:

> I found it smart to prepare before entering the exam, *for fear of a disappointment that I did not want to befall my well-being (khatir)* after having invested all this effort. For that reason, I entered a private school to practice, so I would not be imperiled, especially that the first thing they ask for is to draw the naked human body, then anatomical knowledge of the bones and joints and all miscellaneous details related to that, as well as some knowledge of art history and its schools.[30]

Farrouk looked at the nude as an emotional practice toward gaining an artist's certificate. Protecting his well-being involved attaining the skills that the 1921 Beirut Fair reviewers lauded when reviewing Saleeby's *nu au dos, Carrie*, but more now, it involved restructuring the emotions of this "young man whose lifestyle was formed [...] in the Basta Tahta [Beiruti suburb] quarter," as Farrouk describes himself.[31] The first time he actually encountered a live female model in his drawing class, he trembled so much he could not draw, and, despite "trying his hardest to avoid that annoying, most unwelcome reaction," he candidly admits he had an erection. What follows is doubtlessly one of the funniest passages in the history of modern art:

> I decided internally, fearing a scandal, to admit the reality of the situation and surrender. I exited to the waiting hall, refreshing my spirit and relieving my poor nerves. After my spirit had settled slightly, I scolded it for its weakness *relative to its peers* working in the atelier. Then I returned the serve and re-entered the atelier. *The impact was, naturally, less,* and I was able at least to draw some broad outlines. I left the school that day to my room safe ... content with this outcome. However, I did not stop there, of course, but followed through with a shower of cold water. It was at the end of September, and September [in Italy] has biting cold days. So, this punishment was somewhat harsh. Often punishments have some zing in them, *so as to change people at their core (albab).*[32]

Following the shower with a reading from the Qur'an, and subsequent days of labor, shower, and scripture, Farrouk passed the exam without the interruption of unfortunate reactions, physiological or emotional.

Recalling the concerns of the audiences before *Carrie*, he asserts his ability to comport himself like his peers and become a professional man defined by skill and self-control.[33] As an emotional practice, looking at nudes could dissociate one from the apparent destiny of place.

Transitive Emotional Practices: Nudes as a Space of Imagination

Yet, for Farrouk and fellow painters, self-transformation was just the beginning. Farrouk believed *The Two Prisoners* could convey the same result to his audiences in Beirut. It was not merely a *communicative* display of accomplishments, a modern painting; it was *transitive*, a modern way of becoming dissociated from local destiny while contributing to local progress. Looking at nudes conveyed "culturing" (*tathqif*) by reenacting encounters and experiences, or looking at how oneself looked at nudes. An acerbic account young journalist Kamal al-Naffi published in *al-Ahwal* suggests Farrouk succeeded:[34]

> With the picture, *The Two Prisoners*, you are in front of an Eastern woman stretched out on a couch covered with sumptuous silk brocade. She glances at her companion in prison, a small bird placed in a cage who sings sad songs that bring pain to the heart, the songs of the eternal prisoner. For they are both, verily as is said, prisoners whose counsel still to this very day fights to defend their cause before public opinion.[35]

Al-Naffi describes the figure as an "Eastern woman," treating the representation improbably as accurate, although any reader of his column would know that women in Beirut did not live like that. Still, by situating this hypothetical "Eastern woman" in a metaphorical prison cell apparently found in a modern-day Beiruti apartment, al-Naffi appeals to a local audience then embroiled in debates over women's suffrage.[36] Locality comes to dominate the critic's interpretation of the scene, even though the figure he describes has neither the clothing, home decor, nor body of a local woman.

Al-Naffi's way of looking moves deliberately between locality and dissociation. Paradoxically he opens his essay by rejecting the possibility of an exhibition of fine art in Lebanon, challenging the person who invites him to the show, "Are you crazy? Do you think we're in Venice or one of the elevated cities of the West?"[37] Even as he undertakes reviewing the show, he remains skeptical about its existence, saying, "The arts are to us almost *something completely forgotten* (*nasiyan munasan*), so much are they unknown to us and their value unappreciated."[38] Importantly, his phrase, "*nasiyan munasan*" parrots the Virgin Mary's response to the Annunciation, as recorded by the Prophet Muhammad in "Surat Miryam" of the Qur'an. By echoing this hallowed—and multidenominational—source, al-Naffi renders Farrouk a modern-day prophet sharing divine revelation while also enunciating familiarity with Islamic strictures. Al-Naffi deftly blends cultures, Islamic/Christian and Venetian/Eastern—which others may then have seen as opposed (and may still)—to advance the possibility, if only barely, of a very different local society.

Al-Naffi's cultural blending occurs through a carefully calibrated emotional practice which requires reveling in a picture, just as the 1921 fair attendees cultivated delight and admiration in the Fine Arts stand. Additionally, it involves imagining how unlikely the picture is to have been made—ironically due to an alleged lack of local resources rather than a realistic basis—and how fragile its future remains. Thus, the emotion al-Naffi marshals upon seeing the nude of *The Two Prisoners* is a wincing skepticism that he shares with an audience who "knows" nudes cannot exist here and accepts that this nude symbolizes perpetually oppressed Ottoman-style harem women.

Al-Naffi ushers in the nude as a space of imagination. Strikingly, in closing his lesson on learning to look at nudes, al-Naffi not only disregards Islam's alleged iconoclasm but calls on his readers to pursue aesthetic uplift with a local modern-day prophet "lest they leave it to the foreigners in charge."[39] In "giving Art its due," he concludes, "*they would show* that they are a living people truly striving for freedom."[40] Formed in the subjunctive tense, the sentence conducts a dual emotional practice of mobilizing and communicating emotions. The practice of controlling one's emotions before a woman's naked body that Farrouk's painting provided becomes an opportunity to communicate the new emotional system to onlookers who were assessing demands for a second decolonization—i.e. demanding French withdrawal. Yet, if al-Naffi opened his essay with a Beirut surprisingly like Venice, paradoxically overcoming physical distance with the "birth" of a prophetic painter, his choice to conclude with Farrouk's *Two Prisoners* leaves the city lagging on the singular, teleological march of time.

Out in the Open: From Looking At, to Looking As Nudes

In 1935 the nude expanded its space of imagination from canvases to print media. Its format was a weekly periodical founded by Fouad Hobeiche with the title, *al-Makshuf*, meaning that which is open, exposed, bared, unguarded; but, also, short for the phrase `ala al-makshuf, out in the open. As a young writer, Hobeiche apprenticed in journalism with *al-Ahrar* and *al-Ma`rid*, both of which published his discussions of nudism's benefits and local practitioners. Between summer 1929 and summer 1931 he had published a series of essays in which he railed against social practices he deemed outmoded, from forms of courting to child-rearing to exercise and eating, and encouraged his readers to combat them by stripping.

Now the editor of his own magazine, Hobeiche brought together a sundry array of concerns. Facing pages 10 and 11 of the August 20, 1935 issue of *al-Makshuf* neatly encapsulate the space of imagination the nude carved (Figure 6.4).

Page 10 tells the reader of sex crimes in England that led to trafficking "3000 virgins," while page 11 advertises *al-Ma`rid* newspaper, Savoy Photography Studio, the "modern" painter Sa`adi Sinevi, Ixennol body-slimmer medicine, and last but not least, the editor-in-chief's own publication *Rasul al-`Uri* (The Prophet of the Nude), a guide for would-be nudists (Figure 6.5).

In Hala Bizri's summary, Hobeiche "propagated nudism as a new way of life to bring mankind closer to nature and wellness and to distance it from artifice and lethargy."[41] With articles on nudity in relation to schooling,[42] physical training,[43] childbirth and rearing,[44] premarital sex,[45] women's rights,[46] crime prevention,[47] religion,[48] cinema,[49] Arabic literature,[50] art,[51] and political revolution,[52] as well as famous advocates of the practice in Europe, America, Turkey, and Ancient Greece,[53] Hobeiche and—at least two—other writers associated nudism with vegetarianism, nonconformism, humanism, internationalism, pacifism, and rationalism.[54]

These were global movements. However, the advantage of nudism in contrast to other international imports was that it did not cost practitioners cash. Unlike other kinds of modernism, nudism's practice depends not on goods or class belonging but emotions. Take Hobeiche's reflection from *Rasul al-`Uri*:

This summer I wanted to try experiencing the life of nudism myself. So a friend and I spent twenty days on the beach of `Amshit completely naked, bathing in the sea, exposing our bodies to the sunrays and air currents, and exercising our muscles at the oars. We gained health, vigor, peace of mind, and clarity of thought, which secured our spending the winter season in *a state of physical and mental blessedness* which neither the visitors of `Alay and Sufar nor the frequenters of tea parties and all-night shindigs have ever known.[55]

Figure 6.4 Spread from *al-Makshuf* 1, no. 13, August 20, 1935, 10–11. Dar al-Furat Collection, Beirut.

Figure 6.5 Detail of advertisement for *Rasul al-ʿUri* (Prophet of the Nude), in *al-Makshuf*, 1, no. 13, August 20, 1935, 11. The phrase *ansar al-ʿuri* (partisans of the nude) appears in the last line. Dar al-Furat Collection, Beirut.

Hobeiche's text lays out the steps for attaining that state of physical and mental blessedness, and anyone can imitate them. The text also counterposes those steps to the riches spent by resort-goers and denizens of Lebanon's already infamous nightlife. Art, however, could aid in remapping the space of imagination. From erotic literature to painted canvases, art provided through its material form a venue for nudist emotional practices, a space of imagination that differed substantially from al-Naffi's deferred Venice. Art brings distant places into the local viewer's realm and enables physically improbable experiences.

The year Hobeiche released *Rasul al-'Uri* he visited Cesar Gemayel's studio near the Place de l'Étoile.[56] Gemayel, too, was a newly returned artist, having studied in Paris for three years on a Ministry of Education bursary. Starting with his article's title, "An Hour in Gemayel's Studio, You Imagine Yourself in a German Nudist Colony,"[57] Hobeiche calls on the reader's capacity to migrate imaginatively, complementing the artist's peregrinations. He repeats this claim—or command—three times and compels readers on the trip by listing the contents of the studio's pictures and by allowing his pen to rival their verisimilitude:

> Here is a maiden lying on her back, eyes closed, a deep smile on her lips, clearly showing you that the source of this picture is drunk with the intoxication of delight. This [other picture] represents a lass less beautiful than the first, a lass whose fiancé has broken their engagement and left her at the last minute. She is confused, lost, and knows not what to do with her heart after she offered it such a wretch. As you tour Gemayel's studio you imagine yourself in a German nudist colony. [...] Here is a maiden spread among the grasses on the sea's coast, gazing at the crescent rising on the horizon, while the arc of her body a crescent makes ....[58]

The narration proceeds casually as if writer and reader are accustomed to cavorting with fellow nudists. By imitating Gemayel's visual verisimilitude with his language, Hobeiche makes peership an issue of temporality. His language subtly suggests, contra al-Naffi's certitude, that if Beirut is not Venice "to this very day," it very well *could be*.

The temporal difference between al-Naffi's and Hobeiche's approaches is the cultivation of *al-'uri* as an emotional practice: looking at nudes in this present becomes *looking as a nude*, toward a future, one intertwining the possibility for self-awareness with emerging bodily disciplines. At the end of his essay, Hobeiche appends a provocative quote from the painter: "As for me, I consider figurative art to be a language through which the picturer expresses the emotions and reactions produced within himself."[59] In other words, the production of nudes, which epitomized Gemayel's oeuvre for Hobeiche, and marked his fame for the Beirut public, is an emotional practice, involving naming, communicating, and mobilizing emotions. With this quote, we directly confront the notion of an internally changing self, effected through one's relation to an uncovered body. Gemayel's pictures allow a viewer to practice at being a nudist, comfortable with uncovered truths, fearing and hiding nothing. He is not just looking *at* nudes but *as* a nude. The self-focus shifts markedly from the 1921 national pride at foreigners' recognition of peership among "local sons." In this approach to nudes we have a concern instead for how "local sons" experience motivation.

Hobeiche warned that the social costs of emotional suppression were tremendous. In the summer of 1931 he reported on the recently executed Peter Kürten (1883–1931), known as the "Monster of Düsseldorf," for the brutality he inflicted on his many young victims.[60] Hobeiche held that society was to blame for Kürten's crimes, by falsely teaching that instincts must be suppressed "by whatever means necessary" and leaving the mentally unbalanced with no means of release. Familiarity with nudism and the physical training it fosters— including full bodily exposure to nature, sun, cold showers, walks in the fresh air, and so on—would have spared him the overwhelming affect of his "murderous" lineage—by which Hobeiche referred to the killer's abusive upbringing. Explicitly presenting nudism as an emotional practice, Hobeiche summarized that it had a role in disciplining (*tahdhib*) and cultivating (*tathqif*) society physically and mentally.

In *al-Makshuf*, Hobeiche would offer a trove of erotic short stories toward familiarizing readers with sexual possibilities and outcomes.[61] Others made a similar case for nude cinema, *al-ashrita al-`uri*. Muhyi al-Din al-Tawil reported in the same newspaper that The High Council for Cinema had convened in Paris at the end of 1931 to award prizes to the best "beneficial, educational" films.[62] After noting that most attendees agreed that documentaries of nudist colonies had much more to offer than the "many geographic reels of which people have grown so weary," al-Tawil recounted the words of director George O'Messerly, who had released *Physiopolis*, a documentary about French nudists, in 1930:

> Many assume that nude films, with their scenes of naked men and women, stir up the psyche's latent depths and corrupt the ethics of young men and women, and even old men. But they do not *lend their attention* to the other films that are produced today in great numbers by most French and American companies. They show us plainly and clearly how some husbands plan to betray their women. They show how they *gradually strip their clothing before acting out the role* of the treacherous man! Films produced in that image are the ones to fear stampeding the lofty edifices of social manners and putting an end to ethics.[63]

In 1934, an "educational" film portraying life in a German nudist colony played at Beirut's Olympia cinema.[64] The film opens with a French psychologist's tirade against the horrors of urban life and culminates in scenes of liberated city-folk dancing naked and painting each other in the nude. This was a common trope of nudist publications, emphasizing the high culture benefits of their project.[65] It is worth lingering on the language of theatricality invoked by al-Tawil's review and undertaken by the film. If clothing is a costume one accepts as real, then stripping it can entrench one all the more firmly in a social role that can undermine the basis of all healthy interactions. In contrast to art that strategically staged the removal of clothing to increase irrational, anti-social responses, proponents of nude art held that regular exposure to naked bodies developed balanced emotions of respect and refinement. The role nudism allocated to its enactors was thus civic and publicly engaged. It constituted a human truth subverted by regular clothing practices.

Ansar al-`Uri: Partisans of the Nude/Nudity

When Gemayel's same nudes inhabited the newly (re-)inaugurated School of Arts and Crafts as part of a massive "First Lebanese Salon for Painting and Sculpture" (December 1930 to January 1931), they joined more than 400 works by dozens of professional and amateur artists. At least twenty of the works on display were nudes, among them perhaps even some photographs and one collectively painted by female high school students (Figure 6.6).[66]

Al-Bashir's short review evinces the new interest in discussing regular people's "internal" changes through the medium of art. It praised the event by way of detailing the facial reactions of an esteemed audience of elites and authorities: "As their eyes fell upon the beauty of the artistic creations, the signs of pleasure and awe were clear on all their faces."[67] In their much longer reviews, both Yusuf Ghussub, in *al-Mashriq*, and Jawaba, in *al-Ma`rid*, applaud Gemayel's anatomical precision. Jawaba additionally states that Gemayel's "worthy nudes," especially one supine woman, "provoke desires and inclinations."[68] Similarly, fellow journalist, poet, and reformer Rushdi Ma`luf (1914–80) would later explain that "the epitome of the successful modern picture" is the painting of *zalitāt* (uncovered feminine things), in their undeniably "desire-provoking positions," because they have "an impact in refining characters that velvet and silken clothes cannot for the way they *camouflage*."[69] The artistic handling of limbs and veins suggests to the critic that he is before a live and pulsing model. It invites emotional responses—desires and inclinations—that are communicated, so as to be regulated. At this

No. d'ordre	TITRE	NOM	No. de peintre
249	Mer agité	Mlle Moubarak	1
250	Mer calme	»	2
251	Paysage de pins	»	3
252	Peintre sur poteries	»	4
253	Cheik en comtemplation	Nadia Baidoun	1
254	Fille nue au bain	Zahret el Ahsan Ecole	1
255	Louqsor ruines	»	2
256	Roc of Eggis	»	3
257	Paysanne près du fleuve	»	4
258	Paysanne qui tricote	»	5
259	Femme tenant une branche fleurie	»	6
260	Coussin 1	»	7
261	Coussin 2	»	8
262	Aquarelle	»	9
263	Tête de Cheik 1	P. Guigues	1
264	Palmyre ruelles 3	»	2
265	Paysage Baalbeck 1	»	3
266	Souk de Beyrouth, 2	»	4
267	Portrait Cheik 1	»	5
268	Paysage fleuri 1	»	6
269	Caravane dans les gorges de l'Anti-Liban	»	7
270	Paysage	»	8
271	Paysage	»	9

ARCHIVES M. ZOUEIN

No. d'ordre	TITRE	NOM	No. de peintre
272	Paysages	Blanche Ammoun	1
273	»	»	2
274	»	»	3
275	»	»	4
276	»	»	5
277	»	»	6
278	Nature morte	»	7
279	Boudah	»	8
280	Portrait du Patriarche Maronite	»	9
281	Fleurs (Pavets)	»	10
282	Nature morte Cactus	Georges Corm	1
283	Portrait du Cheik Jamil El Khazen	»	2
284	Groupe de maisons	»	3
285	Beyrouth vue de Raifoun	Charles Corm	1
286	Têtes de Saints	David Corm	1
287	Têtes de Saints	»	2
288	Tête Portrait	Mlle Choucair	1
289	Tête Portrait	»	2
290	Tête Portrait	»	3
291	Tête Portrait	»	4
292	Tête Portrait	»	5
293	Nature morte	»	6

Figure 6.6 Page from catalogue for "First Lebanese Salon for Painting and Sculpture"—December 1930 to January 1931. Number 254 lists a "Fille nue au bain (Nude Girl Bathing)," by the students of Zahra al-Ahsan school, a girls-only establishment. Gilberte Zouaine Collection, Ma`amaltain. Courtesy of Gilberte Zouaine.

1931 exhibition, we are clearly standing with viewers who did not seek only to look at nudes, to become modern as Al-Naffi had, but now as nudes, or in Arabic *fi `urihi[m]*.

Art and cinema critics' goals for looking *fi `urihi* parallel goals associated with "*ansar al-`uri*," which translates as both partisans of the nude and partisans of nudity. These champions called for removing clothing that camouflaged, in the sense of enabling people to pass for that which they are not. Significantly, for Hobeiche and his followers, nudists developed feelings by removing clothing, perhaps only a few pieces or even just their hats or shoes. For example, in April 1930 *al-Ma`rid* reported that churchgoers in Ma`amaltain were surprised upon coming out of Sunday services to find five young men and a woman running past them in the main street, "stripped (`*urwat*), barefoot, and bareheaded, nothing protecting their bodies *but bathing clothes*, known as `*mayu (maillot).*'"[70] The report emphasizes that these six bodies—remember five of which are male—have rejected the protective tissues they are generally thought to need. Dress/undress always being culturally relative, they are naked by local conventions, and the report deliberately displaces their covering from the local context by invoking a Francophone name, "*maillot*." *Ansar al-`uri* moves into its space of imagination by removing "protection (*sitr*)"—it is the same word for curtain and veil—moving not from the skin out but from added layers off and into unlocal worlds.

Overall, the report indicates that nudism was a process of transitioning with transitive effects. The second paragraph of the report adds that the six strangers, visiting from Palestine, bathed in the sea for an hour and then were seen "rolling in the sand, exposing their rosy bodies to the delicious rays of the sun," according to onlookers.[71] The embedded quote suggests the onlookers were favorably inspired by what they saw. As

Hala Bizri puts it, this nudism was "Less a justification than a rich description of something closer to a philosophical concept: one that dealt with more than simply outward expression in attire or lack thereof."[72] Refining emotions, not merely releasing them, is this nudism's goal, for refined emotions will make Venice here, and here still local at once.

Proponents adopted divesting the body of clothing and regarding undressed bodies interchangeably to enhance their rationalism. The project of developing emotions proliferates in articles discussing al-`uri. An unsigned 1930 article in al-Ma`rid invokes Lycurgus of Sparta's promotion of nudism to counter shame and fear among young women.[73] Another report on schools from 1931 concludes with the question, "When will we in the East *feel* this need to strengthen our youth from its very beginning, that we might make of it a generation of the future, strong, courageous, and corrected (*sahih*) from all kinds of maladies?"[74] Clearly the authors were not waiting for the feeling to percolate. They were investing in emotion's emergence by describing, reproducing, and creating encounters with nudes. Promoting "nude literature," nude paintings, and nudism, *ansar al-`uri* called on readers to show their true selves, explain their vices, and know how to avoid them. Then they would become contented and healthy like the unabashed woman on Gemayel's canvas.

Paintings of Nudes for Looking as Nudes

I have argued that art had a special role for *ansar al-`uri* in Lebanon because it combined space in otherwise unmappable ways. It was important for a second, experiential reason; one alluded to by the embedded quote of the report from Ma`amltain above. I posit that artworks modeled, like figures on a catwalk, what nudism could entail and endow, to those who live as nudes. I close with a few artworks from the early 1930s that I take as providing people with the chance to look not simply at nudes but as nudes. In 1932, Omar Onsi painted a composition he called simply, "*A l'exposition*" (At the Exhibition) (Figure 6.7).

Figure 6.7 *A l'exposition*—also known as Young Ladies Visiting an Exhibition—Omar Onsi, 1932. Oil on canvas, 37 x 45 cm. Collection Samir Abillama. Courtesy of Samir Abillama.

One contemporary art critic described it as showing "several young women flocking to gaze at an artistic picture that represents naked women."[75] In the foreground are six women and one small boy seen from behind, grouped around a framed image of two nudes in poses straight out of a studio art class. The women wear short black taffeta frocks, silk stockings, high heels, a *pelerine* (cape), and the *yachmak*—an Ottoman-style head covering common among Beirut's well-off Sunni families.[76] In the background an amorous couple engage in earnest conversation, not apparently acknowledging the pictures on display. The man sports a suit and a fez; the woman dons the latest Parisian fashion, including a turban *à l'orientale*. What is most interesting in terms of the clothing-unclothing mélange produced in this *tableau vivant* is how it foregrounds each wearer's own interpretation of their dress, particularly the young female viewers. Though all wear the prescribed, historically validated dress, they each modify it in their own way, filling out its contours differently, adding a sash, wearing the cape high or low on the arms.[77] The clothing seems as mobile as they are in their act of thrusting themselves toward the canvas to consider its contents.

Painted after Onsi's participation in his first exhibition among his compatriots, at the School of Arts and Crafts in December 1930, and referencing works Onsi showed then, this composition wedges art as a genre for self-awareness into Onsi's society. *À l'exposition* both explores and induces transformations in urban public behavior by impacting the act of viewing. In it, nudity is *in* the jauntily depicted canvas, while the viewer of it is called by its composition to identify with the feminine vectors of visual attention—the six women to the left and not the heterosexual couple to the right. The catalog from 1932, when Onsi next showed in Beirut, again at the School of Arts and Crafts, suggests that it hung at the very entrance to the show, following a now-lost *Allegory: Phoenicia Presenting Oranges*, also a nude representing the gifts of the East to the West (Figure 6.8).[78]

Upon seeing the full-length nude and then an image of looking at nudes, visitors could have become exceptionally aware of themselves as embodying categories of viewing. They would likely attain a heightened sense of being seen rather than being the one seeing, of having to observe developing social codes as well as pictures.

Figure 6.8 *Allégorie: Phénicie présentant les oranges (Allegory: Phoenicia Presenting Oranges)* Omar Onsi, 1932. Oil on canvas, size and whereabouts unknown. Reproduced from *al-Maʿrid* 11, no. 988, February 28, 1932, 20. Dar al-Furat Collection, Beirut.

The respect Onsi demonstrates for women who attend carefully to nudes, as art forms, contrasts drastically with the critique he makes in his next canvas on display, of a male viewer peeking surreptitiously at women as naked bodies. Titled *Imru al-Qais*, it depicts a popular episode described by the sixth-century pre-Islamic poet Imru' al-Qais, from his courtship of Unaizah, when he secretly follows her and two friends to a bathing pool where he steals their clothes. In the poem Qais then demands that each woman leave the pool and ask him for her clothes back, which they resist until they are faint with hunger. A reviewer of Omar Onsi's version of this episode, shown in 1932, explains: "[Qais] stands awaiting their exit to the shore to enjoy the view of their nakedness."[79] Unlike nudes, the naked women fixed by Qais's stare have not undergone art's idealizing, intellectual process. Whereas a gilt frame around a canvas of a nude provides audiences with dignifying assurance that they are observing an abstraction from real life, the flimsy palm fronds framing Qais's gaze proclaim that he has adopted an improper position for viewing nakedness. This is a sort of looking that stands resolutely outside social interactions and social progress, pre-Islamic as it were.[80]

Clearly, social ills remained if audiences failed to learn to look as nudes. A year after Onsi painted his critique of backward masculine ways of looking, Farrouk inked a caricature of regressive, rural ways of looking (Figure 6.9).

The title, *Souvenir de l'exposition Farrouk (1933–1934)*, suggests it summarizes the character of the audience at Farrouk's show a few weeks earlier. It depicts a peasant couple whose questioning gestures and passive stance mark their bafflement. The man's mix of Ottoman-era *shirwal*, antique multi-buttoned chemise, contemporary suit jacket, slippers, and *tarbush* (brimless hat) hang heavily on his body, emphasizing his pencil-thin neck and protruding, outdated mustache. Behind him, his spouse seems to shrivel under a hefty, woolen robe with an overwhelming collar and enveloping veil; her flat shoes have curled up at the toes. The couple seems trapped in their clothing, completely lacking the fluidity and flourish of Onsi's young women. The composition draws a stark division between the slovenly, stooping character of the visitors and the geometrical rationality of the art on display. Worse, the visitors actually darken the art, casting their shadows across the viewing balustrade, rather than receiving its enlightenment. Unsurprisingly, the picture challenging their backwardness is an academic nude. By aligning confusion over how to understand and respond to an academic painting with signs of pastoral lifestyle, Farrouk equates, by corollary, the appreciation of this fine art genre with urban, technologically modern lifestyles.

The picture taunting the peasant couple specifically refers to *Au crépuscule* (c. 1905), a famous work by Farrouk's French mentor Paul Chabas (1869–1937), member of the French Academy of Beaux-Arts and President of the National Society of French Artists, in whose annual exhibition Farrouk participated in 1931. A similar work by Chabas, titled *September Morn*, had prompted public outcry and a nationwide anti-vice campaign when displayed in a gallery window in New York in 1913. Displaying his homage to Chabas' oeuvre in Beirut, Farrouk articulated his affiliation with a beleaguered lineage of academic artistry. He also extended the challenge of aesthetic enlightenment to his compatriots. Thus, the peasants standing before the picture are a cosmopolitan problem and not categorically a "Lebanese" or "Arab" one. Given that Farrouk consistently created ennobling pictures of peasants throughout his career, one can assume that his critique of the couple did not attribute their backwardness to an inherent cultural cause. Moreover, the signatures in his 1933 exhibition registry place his audience firmly in the urban milieu, and their comments attest to their labor to be enlightened by the art.[81] These facts set Farrouk's ink-drawing in the realm of fantasy rather than memory. In other words, the image alerts upcoming audiences to the potentiality of peasanthood—now the state (emotion?) of not deserving membership in modern urbanity—still present in those who do not cultivate looking at and as nudes. They cannot enter the space of imagination that is modernity.

Figure 6.9 *Souvenir de l'exposition Farrouk (1933–1934)* (Souvenir of Farrouk's Exhibition [1933–1934]), Moustapha Farrouk, 1934, printed postcard. Hani Farrukh Collection, Beirut. Courtesy of Hani Farrukh.

Conclusion: Nudes as a Lesson for Scholarly Imagination

The problem scholars confront in approaching such material today is that there are no clear outcomes or meanings to all this social effort, whether in art hung in salons or nudists cavorting on the beach. Farrouk's image recalls the theatrical language deployed by al-Tawil for his discussion of the effort one makes to take up a social role. If film critic al-Tawil grappled with the dilemma of undressing, Farrouk describes that of cross-dressing. For cross-dressers the existential dilemma lies in negotiating binary oppositions, neither term of which fully sums up their identity or experience.[82] Here the poorly matched clothing indicates people who have, like al-Tawil's socially reputable husbands, found refuge in customs; when asked to see the world as nudes, they reveal their lack of comfort with themselves. Fashion and fine art are both frequently accused of providing merely "solace, illusion, and escape."[83] Yet, nude paintings and bodies of the Mandate era provided means to engage and inspire ways of thinking by deploying one's body differently.

More and more in the 1930s, the discussion of nudes becomes discussion of art as a medium not for gaining external admiration but for *self-exploration*, not only for artists but also for audiences who could seek out such works. With this type of criticism, the nude gets taken up into large-scale social projects and becomes a medium for discussing the possibility of deep social change, rooted in the nerve fibers of the artist and viewer. Paying attention to the investment in a movement for self-divestment helps us rethink the boundaries, polarities, subjectivities, and imaginations that developed during the period. Whether deployed on canvas, in literature, on the street, or at the beach, nude bodies, in their very materiality, intervened in and proposed a new space for imagination. These social agents help us review the commonly relied upon boundaries of society, politics, and possibility, and lay out a space of imagination to which we otherwise have little access today. Foreclosing our awareness of its existence truncates our appreciation of the creative capacities of the people who grappled with colonialism and conceived of new subject-positions for themselves not bounded by passports and the identity-politics familiar to us today.

Notes

1   "*Fi al-Ma`rid: Rusum al-Salibi*" (At the Fair: Saleeby's Pictures), *Lisan al-Hal* 44, no. 8314–664, May 17, 1921, 2.

2   In line with Woodrow Wilson's 14 Points and following the loss of legitimacy of colonial rule after the Great War (the First World War), the League of Nations created a new legal status—Mandate Territory—for territories that had been under Ottoman or German imperial rule and sought sovereignty. "A hybrid, a halfway house between colonial rule and independence," the Mandate system impeded direct rule of Arab, African, and—later—Pacific populations by British, French, or—later—Australian and American authorities but maintained control until said populations could demonstrate their "fitness" for self-rule, that is, amenability to the Mandate authorities' priorities. See Nadine Méouchy and Peter Sluglett, "General Introduction," in *The British and French Mandates in Comparative Perspectives*, eds. Nadine Méouchy and Peter Sluglett (Leiden: Brill Publishers, 2004), 10–11.

3   M.V. [Max Villard], "*Nudisme …*," *L'Orient* 10, no. 22, June 7, 1934, 2.

4   One could engage in "nudity" by wearing less clothing than usual. Cartoonist Ra'fat Buhairy's sketches from the Beirut beach in July 1931 purported to show current practices of nudism. See Ra'fat Buhairy, "*Bayrut fi al-Bahr, Afkar wa Mushahidat `Ariya*" (Beirut at Sea, Nudist Thoughts and Scenes), *al-Ma`rid* 11, no. 959, July 19, 1931, 9.

5   See "*Al-Sair taht al-Shams (La Marche au Soleil)*," advertisement, *al-Nahar* 1, no. 203, April 19, 1934, 6.

6   Editorialists of rival journals appealed to "moral" readers to avoid these images, warning they would lead to abomination. For example, see unsigned editorial "*Mahaliyyat* (Local issues)," *al-Bashir*, January 22, 1931, 1 and editorial, "*Bu'rat Fasad* (Wasteland of Corruption)," *al-Bashir*, May 5, 1935, 1). Their success was at best spotty. Whereas a 1931 journal called *al-Nassim* did not last, *al-Makshuf* had a wide readership which indisputably included men and women. See *al-Makshuf*, no. 42 (March 23, 1936) which announces that "female virgins" can continue reading the magazine but now more publicly, knowing they are contributing to national development, "and legitimate

hopes for life and liberty." See Hala Bizri, "The Nudism of Sheikh Fouad Hobeiche," trans. Elisabeth Jaquette, in *Art, Awakening, and Modernity in the Middle East: The Arab Nude*, ed. Octavian Esanu (London: Routledge, 2018), 86–96.

7   Ibid., 93.

8   The word "*al-ʿuri*," usually translated as "nudity," comes from the root ʿa-r-y which references stripping down, cutting back, or removing protection.

9   Monique Scheer, "Are Emotions a Kind of Practice (and is that what makes them have a history)? A Bourdieusian Approach to Understanding Emotion," *History and Theory* 51, no. 2 (2012): 193–220.

10 The practice spread widely, including among female artists, most notably Marie Hadad (1889–1973), but documentation of their work has been dispersed and impedes extended analysis.

11 See Jawaba—a pen name, probably for Hobeiche—"*Al-Musawwirun al-Wataniyyun wa al-Ajanib Yuʿariduna Atharihim* (Local and Foreign Artists Display Their Works)," *al-Maʿrid* 9, no. 935, January 22, 1931, 8–9.

12 For more on the ideologies proliferating in the period, see Fawwaz Traboulsi's chapter "From Mandate to Independence (1920–1943)," in his volume *History of Modern Lebanon* (London: Pluto Press, 2012), 88–109; Christoph Schumann, "The Generation of Broad Expectations: Nationalism, Education, and Autobiography in Syria and Lebanon, 1930–1958," in *The Making of the Arab Intellectual*, ed. Dyala Hamzah (London: Routledge, 2013), 188–211; and Jennifer Dueck, "A Muslim Jamboree: Scouting and Youth Culture in Lebanon under the French Mandate," *French Historical Studies* 30, no. 3 (2007): 485–516.

13 "*Hawl al-ʿUri*" (About Nudity), *al-Maʿrid* 9, no. 886, January 1, 1930, 11.

14 At least one review referred to the image as showing Saleeby's wife. (See "*Fi al-Maʿrid* (At the Fair)," *Lisan al-Hal*, 44, no. 8332–672, May 30, 1921, 2. Insufficient information precludes knowing how awareness of the model's identity may have impacted viewers. Perhaps one could read the staunch but dispassionate support for Saleeby's work as a defensive posture against recriminations which have not been recorded in the press. Clearly publications that made it their business to guard public morals, such as the church-produced *al-Bashir* and *al-Mashriq*, and could be expected to denounce the pictures, did not.

15 Also mentioned as participating were Salim Samra, a Damascene painter, a Mr. Humsi and a Mr. Kujaz. For participants, see "*al-Maʿrid Aidan*" (The Fair Again), *Lisan al-Hal* 44, no. 8304–654, May 5, 1921, 2; "*Maʿrid al-Funun Al-Jamila*" (The Exhibition of Fine Arts), *al-Maʿrid* 1, no. 4, May 12, 1921, 3; "*Qasr Bayrut: fi al-Maʿrid*," (Beirut Castle: at the Fair), *al-Maʿrid* 1, no. 5, May 15, 1921, 4; "*Fi Maʿrid al-Manshiyya*" (In the Industrial Fair), *Lisan al-Hal* 44, no. 8315–665, May 18, 1921, 2; "*Jawaʾiz al-Maʿrid*" (Prizes for the Fair), *Lisan al-Hal* 44, no. 8358–698, June 30, 1921, 2; "*Lamha Taʾrikhiyya ʿan Maʿrid Bayrut* "(A Historical Glimpse of the Beirut Fair), *al-Mashriq* 21, no. 7, July 1921, 528–535.

16 See, for example, "*Iftitah al-Maʿrid*" (The Fair Opening), *Lisan al-Hal* 44, no. 8301–651, May 2, 1921, 2; "*Fi al-Maʿrid*" (At the Fair), *Lisan al-Hal* 44, no. 303–653, May 4, 1921, 3.

17 Ibid.

18 "*Qasr Bayrut: fi al-Maʿrid*" (Beirut Castle: In the Fair), *al-Maʿrid* 1, no. 5, May 15, 1921, 4.

19 "*Fi Maʿrid al-Manshiyya*" (In the Industrial Fair), *Lisan al-Hal* 44, no. 8315–665, May 18, 1921, 2.

20 Commenting in *al-Mashriq*, one reporter meekly remarked of Yusuf Huwayyik's sculpted female nudes: "It would not have been wrong if their nakedness were covered with a bit of clothing!" "*Lamha Taʾrikhiyya*," *al-Mashriq* 21, no. 7, July 1921, 528–35.

21 "*Hafla fi al-Maʿrid*" (Party at the Fair), *Lisan al-Hal* 44, no. 8332–672, May 30, 1921, 2.

22 "*Fi al-Maʿrid: Rusum al-Salibi*" (At the Fair: Saleeby's Pictures), *Lisan al-Hal* 44, no. 8314–664, May 17, 1921, 2.

23 Ibid.

24 "*Hafla fi al-Maʿrid*," *Lisan al-Hal* 44, no. 8332–672, May 30, 1921, 2. I settle on this interpretation by contextualizing the text amidst contemporary advertisements for goods from "the West," but I acknowledge the text is ambiguous. "*Ibn al-maghrib*" currently reads as "son of Morocco," which has no relation to the context. The same phrase carries an older, religious meaning of "one from the west." It could simply be a typo; or the print ligature may appear to add the "m" letter.

25 Scheer, *Are Emotions a Kind of Practice*, 193.

26 "*Rusum Jamila wa lakan Hathuha Qalil*" (Pretty Pictures but Bad Luck), *Lisan al-Hal* 44, no. 8333–673, May 31, 1921, 1.

27 Michael Jackson, *The Work of Art: Rethinking the Elementary Forms of Religious Life* (New York: Columbia University Press, 2016), xv.

28 Mustafa Farrukh, *Tariqi ila al-Fann* (My Road to Art) (Beirut: Dar Naufal, 1986), 171–72.

29 Kirsten Scheid, "Necessary Nudes: *Hadatha* and *Mu'asara* in the Lives of Modern Lebanese," *International Journal of Middle East Studies* 42, no. 2 (2010), 203–23.

30 Farrukh, *Tariqi*, 63, emphasis added.

31 Ibid.

32 Ibid., 65, emphasis added.

33 Ibid., 63.

34 Kamal al-Naffi, "*Ma'rid Farrukh fi al-Jami'a al-Amrikiyya*" (Farrouk's Exhibition at the American University of Beirut), *al-Ahwal*, June 1, 1929 (Hani Farrukh Archives, Beirut).

35 Ibid.

36 For more on these debates, see Elizabeth Thompson, *Colonial Citizens: Republican Rights, Paternal Privilege, and Gender in French Syria and Lebanon* (New York: Columbia University Press, 2000).

37 Al-Naffi, "*Ma'rid Farrukh fi al-jami'a al-amrikiyya*".

38 Ibid.

39 Ibid.

40 Ibid., emphasis added.

41 Hala Bizri, "Introduction," in *Rasul al-'Uri* (The Prophet of the Nude), ed. Hala Bizri, 2nd edn (Beirut: Editions Snoubar Bayrout, 2014), 10–12.

42 "*Madaris al-Ulad fi al-Hawa' al-Talaq*" (Children's Schools in the Open Air), *al-Ma'rid* 9, no. 955, June 21, 1931, 10.

43 "*Hawl al-'Uri* (About Nudity)."

44 Ibid.

45 Fuad Hubaysh, "*Huquq al-Mar'a fi al-Hubb*" (Women's Rights in Love), *al-Ma'rid* 9, no. 901, April 20, 1930, 8.

46 Ibid.

47 Fuad Hubaysh, "*Fawa'id al-'Uri fi Mu'alajat al-Fasad*" (Benefits of Nudism in Treating Perversion), *al-Ma'rid* 10, no. 954, June 14, 1931, 10.

48 "*Al-'Urwat al-Alman Yusaluna*" (German Nudists Pray), *al-Ma'rid* 11, no. 981, December 25, 1931, 17.

49 Muhyi al-Din al-Tawil, "*Fa'ida Ashrita al-'Uri*" (The Benefit of Nudist Cinema), *al-Ma'rid* 11, no. 980, December 13, 1931, 16.

50 Ilyas Abu Shabaka, "*Al-Failasuf al-Sha'ir Rida Tawfiq*" (The Philosopher-Poet Rida Tawfiq), *al-Ma'rid* 11, no. 1001, May 29, 1932, 7–19.

51 E.g. Jawaba, "*Al-Musawwirun al-Wataniyyun*."

52 Abu Shabaka, "'*Inda al-Failasuf Rida Tawfiq*" (At the Home of Philosopher Rida Tawfiq).

53 "*Intishar al-'Uri fi al-'Alam*" (The Spread of Nudism through the World), *al-Ma'rid* selections republished by *al-Nahar* 2, no. 33, August–October, 1931, 15; "*Al-'Uri fi Khudr al-Hasan*" (Nudity in the Torpor of Young Women), *al-Ma'rid*, selections republished by *al-Nahar 2*, no. 33, August–October, 1931, 15; *al-Tawil*, op. cit.; "*Madaris al-Ulad*," op. cit.

54 Muhyi al-Din al-Tawil and Elias Abu Shabaka also published on nudism. Interestingly the constellation of concerns they generated is isometric with that of contemporary nudists in Europe and America, albeit avoiding the rigid nationalist essentialization of some German currents. See Chad Ross, "Building a Better Body: Nudism, Society, Race and the German Nation (1890–1950)," PhD diss. (University of Missouri-Columbia, 2003); Brian Scott Hoffman, "Making Private Parts Public: American Nudism And The Politics of Nakedness, 1929–1963," PhD diss. (University of Illinois at Urbana-Champaign, 2009); Merrill and Merrill, *Among the Nudists – Early Naturism*, rep. edn (Redditch: Read Books Ltd 2013 [1930]).

55 Fu'ad Hubaysh, *Rasul al-'Uri* ("The Prophet of the Nude") (Beirut: Dar Sader, 1930; republished by Editions Snoubar Bayrout, 2014), 43.

56 Fu'ad Hubaysh, "*Sa'a fi Studyu al-Fanan Qaysar al-Jumayyil*" (An Hour in Cesar Gemayel's Studio), *al-Ma'rid* 10, no. 912, July 5, 1930, 8.

57 Ibid.

58 Ibid.

59 Ibid.

60 Hubaysh, "*Fawa'id al-'Uri*."

61 For more on *al-adab al-'uri*, see Bizri, "Introduction," in *Rasul al-'Uri* (The Prophet of the Nude).

62 Al-Tawil, "*Fa'ida Ashrita al-'Uri*."

63 Ibid., emphasis added.

64 Under the title, "*Al-Sair taht al-Shams*," as advertised in *al-Nahar*, for example, April 19, 1934, 1, no. 203, April 19, 1934, 6.

65 See also the illustrations in Merril and Merrill's *Among the Nudists*.

66 I infer this number from both the titles in the catalog and the photographs of the event.

67 "*Ma`rid al-Naqsh wa al-Taswir*" (Exhibition of Sculpture and Painting), *al-Bashir*, December 20, 1930, 61, no. 4190, 1.

68 See Jawaba, "*Al-Musawwirun al-Wataniyyun*."

69 Rushdi Ma`luf, "*Jawla fi Ma`rid Qaysar al-Jumayyil*" (A Tour of Cesar Gemayel's Exhibition), *al-Makshuf* 3, no. 96, May 19, 1937, 9.

70 "*Badirat al-`Uri fi Lubnan*" (Nudism Initiatives in Lebanon), *al-Ma`rid* 9, no. 901, April 20, 1930, 16, emphasis added.

71 Ibid.

72 Quoted by Bizri, "The Nudism of Sheikh Fouad Hobeiche," 89.

73 "*Hawl al-`Uri*" (About Nudity).

74 "*Madaris Ulad fi al-Hawa' al-Talaq*," 11.

75 Jawaba, "*Ma`rid al-Fannan `Umar al-'Unsi* (The Exhibition of the Artist Omar Onsi), *al-Ma`rid* 11, no. 988, February 28, 1932, 20.

76 I use clothing terms supplied by oral history interviews I conducted with `Awatif Sinnu Idris (Beirut, July 21, 2000) who wrote about the history of her family and Beirut social trends of the 1930s and 40s in several novels, and Umayma Ghandur Idris (Beirut, July 27, 2000) who spoke from personal experience of the era.

77 I thank Reina Lewis for pushing me to see the very modern approach adopted by these wearers and their painter to this Ottoman garment.

78 Exposition Omar Onsi, School of Arts and Letters, [sic], exhibition brochure, February 21-28, 1932 (Archived material, Joseph Matar Archives, 'Idda, Lebanon).

79 Jawaba, *Ma`rid al-Fannan*.

80 Moustapha Farrouk and Cesar Gemayel both painted this topic in the same period. However, they adopt a very different viewing position, placing the audience behind the unclothed bathers looking at Imru' al-Qais. I have not discovered a specific reason for their convergence on this scene.

81 See the registry analysis in Kirsten Scheid, "Divinely Imprinting Prints, or, how pictures became influential persons in Mandate Lebanon," in *The Routledge Handbook of the History of the Middle East Mandates*, eds. Cyrus Schayegh and Andrew Arsan (London: Routledge, 2015), 371–91.

82 See Reina Lewis, "On Veiling, Vision and Voyage: Cross-cultural Dressing and Narratives of Identity," *Interventions: International Journal of Postcolonial Studies* 1, 4 (1999): 500–20.

83 For example, Judith Naeff, *Precarious Imaginaries of Beirut: A City's Suspended Now* (Cham, Switzerland: Palgrave Macmillan, 2018), 163, quoting Lebanese artist Zena Khalil 2009: 107.

CHAPTER 7

ANOTHER LOOK: "THE BODY THAT IS," GENDER, SEXUALITY, AND POWER IN POST-OTTOMAN EGYPT

Wilson Chacko Jacob

Introduction

With this chapter, I begin a journey back to where I started my intellectual career—thinking about gender, sexuality, and power in the context of Middle East history—and by way of retracing my steps I hope to find a new path to follow within this rich area of research. Specifically, the journey back is to my 2011 book *Working Out Egypt: Effendi Masculinity and Subject Formation in Colonial Modernity, 1870–1940*, which started out as a doctoral dissertation and took a decade and a half to complete.[1] In the meantime I've taken a detour through Indian Ocean history, researching forms of power and authority in the transregional, mobile life of a Hadhrami[2] Sufi *sayyid*[3] by the name of Fadl Ibn Alawi (c. 1824–1900). His was a life that intersected with multiple imperial bodies heralding new claims of sovereignty.[4] In this reflection back on the starting point, the insights gained by taking the detour through transoceanic spaces, fluid bodily borders and cultures, and imperial reformulations of sovereignty cannot but be brought to bear on thinking the limit of the body that formed the basis of gender and sexuality in colonial modernity. Arriving at such a frontier post, as I picture it, we might reconceive the self-sovereignty that was a condition of postcolonial ethical and political claims. With this aim and in order to flesh out an argument about, what I'm calling here, "*the body that is*" and its regular disappearance, a brief survey of a stark faultline in Egyptian historiography will be followed by a re-reading of a particular moment from *Working Out Egypt*. The conclusion will draw out more explicitly the stakes involved in reconceiving the body of history in terms of *the body that is*.

Returns and Revisions: Egypt and Beyond

Since the governorship of Mehmed Ali (1805–48), Egypt carved out a place for itself as a semi-autonomous province within the Ottoman Empire. That status was reaffirmed under the rule of his grandson, Ismail, who negotiated the title of *khedive* (viceroy) for himself making Egypt the peculiar entity known as the *khedivate*. That entity, within which a territorial and cultural nationalism would be imagined and advocated by Arabic-speaking Egyptians—the emerging *effendiyya*—lasted until 1914. At the start of the First World War, the British Empire, which had invaded and occupied Egypt in 1882, made a unilateral declaration of protection that severed all legal and political ties between Egypt and the Ottomans. The tale of Egypt's semi-independence from the British in 1922, the result of another unilateral declaration, is also the tale of a post-Ottoman Middle East. In that world, grasping for a new cultural—as well as political, economic, and ethical—matrix within

Transliteration in this chapter is a simplified version of the system recommended by the *International Journal of Middle East Studies*.

which to locate people who had belonged to a specifically Ottoman ecumene for four centuries or more, (un)dress played a vital role in differentiating new from old and self from other. In my book, I traced in part the gendered, sexualized, and classed trajectories of this quest for a *post*-Ottoman culture, which sometimes leaped forward, other times fell backwards, and yet on other occasions stayed perfectly motionless; of course, deciding which was which—progressive, regressive, stagnant—was tantamount to claiming power and authority in an uncertain, new world.

We now have a fairly developed sense of how much Egypt remained a part of the Ottoman imperial world even as it began to drift toward other worlds of thought, practice, and feeling by the last third of the nineteenth century, with publication of works like the now classics, *State and Society in Mid-Nineteenth-Century Egypt* by Ehud Toledano from 1990, *All the Pasha's Men: Mehmed Ali, His Army and the Making of Modern Egypt* by Khaled Fahmy from 1997, and the more recent continuation of that line of analysis by Adam Mestyan in a 2017 monograph *Arab Patriotism: The Ideology and Culture of Power in Late Ottoman Egypt*, and the excellent dissertation by Aimee Genell, "Empire by Law: Ottoman Sovereignty and the British Occupation of Egypt, 1882–1923."[5] These social, political, cultural, and legal histories explain how Egypt's modern transformation was as much due to its incorporation into the world economy as it was due to the continuation of Ottoman political and elite cultural traditions. These traditions themselves had been revised and opened up by global crises faced in the seventeenth and eighteenth centuries, which witnessed the emergence of new players and new modalities of play. To this mix we might add the works of gender historians like Judith Tucker, Lisa Pollard, Hanan Kholoussy, Liat Kozma, Hanan Hammad, myself, and others. However, the former are rarely in conversation with the latter; they are as two approaches proceeding on parallel tracks, exploring separate and divided domains: the one seemingly seeking material histories and the other immaterial pasts.[6]

Terms of Debate: Oversight and Insight

I use "history" and "the past" advisedly here and mainly heuristically in order to signal what I have come to suspect is a subtle yet deeply ingrained distinction between sociopolitical and gender historians. There are surely many explicit and substantive differences as well as similarities between these historiographical fields. However, the distinction—between history and past—that indexes and simultaneously hails different kinds of intellectual postures vis-à-vis our accounting of the passage of time itself might be said to have a gendered dimension. Masculinities and femininities—not to be read off of normative, biological sexes—are performed and reproduced in the process of identifying properly historical treatments of the past. So, it's not that Middle East social history is an exclusively male domain and gender history female. Rather, I am suggesting that there is a peculiarly masculin*ist* positioning to certain materialist perspectives regarding historical temporality, wherein the measure of change is pegged to structures, the state, and collective struggles narrowly conceived. The specter of idealist forms haunts this position even as, or especially when, it relegates other positions to the level of superstructure or ungrounded, timeless theories.[7] The use of class, for example, by social historians of the Middle East was quite some time ago subjected to the postcolonial critique that un-self-reflexive deployments of analytical categories developed in a European context unwittingly reconstituted Eurocentric narratives of historical change.[8]

In other fields, feminist and anthropologically informed interventions had already begun to demonstrate that the *body* forms the most material basis of any Marxist/ Marxian or liberal contractarian deliberation.[9] In the intervening time very sophisticated understandings of the body itself have emerged at the intersection of the materialist/idealist debates. Some of the contributors to this advancement in the Middle East field such as Paula Sanders for medieval history, Reina Lewis and Afsaneh Najmabadi for modern history, and Saba

Mahmood in anthropology have been marvelously innovative in their development of sources and arguments and have in turn had an impact on other fields.[10] We have learned over the years from them and others that the body is not a transhistorical given, an instrument to be wielded, a vessel for ideas and movements, a bearer of tradition or modernity.[11] Rather, and I'm jumping over a few turns here, in perhaps the most radical and deceptively simple reading: the body is. *The body*, simply and with great complexity, *is*, and as such it is neither a vehicle of language and symbols nor a site of affect, emotion, memory, power. The body's radical materiality is in its skin, its hair, its organs, its fluids, its muscles, its permeability, and in the latest scientific jargon in its "gene expression signatures."[12] This list does not exhaust the range of body matters, as my own recent inquiry into Sufi mystical approaches to embodiment and intertwined bodies reveals and as current queer and feminist investigations of non-human animal and machine bodies demonstrate.[13] Nor does it mean reducing to and freezing the body in its parts with no change over time; since an aspect of its radical materiality is the fact of the body's growth under all kinds of conditions and its gradual or tragically sudden degeneration under a narrower set of conditions—an aspect nineteenth-century social and political theorists as well as historians ironically borrowed to model abstract forms of life.[14]

This *the body that is*, the body predicate, rather than the body prepositional—the body of, the body to, the body for, the body as—the body that simply is, the body that complexly is, radically disrupts the aims of Western metaphysical thought and its attendant practices, which together have arguably played the most significant role in our modern times in re-ordering life and non-life, the interconnected worlds of humans, animals, and things. In this new order of modern life that was at once the basis and the object of a worldly sovereignty, *the body that is* constituted a life not worth living or was slated for "cheapening"; accordingly, bodily life was subjected to a new politics that made it its object to re-form and re-shape.[15] I don't mean to suggest that there was a "time before" when *the body that is* existed as pure predicate and a "time after" when it undergoes a prepositional transformation. The body's radical materiality was always and everywhere mediated by other forms—social, cultural, economic, and political abstractions serving particular ends or interests in human time and environmental and extra-planetary forces in the pre-Holocene. The turn to the Anthropocene among scholars and others to account for the deep structures of historical change at a planetary level does to some extent attend to *the body that is*, as both a source and a consumer of energy, at one with nature. Though for the Middle Eastern context, particularly when considering the transformation of agricultural life, I find Jason Moore's corrective more compelling. Under the ugly label "Capitalocene," he re-centers capital accumulation and labor in and through the physical expenditures of bodily energy, whether of increasingly cheap human bodies or of non-human bodies such as trees and rocks (coal) since the fifteenth century.[16] Islam's coeval globalization intersected with the Capitalocene in ways that have yet to be fully explored, but it brought simultaneously commensurate, oppositional, and radically other bodily conceptions.

Rather than open an inquiry into transhistorical bodies or engage the above frameworks, my question is specific to my previous work and is twofold: 1) Does *the body that is* assume a new position globally in relation to life after the consolidation of modern abstractions and technics of sovereignty at the end of the long nineteenth century? 2) Does seeing the body as radical materiality—defined in terms of *the body that is*—broaden and deepen our understanding of the specific conditions of modern life in a post-Ottoman, semi-colonial Egypt in the 1920s and after, when the politicization of bodily life, through its attachment to the emerging state, was already a century old or more? In other words, I am trying to think out loud about niggling concerns I've had in the years since finishing my first book. Regarding the bridge across, or hyphen between, Ottoman and its after-time, I find myself asking whether the latest revisions that insist on various continuities and fewer ruptures, perhaps unwittingly reinforce Orientalist narratives of an exceptional Middle East. This geographically vague formation was born anew as a deviant and defective body from the ashes of empire. Here, the materiality of *the body that is* might be seen to mark a universal radical alterity that questions the solidity of "Ottoman/post-Ottoman" periodization. This enables us to regard those temporal and spatial appellations as also acts that discipline and delimit the boundaries of bodies that were never really, by which I mean materially, identical to the bodies that were objects of government, or for that matter, of history. Rather than pick on others, I will implicate myself.

In 2011, in my book *Working Out Egypt*, *the body that is* constantly disrupted my efforts to map the body's transformation as a gendered and sexualized subject of colonial modernity—the lens I developed for regarding the Ottoman/post-Ottoman divide on a broader, global scale. My strategy in those interruptive moments, I realize now, was to ignore or to discipline that body, in effect repeating the terms of the historical narratives, however revisionist, of Egypt's becoming post-Ottoman, national, and modern. In this chapter, I revisit one of those moments from the book with an eye to the act of erasure. In turn I suggest that self-declared materialists and gender/sexuality historians might productively work together to rethink the boundaries of the material, of bodies, and in turn bring to crisis and displace for good Middle Eastern exceptionalism.

"The Body That Is": Disrupting and Displacing

How did the disruptions occur? Perhaps the most obvious manner, given my investigation into masculinity, was the paradox of the body literally muscling forth—as bodies everywhere and in every time have done— on the one hand, as simple and similar to one another in constitution, and on the other hand, as complex and highly differentiated. Unsurprisingly, I was drawn to the appearance in time and space of the complex, dressed-up body. *Riyada al-Badaniyya* (Physical Culture), an incredible source my colleague and friend the gender historian Laura Bier acquired for me from a used bookseller in Cairo, provides an example of the way the body was seen, and not seen. It was a moment of disruption controlled and repeated.

Physical Culture, the brainchild and business venture of a group of brothers from Cairo, formed part of a socially expansive and variegated interventionist agenda emerging in the last years of the 1920s. The timing of the uptick in sociopolitical and generational consciousness was not accidental. After four tumultuous, for many traumatic, years of war which saw enormous deprivation at home and the disappearance of the 400-year-old Ottoman Empire of which Egypt had been an integral part, larger numbers of the new *effendi* "middle class" asserted themselves in the political and cultural spheres with renewed vigor, especially as opportunities within the economic sphere did not expand so rapidly.[17] The energy and momentum of the 1919 revolution, which brought Egypt a nominal form of independence from British rule in 1922, quickly gave way to old problems while inscribing newly created problems, namely of broader political representation, within an exclusive territorial, nationalist framework. Egypt was still compelled to prove itself worthy of total self-determination—only now the external and internal audience was larger. A broader range of cultural and political agents among the effendiyya began to contest elite claims to being the rightful representatives of the nation. One of the modes in which this contest was carried out was pedagogy. During the interwar period there was a marked proliferation of conventional educational institutions as well as independent print and other media dedicated to the dissemination of nationalist and modernist lessons.[18]

At the end of 1927 the lawyer Muhammad al-Jawhari and his brothers, Mukhtar and Ra'uf, had opened the Physical Education Institute (ma'had al-tarbiyya al-badaniyya). In the same year, the Young Men's Muslim Association, with its own athletic facilities, opened its doors not far from their location at 28 Sharia Fuad, in Cairo.[19] The following year the brothers launched the monthly magazine *Physical Culture*. Its main focus was the care of the body—the literal translation of the Arabic expression *al-riyada al-badaniyya*. Under this rubric, the editor Muhammad Fa'iq al-Jawhari made it the magazine's mission to educate the Egyptian reading public about sex, love, and physical beauty. Although the figure of the nation certainly made regular appearances as a legitimizing trope, the magazine represented a much broader, global modernist project and was intensely conscious of its role as a new technology of modern self-fashioning and hence as a herald of the future.

In this vein the new magazine *Physical Culture* displayed a keen interest in sex education (*al-tarbiyya al-jinsiyya*). The appearance of "sexuality"[20] as an object of pedagogy in Egypt was coincident with global economic crises. I placed sexuality in quotes to signal a possible misfit in the translation into this name of a field of knowledge that was still in a nascent stage in Egypt even by the interwar period. Hereafter, the word will appear without quotes, in part because of stylistic demands, but also because the makings of sex as discourse was the *sine qua non* of *Physical Culture*. To some extent, sexuality's development as a discursive and disciplinary apparatus indexed the beleaguered condition of middle-class effendi masculinity as the economy worsened, political negotiations stalled, and contentious women were running amok.[21]

At the same time, the reiterations in *Physical Culture* of what was a proper sexual subjectivity and how to inhabit this normative condition, or be inhabited by it, were culturally productive in ways that were subtle and never fully predictable. Indeed, in the spaces between pedagogy and performativity may reside *the body that is*. In any case, the asymmetries of a global and still colonial political economy did not singularly determine Egyptian performances of masculinity and sexuality, even if one can show, as I do, that they actively engaged coeval Euro-American discourses of physical culture and sexuality.

A primary concern—it would not be an exaggeration to say an obsession—of the magazine evident in practically every issue was the problem of abnormality and the possibility of straight sex. In general, *Physical Culture* defined a domain of "sexual deviancies" according to its mission to promote sex education (*al-tarbiyya al-jinsiyya*).[22] Unsurprisingly, the targets were most often masturbation and venereal diseases. Medical expertise—foreign and Egyptian—was regularly marshaled to demonstrate the harms of sexual activity outside of the legitimate bonds of marriage. Dr. Fakhri Faraj and Dr. Sabri Jirjis became familiar household names and images through the frequent appearances of their articles and interviews in the magazine.[23]

In a 1932 interview with Dr. Faraj, he was presented to the readers as a pioneer in Egyptian medicine who had long called and worked for sex education.[24] He launched his crusade in 1921 with a lecture at the Egyptian University, which apparently was not well received. For years after, the only venue that allowed him to lecture about sexual health issues was Ewart Hall of the American University in Cairo.[25] However, he was not prevented from publishing extensively before he became a regular contributor to *Physical Culture*. He had written several volumes on female sexuality, reproduction, prostitution, venereal diseases, the woman question, and sexual impotence.[26]

When the interviewer asked whether his efforts had made a difference, he admitted that both at the government and popular levels only limited progress had been made. In a report on the spread of prostitution and ways to combat it, which he had submitted to King Fuad and to the first parliament in 1924, he recommended sex education programs in government schools. His plan was partially implemented by the Ministry of Education: lessons on plant and animal reproduction were added to the primary school curriculum but the human reproduction component, which was meant for secondary schools and university, was not incorporated. Although he performed what he termed his "civic duty" (*wajibi al-ijtima'i*) through his public lectures delivered at the American University, he acknowledged that the audience was not the mass of the population.

For the masses, especially the young, cases of sexually transmitted diseases were on the rise.[27] According to Dr. Faraj, this was commensurate with their total ignorance about sex: "I am probably not exaggerating if I said that they don't know any of its details except for what is [necessary] to fulfill their sexual cravings. They are not different in this respect from their companions—wild animals."[28] Despite this state of sexual ignorance inhabited by the majority of Egypt's—peasant—population, Dr. Faraj expressed his abiding confidence that "the spirit of Egypt's intellectual renaissance" and "the spirit of [its] leap forward" could not but address this problem too. He cited anecdotal evidence of doctors in the provinces imbued with this spirit, who were undertaking on their own initiative programs to educate the people about sex and sexually transmitted diseases.

Although the politics of sex education was not addressed directly in this interview, it did rear its head when Dr. Faraj mentioned in passing opposition from "the guardians of public morals." According to the editor, *Physical Culture* was constantly subjected to charges of encouraging immorality.[29] Interestingly, criticism also seems to have been launched against it from a third position that found the magazine's message of chastity puritanical and outdated.[30] Essentially, the magazine maintained that knowledge about sex would encourage self-control, *which was what distinguished humans from animals*. An important component of their philosophy was the belief that there was a causative element to sex knowledge and the outcome was ultimately empowerment.

Thus, in the magazine's discourse a secular concept of self-sovereignty was fundamental to individual, social, and ultimately national progress. It was that connection that absorbed me in my original treatment of the magazine. The highlighted clause above on the distinction between humans and animals did not give me much pause other than to appreciate that urban elites had long before drawn stark lines between effendi and *fellah* (peasant) cultures and ontologies. Such an opening to reconsider the relationship between the newly politicized life and *the body that is* was mediated and foreclosed by this historian's explanatory rubric.

Muhammad al-Jawhari introduced his editorial comments a few months after the interview with Dr. Faraj by reflecting on the historical case of the European Wars of Religion as an example of fighting for a cause—of the principled assault. He contrasted this to the attacks on the magazine, which he deemed hypocritical because of their intentional misrepresentation of its educational mission to enlighten people about the dangers of abusing their bodies sexually. It is when one wonders who was doing the attacking—since they go unnamed—that the example drawn from European history becomes intelligible. Unlike the Wars of Religion, wherein questions of belief were ostensibly at the heart of conflict, the editor of *Physical Culture* was suggesting that his magazine was being attacked in the name of religion by people who should and did know better. In other—unuttered—words, Islam was being twisted to meet ends that were not necessarily Islamic. This reading is supported by the magazine's inclusion of religious experts alongside the medical experts to opine on issues related to sexuality and the right to research and discuss them publicly. Another likely proposition is that the editor was manipulating religion just as interestedly as his opponents in order to enhance magazine sales that depended on "sexual" content.

All of these interpretations are possible, hence my retrieval and re-presentation of them in the book. However *the body that is* troubles the discourses signaled above—secularism, religion, capitalism—by its irreducibility. And yet it disappears into those discourses. The disciplined or desirable body historically pursued by governments, social reformers, *ulama* (Muslim scholars), and businessmen was trackable and tracked precisely because historical change is measured and recorded in discursive and not bodily terms, whether the historian does social or gender history. My original analysis followed the reasons for Dr. Faraj's legal troubles after lecturing at the American University in Cairo in 1931. His stance on religious personal status laws needing reform landed him in court. My focus was on the secular, medicalized erosion of religious authority and the lack of genuine concern for gender equality. I did not investigate the body and its boundaries as they were conceived within religious traditions and, as I will argue below, this is one route by which *the body that is* disappeared.

On the issue of equality between men and women, Faraj expressed indignation at those who would even pose such a question and accused them of living in a "fantasy world." Ostensibly, the little political responsibility women already had was a burden too heavy for them. Echoing the late nineteenth-century discourse on motherhood, Dr. Faraj points to Egyptian men marrying foreign women as a sign of the failure of Egyptian women in their nationalist duty to raise sons with good nationalist values.[31] In any case, according to Faraj, *nature* and *biology* had already invalidated the very possibility of equality. For motherhood was a natural right given only to women, through which, they had power over others: children, husband, family. Men could never possess this right, thus denying them that route to power.

As a medical expert assessing women's mental and physical capacity, he granted that there was the potential for a certain level of equivalence with men if these aspects were allowed to develop. The problem was that such a development would undermine the biological basis of personhood and contradict the social aspects of the woman's role as spouse and mother. According to Faraj, practicing sports that resulted in building musculature could introduce masculine elements into her body that would affect her chances for marriage, her sex life, and her reproductive ability. So, only properly feminine activities such as tennis, calisthenics, and jumping rope were recommended. In this recommendation, he was merely following international standards that had been scientifically established in preceding decades concerning women's physical exercise. According to the program of sessions held at the 1905 International Congress on Sports and Physical Education in Brussels, women's exercises would be discussed as "*exercises propres à developper sans danger la jeune fille et la femme*"[32] (appropriate exercises for the development of girls and women without causing harm). Global circulation of the normative gendered body was made possible by the gradual internationalization of disciplinary regimes, which had a pre-First World War genealogy.

Fantasies of Sovereignty

The legal and political distinctions between colony and metropole may have slowed the progress of this order, but it could not stop it. *Working Out Egypt* traced specific historical manifestations of the global and the international in the formulation of gender norms. However, in that process of retrieval and representation, *the body that is* became Other despite, or precisely because of, the historiographical dictate—and at the time, I thought, political urgency—of locating and explaining shifts in the way sovereignty of self and state were performed.

I argued that the creeping masculinization of women and the threat this posed to social order was a phenomenon that deeply concerned the Egyptian middle class, including the feminists that sought to challenge the status quo. As Margot Badran points out, although education was one of the areas in which Egyptian feminists had made major gains, by the mid-1930s there was growing unease about the inability of educated women to fulfill their roles as mothers and daughters. So much so that even feminists articulated the need for more home economics courses and supported the Ministry of Education's establishment of "schools of feminine culture" in 1938 as an alternative route after finishing primary school.[33]

On the other hand, the family was an arena in which feminists had failed to achieve any significant advances, but in the 1930s they shifted strategies from seeking change through legal reform to instructing women on ways to run a more efficient household and to obtain better conjugal relations with their husbands. Badran explains this move in terms of economic need and political expediency:

By the late 1930s middle-class women had broken into new professions, entering the workplace in significant numbers and often competing with men for jobs. The influx, which made many men uneasy, was exacerbated by the persisting economic recession. As working women came under increasing attack as wives and mothers who neglected their home and "natural" roles, feminists stepped up the discourse on the importance of women's family roles.[34]

I previously argued that the fear of women's denaturalization was not just a question of the failure to fulfill roles as Badran suggests. There was a more fundamental questioning of the boundaries between masculinity and femininity that was brought to the foreground by the factors Badran identifies but whose implications were problematic for both men and women. The political cartoons of this period satirize both the masculinization of Egyptian women and the emasculation of Egyptian men. Men were depicted as fighting—poorly—on two fronts to maintain their honor: against persistent colonial relations and the feminist onslaught. Women are depicted mainly as fighting Egyptian men for supercilious gains. The figuration of the political context is shot through with explicitly gendered tropes. In the cartoons I have tracked from the early 1920s—including Figures 7.1 and 7.2—to the late 1930s, it is possible to get a sense of the growing unease over women becoming more like men and even culminating in corporeal sameness.

Figure 7.1 The Arabic sentence in the image reads: "Women Lead the Men." The first line of the Arabic caption reads: "Women advance and men regress." The next line: "Ms. Huda Sha`rawi issued a general call for the ladies to look into the question of Sudan." Cover of the magazine *Khayal al-Zill* (October 30, 1924). Courtesy of The National Library and Archives of Egypt.

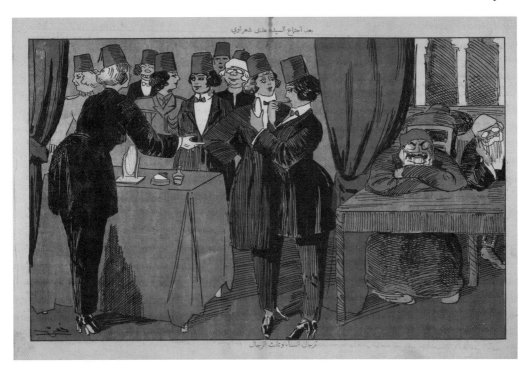

بعد اجتماع السيدة هدى شعراوى

رجل النساء. وثأث الرجال.

Figure 7.2 The Arabic at the top reads: "After Huda Sha`rawi's Meeting." At the bottom: "The Masculinization of 7.2 Women and the Feminization of Men." Illustration in the magazine *Khayal al-Zill* (November 6, 1924): 8-9. The National Library and Archives of Egypt.

The perceived sense of women's growing identity with men—in corporeal and social terms—as an unnatural occurrence was not expressed simply as a critique of the feminist movement. Implicit in it were significant anxieties about men's ability to lead the new nation to complete freedom and to lead the new middle-class households—based on companionate marriages—to happiness. Against this critique of secular middle-class masculinity from various corners, *Physical Culture* stood as a response and a program for the rehabilitation of Egyptian men.

Piercing Fantasies of Sovereignty: Tracing the "Body That Is"

The failure to recognize that these frameworks of interpreting the body and my own ostensibly critical historicization of them were not entirely dissimilar rested on how the fact of the body was conceived. The conception of the body as object and the historicization of this objectification did not only raise the problem of the body's assimilation to discourse but the very move at either level of representation was contingent on erasing real bodies. In part, this failure of recognition is symptomatic of the ineluctable Cartesian split that reproduces itself in every moment of knowing.[35] Accordingly, a direct line might be drawn between my attempts to know Egypt and the interwar Egyptian knowledge projects like *Physical Culture*, and points before and after each, wherein there are always bodily casualties. In some sense, the failure of knowledge and erasure of the body seems inevitable when language is considered superior to, say, gesture. Representation and re-presentation as Gayatri Spivak famously argued are linguistic, ethical, and political acts, and as they are performed and repeated across temporal and spatial grids divided by asymmetries of power they cannot not produce certain silences.[36]

That my project of historicization and the reform project of *Physical Culture* were more intimately entwined than I realized becomes clear when I revisit my treatment of the other regular contributor to the magazine's pedagogic mission, Dr. Sabri Jirjis, who offered his expert knowledge on abnormal and deviant sexuality. He was first introduced to the readers of the magazine in August 1931 as a new "volunteer" member of the "*Physical Culture* family." Dr. Jirjis practiced at the VD clinic in Bani Suwayf, south of Cairo.[37] The editor described him as a "young sportsman" (*shab sbur*).

Jirjis supplemented his medical knowledge with a critical social-scientific lens for better viewing the relationship between sex-gender and social progress. The intellectual tools available to the good doctor were revealed in a very interesting article titled "On Politics and Political Economy."[38] He began by explicating the difference between the two:

> Power and wealth were always the two objects targeted by politics. However, political economy (*al-iqtisad al-siyasi*) is a science that studies the different conditions of [groups of] people, and all of its theories are based in history, statistics, and observations. Its aim is to determine laws for organizing production and distribution of products, for the division of labor, and for the social regulation of peoples in terms of public health, population (over or under), and rates of birth and death (increase or decline).[39]

He proceeded to identify a significant absence in political economy, which he labels "natural history"—by this he meant the history of the body and psychology as they related to sex and reproduction. It was this lacuna that undermined the ability of political economy to produce solutions for the imminent population crisis. His next move was to trace the roots of eugenics to Malthus and theories of rational selection, agreeing with the contemporaneous view that people like the Chinese posed a threat to humanity's future if they continued to breed like rabbits. It was on a social Darwinist basis that Dr. Jirjis advanced his support for sex education and women's rights.

He rejected what he termed was the traditional tendency to explain any strange or extraordinary social developments with an injunction to "examine women" (*ibhath 'an al-mar'a*). Women were not left out of the equation altogether, but the starting point, according to Dr. Jirjis, should be to "examine the sexual impulse" (*ibhath 'an al-dafi' al-tanasuli*). Such an investigation was warranted, he maintained, since desire and emotion (*ahwa' wa 'awatif*) were more common determinants of human action than reason and logic, with the sexual impulse being the most powerful. The "role of women" was essential here in connecting sex to the social and political. Only through the liberation of women (*tahrir al-mar'a*) would society advance. Reversing Faraj's argument, Jirjis maintained that making women equal partners with men in social life by encouraging their participation in work and granting them the right to vote and be elected, the sexual relationship would necessarily be transformed as her object status was eliminated. Moreover, as the sex act duly became elevated from the depths of selfish lust and was redirected at smart reproduction, it would be aligned more with the social good.[40]

My prior conclusion was that Dr. Jirjis' writing on sexuality and deviance exemplified the work of *Physical Culture* toward the normalization of heterosexuality as a key to Egyptian modernity. Essential to this goal was the constitution of society as an object that could be acted upon by its localization in the individual human body, namely in the male sex.[41] The male subject of Egyptian modernity had been problematized since the late nineteenth century as lacking the proper qualities of masculinity. After a lull in the discourse around the revolutionary years following 1919, Egyptian masculinity returned in the pages of *Physical Culture* facing a new endangered future, sapped by excessive masturbation and the contraction of venereal diseases.

A global agenda had been consolidated by the interwar period: the libidinal, diseased, fertile, muscled, weak, rebellious, and natural body was to be fixed with the aim of serving modern, secular, rational, and national ends. My focus in *Working Out Egypt* was on this fixing of life through discourses of gender and sexuality and the form(s) of sovereignty it implied. However, the detour I took through the Indian Ocean world and Sufism in my recent work, also investigating the question of modern sovereignty, raised for me another question of the body. Exploring the Sufi conception of life/death as interconnected phenomena with a thin veil separating the spaces and times of the living and the dead—and other spiritual beings—opened the body to another conceptualization that had the power to decenter or re-ground sovereignties of state, self, and even the divine. This body has permeable borders, making its representation in both language and institutions of power impossible. This is *the body that is*; it is human/non-human, life/non-life, seen/unseen, in time/out of time, material/immaterial. *The body that is* unfolds and is neither born nor dies; it is always in a state of return.[42]

From this mystical—for lack of a better term—perspective, gender and sexuality as discourses imbuing and imbued with secular power that targeted Egyptian bodies in the post-Ottoman period with renewed vigor can be seen as mere nodes of a much wider web of bodily being and becoming. At the very least, this perspective, of *the body that is*, reveals an anthropocentric bias in the original work and, at the very extreme, points to this researcher's own assimilation, along with *effendis* like Drs. Faraj and Jirjis, into the power of and over life inhering in modern sovereignty.

Conclusion

What is a body to do when the circuits through which it was made legible were garbled and ultimately ditched? This was the fundamental question for social and political reformers of post-Ottoman Egypt learning to map the "time after"; since the "time before" could now only be regarded as outmoded, in need of overcoming. In the process of my retracing those maps, "the body that simply is" necessarily receded from the horizon, because, from a practical standpoint, the historian can only ever regard the body that was doing and to some extent the body being done. The visible body in various states of dress and undress, literally and guratively, seemed the story of post-Ottoman cultural politics in Egypt, which was always already also a transregional space.

Between disclosing the innermost recesses of the body that once remained the secret of self and debating what should adorn the tops of heads, a modern public culture emerged that was simultaneously national and global as well as gendered, sexualized, and classed. In the process of tracing this dressed/undressed body, *the body that is* disappeared.[43]

Admittedly, *the body that is* is not exactly what troubled the contributors to *Physical Culture*. Rather it was a body that had already been socialized and politicized into a prior regime of life that needed reform. It is here that Sabri Jirjis suspected that the act of approaching the body was always already political and economic; accordingly, the tools of a discipline calibrated to tracing those relationships were necessary. As a practicing physician and social Darwinist, he offered the critical intervention that the biological body was dangerously absent from political economy; this absence ultimately threatened the future of Egypt and of the world.[44]

When reading Jirjis, it would be hard not to hear Foucault's often quoted line from *The History of Sexuality*: "For millennia, man remained what he was for Aristotle: a living animal with the additional capacity for a political existence; modern man is an animal whose politics places his existence as a living being in question."[45]

Figure 7.3 Arabic heading reads: "The Shaykhs and The Hat." Arabic caption: "Al-Shaykh Bakhit—We prayed with the Afghan King and he was wearing a hat! What are we going to tell the people?" Second missing Arabic caption: "Al-Shaykh Shakir—We'll tell them that when a Muslim king wears the hat it becomes halal but when we or anyone else wears it, it becomes haram." Illustration in the magazine *Al-Kashkul* (January 1, 1928): 20, which appeared on the occasion of the modernizing Afghan sovereign Amanullah Khan's visit to Egypt. Courtesy of The National Library and Archives of Egypt.

In my initial reading of gender, sexuality, and the body in Egypt under colonial modernity, I followed the trajectory of what Foucault termed "bio-power." He argued:

> Power would no longer be dealing simply with legal subjects over whom the ultimate dominion was death, but with living beings, and the mastery it would be able to exercise over them would have to be applied at the level of life itself; it was the taking charge of life, more than the threat of death, that gave power its access *even to the body* [emphasis added]."[46]

However, the radical materiality of *the body that is*, escapes this history and remains to be accounted for; Foucault himself noted the tendency of bodily life "[o]utside the Western world" to evade biopolitical capture—albeit in crude developmentalist terms that cast the non-West as the site of famine and species-threatening epidemics. In some ways this failure of French theory and of conventional historiography is what Spivak glossed in her now classic—and to some, incomprehensible—query, "Can the Subaltern Speak?" Though this question and its treatment is often the subject of historians' misunderstandings and resultant caricatures, *the body that is* might be read along the lines of the subaltern limit to representation, which Spivak glosses as inextricably intertwined linguistic, ethical, and political acts.

If we take our cues from Spivak and a decolonial Foucault, then considering *the body that is* in a post-Ottoman Egypt might show us that the efforts of power in its thick sovereign and thin biopolitical forms could only ever subordinate and subjugate within limited domains. It is in the spaces and temporalities of *the body that is* that the hope of the political may reside. The radically material, porous body is not the excluded as it often appeared in *Working Out Egypt*. It is rather an unacknowledged or perhaps invisible political life, on the one hand, and the grounds of all (non-)life on the other.[47]

Judith Butler's recent attempt to think about the popular protests that swept the Middle East and the world in our age of austerity and right-wing resurgences offers a cautionary tale about the Arendt-Foucault-Agamben trajectory of locating political life in the visible/representable, that is, the public, and locating bare, naked, or mere life among the invisible and excluded. Using the figure of the destitute, she notes:

> At stake is the question of whether the destitute are outside of politics and power or are in fact living out a specific form of political destitution *along with* specific forms of political agency and resistance that expose the policing of the boundaries of the sphere of appearance itself. If we claim that the destitute are outside of the sphere of politics—reduced to depoliticized forms of being—then we implicitly accept as right the dominant ways of establishing the limits of the political.[48]

At stake then in recasting Middle East history as not "really" hinging on a time before and a time after, indexed in the post-Ottoman marker, is the radical political and ethical potential of *the body that is*. For even as its radical materiality is continuously and constantly mediated by social, political, and cultural forms—not to mention world ecologies of nature, capital, God—whenever *the body that is* appears with other bodies that are, then the potential for political life is also present.

What Butler has tried to do and what other critical scholars have done in the face of what is an imminent planetary catastrophe is attempt to clear space within old traditions of thought for new perspectives to emerge on the relations among bodies human and non-human such that an effective politics might become possible.[49] Whether it is in the intractable grounding of Western political philosophy in Ancient Greek thought or the equally intractable grounding of Islamic thought in an early textual canon, there is an urgency for rediscovering genealogies of the borderless, non-sovereign body. Thus, the body of the *khawal* (male drag performer), for example (see Figure 7.4), may have undergone disciplining and legal regulation in post-Ottoman Egypt, making it spectral as I argued previously, but mapping this route of social exclusion should not have to agree with the dominant regime that these are "deanimated 'givens' of political life." The khawals ("faggots") return and the persistence of Sufis and mystics in the present might appear more comparable and intelligible, and as potential vectors of other political imaginaries when they are regarded as bodies without boundaries; such bodies do not belong exclusively to any one culture or history or species. Here gender and sexuality as discourses of power that were routed through histories of divine, imperial, state, and self-sovereignty cannot in themselves also form an analytics of power that would make *the body that is* legible. Refusing the dominant and hegemonic terms of the political and its location, however, is no easy task. It may in fact require undressing and unlearning many basics of history—from periods, regions, events, structures, and agency to definitions of putatively self-evident categories, such as the body.

Figure 7.4 The Arabic in the image reads "In Egypt, khawal" and the French caption is "Eccentric cross-dressing dancer." Postcard dated 18 December, 1906. Collection of Max Karkegi.

Notes

1   Wilson Chacko Jacob, *Working Out Egypt: Effendi Masculinity and Subject Formation in Colonial Modernity, 1870–1940* (Durham, NC: Duke University Press, 2011).
2   Hadhramis are from the southern Arabian Peninsula; their region, Hadhramawt, is a province within the modern state of Yemen.
3   Sayyid as a common honorific today means something like the French "monsieur;" however, in this specific case, it denotes a descendant of the Prophet Muhammad and is closer in meaning to "The Most Noble" or "His Grace."
4   Wilson Chacko Jacob, *For God or Empire: Sayyid Fadl and the Indian Ocean World* (Stanford, CA: Stanford University Press, 2019).

5   Ehud Toledano, *State and Society in Mid-Nineteenth-Century Egypt* (New York: Cambridge University Press, 1990); Khaled Fahmy, *All the Pasha's Men: Mehmed Ali, His Army and the Making of Modern Egypt* (New York: Cambridge University Press, 1997); Adam Mestyan, *Arab Patriotism: The Ideology and Culture of Power in Late Ottoman Egypt* (Princeton, NJ: Princeton University Press, 2017); Aimee Genell, "Empire by Law: Ottoman Sovereignty and the British Occupation of Egypt, 1882–1923," PhD thesis (Columbia University, New York, 2013). Also see Ken Cuno, *The Pasha's Peasants: Land, Society and Economy in Lower Egypt* (New York: Cambridge University Press, 1992).

6   Judith Tucker, *Women in Nineteenth Century Egypt* (New York: Cambridge University Press, 1985); Lisa Pollard, *Nurturing the Nation: The Family Politics of Modernizing, Colonizing, and Liberating Egypt, 1805–1923* (Berkeley: University of California Press, 2005); Hanan Kholoussy, *For Better, For Worse: The Marriage Crisis That Made Modern Egypt, 1898–1936* (Stanford: Stanford University Press, 2010); Liat Kozma, *Policing Egyptian Women: Sex, Law, and Medicine in Khedival Egypt* (Syracuse: Syracuse University Press, 2011); Hanan Hammad, *Industrial Sexuality: Gender, Urbanization, and Social Transformation in Egypt* (Austin: University of Texas Press, 2016); Jacob, *Working Out Egypt*. For a recent example of recapitulating this divide, see Mestyan, *Arab Patriotism*, 5–6.

7   Hegel's snarky rebuke of empiricists who dismiss philosophy in his reflections on world history comes to mind. G. W. F. Hegel, *Reason In History, a general introduction to the Philosophy of History*, trans. Robert S. Hartman (A Liberal Arts Press Book, New York, The Bobbs-Merrill Company, 1953), Part IV, no. 3. Available online: https://www.marxists.org/reference/archive/hegel/works/hi/introduction.htm (accessed November 9, 2018).

8   I am thinking here of the productive exchange between Middle East and South Asian scholars from the mid- to late-1990s. Dipesh Chakrabarty, "Labor History and the Politics of Theory: An Indian Angle on the Middle East," in *Workers and Working Classes in the Middle East: Struggles, Histories, Historiographies*, ed. Zachary Lockman (Albany, NY: SUNY Press, 1994). See also Timothy Mitchell, ed., *Questions of Modernity* (Minneapolis: University of Minnesota Press, 2000).

9   In addition to the very early efforts of Engels, Goldman, de Beauvoir, et al. to theorize the family, women, and (re)production, see Carole Pateman, *The Sexual Contract* (Cambridge: Polity Press, 1988); Judith Butler, *Gender Trouble: Feminism and the Subversion of Identity* (New York: Routledge, 1990) and *Bodies That Matter: On the Discursive Limits of "Sex"* (New York: Routledge, 1993); and Elizabeth Grosz, *Volatile Bodies: Toward a Corporeal Feminism* (Bloomington: Indiana University Press, 1994). Though the body would largely disappear in the groundbreaking combinations of feminism and marxism, for an archive of these earlier interventions see Rosemary Hennessy and Chrys Ingraham, eds., *Materialist Feminism: A Reader in Class, Difference, and Women's Lives* (New York: Routledge, 1997).

10 Paula Sanders, "Gendering the Ungendered Body: Hermaphrodites in Medieval Islamic Law," in *Women in Middle Eastern History: Shifting Boundaries in Sex and Gender*, eds. Nikki R. Keddie and Beth Baron (New Haven: Yale University Press, 1991), 74–95; Reina Lewis, *Gendering Orientalism: Race, Femininity and Representation* (New York: Routledge, 1996); Afsaneh Najmabadi, *Women with Mustaches and Men without Beards: Gender and Sexual Anxieties of Iranian Modernity* (Berkeley: University of California Press, 2005); and Saba Mahmood, *Politics of Piety: The Islamic Revival and the Feminist Subject* (Princeton: Princeton University Press, 2005).

11 Medieval historiography in particular demonstrates the extensive payoffs of dislodging the body from modernist enclosures. Peter Brown, *The Body and Society: Men, Women and Sexual Renunciation in Early Christianity* (New York: Columbia University Press, 1988). Many of the concerns raised in this paper are mere echoes of Caroline Bynum, "Why All the Fuss about the Body? A Medievalist's Perspective," *Critical Inquiry* 22, no. 1 (1995): 1–33.

12 Ivan Semeniuk, "Genetic study of Quebec residents finds air pollution trumps ancestry," *The Globe and Mail* [Online], March 6, 2018. Available online: https://www.theglobeandmail.com/news/national/genetic-study-of-quebec-residents-finds-air-pollution-trumps-ancestry/article38217989/ (accessed March 6, 2018). Of course, DNA may also be mediated by sociopolitical forms: "This gets to the future of risk prediction," said Stephen Montgomery, a geneticist at Stanford University in California who was not involved in the study. "It's not just what's in your genome, but what you're exposed to."

13 On the drone body, see Cara Daggett, "Drone Disorientations," *International Feminist Journal of Politics* 17, no. 3 (2015): 361–79, DOI: 10.1080/14616742.2015.1075317.

14 Bourgeois economists might have deployed the body as machine, in the case of Andrew Ure imagining a single automaton of man-machine, which seems quite material but even Marx called it out as merely "stupid" bourgeois fantasy. See Andrew Zimmerman, "The Ideology of the Machine and the Spirit of the Factory: Remarx on Babbage and Ure," *Cultural Critique*, no. 37 (Autumn 1997): 5–29.

15 An earlier version of this argument which, however, was not yet attuned to *the body that is*, might be found in Wilson Chacko Jacob, "Overcoming Simply Being: Straight Sex, Masculinity, and Physical Culture in Egypt," *Gender and History* 22, no. 3 (November 2010): 1–19. On the specific sense of "cheapening" as it is used here in relation to bodies in time, see Jason Moore, "Capitalocene, Part I: On the Nature and Origins of our Ecological Crisis," *The Journal of Peasant Studies* 44, no. 3 (2017): 594–630.

16 Jason Moore, *Capitalism in the Web of Life: Ecology and the Accumulation of Capital* (New York: Verso, 2015). Overall, however, the specificities of region, gender, and sexuality necessarily remain opaque in the new meta-frameworks of Anthropocene or Capitalocene.

17 For a reevaluation of the conceptual and social meanings of the *effendiyya* as a collective, and *effendi* as an individual subject, see Lucie Ryzova, "Egyptianizing Modernity through the 'New *Effendiya*': Social and Cultural Constructions of the Middle Class in Egypt Under the Monarchy," in *Re-Envisioning Egypt, 1919–1952*, eds. Arthur Goldschmidt, Amy Johnson, and Barak Salmoni (Cairo: American University in Cairo Press, 2005), 124–63. Also see Israel Gershoni and James Jankowski, *Redefining the Egyptian Nation, 1930–45* (New York: Cambridge University Press, 1995).

18 Barak Salmoni, "Historical Consciousness for Modern Citizenship," in *Re-Envisioning Egypt*, 164–193. For a study looking at schools and the press as sites of gendered and classed instruction for the preceding period, see Lisa Pollard, *Nurturing the Nation: The Family Politics of Modernizing, Colonizing, and Liberating Egypt, 1805–1923* (Berkeley: University of California Press, 2005). For the performative possibilities engendered by the new media in particular, see Walter Armbrust, *Mass Culture and Modernism in Egypt* (New York: Cambridge University Press, 1996).

19 This was the address of the institute in 1938; I was not able to establish whether it was always in the same location. Interestingly, the YMMA continues to exist and operate in the same location while the *ma'had* has disappeared entirely, even from memory.

20 On this point, see Joseph Massad, *Desiring Arabs* (Chicago: University of Chicago Press, 2007).

21 For another set of representations that engaged the same anxieties and in a sense paved the way for *Physical Culture*, see Marilyn Booth, "Un/safe/ly at Home: Narratives of Sexual Coercion in 1920s Egypt," *Gender and History* 16, no. 3 (November 2004): 744–68.

22 This very same source has been read through its visual images of women as peddling soft-core porn in the guise of exercise and health; see Lucie Ryzova, "'I Am a Whore But I Will Be a Good Mother': On the Production and Consumption of the Female Body in Modern Egypt," *Arab Studies Journal* XII, no. 2/ XIII, no. 1 (Fall 2004/Spring 2005): 80–122.

23 Other contributing medical experts included Dr. Husayn 'Izzat, Dr. Muhammad Kamil al-Khuli, Dr. Muhammad Abd al-Hamid Bey, Dr. Husayn al-Harawi, and Dr. Muhammad Shahin Pasha.

24 "Sex Education: An Hour with Dr. Fakhri Faraj, The Famous Doctor of Venereal Diseases," *Riyada al-Badaniyya* (Physical Culture) (hereafter referred to as *RB*) (May 1932): 6–12.

25 Bruce Dunne discusses the role of the AUC and Faraj's lecture series in the dissemination of knowledge about sexual health as part of colonial and national efforts to "civilize" Egyptians in chapter six of "Sexuality and the 'Civilizing Process' in Modern Egypt," PhD thesis (Georgetown University, Washington DC, 1996).

26 Dr. Fakhri Faraj, *al-Mar'a wa falsafat al-tanasuliyyat* [Women and the Philosophy of Sexuality] (Cairo: al-Matba'a al-'Asriyya, 1924); *Taqrir "an intishar al-bigha" wa al-amrad al-tanasuliyya bi al-qutr al-misri wa ba'd al-turuq al-mumkin ittiba'uha li- muharabatiha* [The Spread of Prostitution and Venereal Diseases in the Country of Egypt and the Steps that Might be Taken to Combat It] (Cairo: al-Matba'a al-'Asriyya, 1924); *al-Tanasul fi al-hayawan wa al-insan wa al-nabat* [Reproduction in Animals, Humans, and Plants] (could not locate); *Hal tatasawi al-mar'a bi al-rajul fi al-huquq wa al-wajibat?* [Is the Woman Equal to the Man in Rights and Responsibilites?]; *Al-amrad al-tanasuliyya wa 'ilajuha* [Venereal Diseases and their Treatment] (could not locate); *Al-du'f al-tanasuli fi al-dhukur wa al-anath wa 'ilajuhu* [Sexual Impotence in Males and Females and its Treatment] (could not locate).

27 Given the absence of much statistical data related to sexually transmitted diseases from this period, it is very difficult to corroborate this claim. Making it his life's work suggests at least that it was a major concern for Dr. Faraj and not solely a rhetorical device.

28 *RB* (May 1932): 9.

29 Muhammad Fa'iq al-Jawhari, "The Honorable Attack," *RB* (October 1932): 4–5.

30 For a defense of their philosophy on sex education, see "Girls and Diminished Morals," *RB* (February 1935): 113–14.

31 Hanan Kholoussy, "Stolen Husbands, Foreign Wives: Mixed Marriage, Identity Formation, and Gender in Colonial Egypt, 1909–1923," *Hawwa* 1 (2003) 2: 206–40.

32 Dar al-Watha'iq al-Qawmiyya [The National Archives of Egypt]: Mahfuzat Majlis al-Wuzara', Nizarat al-Kharijiyya 4/9, Mu'tamarat (1905–1923), File 3, 15. Tellingly, the topic of women's physical exercise was the very last entry in the program.

33 Margot Badran, *Feminists, Islam, and Nation: Gender and the Making of Modern Egypt* (Princeton, NJ: Princeton University Press, 1995), 145–46.

34 Ibid., 136.

35 While this re-reading is inspired by my recently completed research into an Islamic form of mysticism, I could just as well have made the decolonial interventions of indigenous scholars the starting point. See, for example, Glen Coulthard, *Red Skin, White Masks: Rejecting the Colonial Politics of Recognition* (Minneapolis: University of Minnesota Press, 2014).

36 Gayatri Spivak, "Can the Subaltern Speak?" in *Marxism and the Interpretation of Culture*, eds. Cary Nelson and Lawrence Grossberg (Urbana: University of Illinois Press, 1988), 271–313.

37 This "location" of Dr. Jirjis in a peripheral community added to his authenticity and authority for a mostly urban reading public. A more likely scenario was that he occasionally visited Bani Suwayf from Cairo and perhaps also offered his medical services. I thank Walter Armbrust for suggesting this reading.

38 Dr. Sabri Jirjis, "On Politics and Political Economy," *RB* (March 1934): 15–21.

39 Ibid., 15.

40 Ibid., 20–21.

41 The use of the body as a social and political metaphor was of course already quite old by then. Its modern use to describe national communities in Egypt can be traced to at least as far back as Rifa'a al-Tahtawi's *al-Murshid al-Amin lil-banat wa al-banin* [The Trusted Guide for Girls and Boys] (Cairo: The Supreme Council for Culture, 2002 [1872]). One of the most explicit and extended treatments of the "organic body" (*jism 'udwi*) as both a metaphor for and constitutive of modern society was Ahmad Amin's *al-Akhlaq* (Cairo: Lajnat al-Ta'lif wa al-Tarjama wa al-Nashr, 1920).

42 While there is some affinity here with the theoretical impulses of postcolonial and queer "necropolitics," it should be obvious that the life/death continuum of Sufism and the potentialities therein for political life are in, and aimed at, an entirely different universe from the geopolitical realities of the post 9/11 period. See J.-A. Mbembé, "Necropolitics," trans. Libby Meintjes, *Public Culture* 15, no. 1 (Winter 2003): 11–40, and Jasbir Puar, *Terrorist Assemblages: Homonationalism in Queer Times* (Durham, NC: Duke University Press, 2007).

43 On the tarbush debates, see Jacob, *Working Out Egypt*, 186–224.

44 On the broader impact of Darwinism in the Middle East, see Marwa Elshakry, *Reading Darwin in Arabic, 1860–1950* (Chicago: University of Chicago Press, 2013).

45 Michel Foucault, *The History of Sexuality: An Introduction*, trans. Robert Hurley (New York: Vintage, 1990), 143.

46 Ibid., 142–43.

47 Though apprehended by the law and sent to the gallows, this invisibility might have been what Natalie Zemon Davis struggled to illuminate in the figure of the lowly impostor that seemed to fascinate the eminent Judge Coras in *The Return of Martin Guerre* (Cambridge: Harvard University Press, 1984).

48 Judith Butler, *Notes Toward a Performative Theory of Assembly* (Cambridge: Harvard University Press, 2015). The quote is taken from proofs circulated at a seminar given by Butler at Cambridge University, May 2013.

49 On the real and present dangers to the life of the biosphere and to all (non-)life by extension, see the 2018 Intergovernmental Panel on Climate Change special report, *Global Warming of 1.5°C*. Available online: https://www.ipcc.ch/sr15/ (accessed January 17, 2020). Also see the argument about the paralysis of politics in dealing with planetary crises within the current framework of sovereignty in Timothy Mitchell, *Carbon Democracy* (New York: Verso, 2011).

CHAPTER 8

THE ARAB GARÇONNE: BEING SIMULTANEOUSLY MODERN AND ARAB IN 1920s AND 1930s PALESTINE, LEBANON, AND EGYPT

Yasmine Nachabe Taan

Introduction

Within the context of the rising debates and tensions around gender norms and breaking them in the circulating press of the 1920s and 1930s Palestine, Lebanon, and Egypt, this chapter examines performance, theatricality, and cross-dressing that work to shatter fixed identities. It explores heterogenous representations of women in photographs during this period not only drawing from gender expressions but also experimenting with identities from different social classes and geographic places. The categories and frameworks developed in this chapter focus on the ways these women challenge social norms both in Europe and in the Arab world while complicating the assumption of cross-dressing as a Western practice and establishing this practice in the context of Lebanon, Palestine, and Egypt as a modality of feminine freedom.

In analyzing how women transformed themselves into different dramatic personae, casting heroic roles and charismatic personalities in search of the New Woman, the chapter highlights a whole range of new social values. The complex practices of cross-dressing and casting heroic persona, not only in photographs but also in Arab women's writings on historical female figures, call for further interpretations that subvert social and political ideologies and contest the limitations of women's roles in the domestic sphere. Women's presence and performance in such photographs and writings is seen as activism, challenging the stereotype of the Ottoman Arab women as passive. I argue that this nuanced gender reconfiguration creates a space for negotiation. By adopting male attire and behavior in the photographs, cross-dressed women diluted the patriarchal values deeply rooted in institutional ideologies. They embody masculine symbols to project a gender with its own cultural history rather than one that is exclusively derived from masculinity. Contested as it may be, cross-dressing offers a chance for terms of ambiguity and contingent performances of self as other. It is evidence of a subversive movement in parallel with the rising feminist movement in Cairo that expresses discontent and political activism through unexpected sartorial choices. By challenging the dress code assigned to women, these women presented an alternative history in staging scenes that resisted their fixed body management.

Women Transforming Themselves into Images

While looking into the large collection of photographs compiled by the Arab Image Foundation in Beirut, I came across a number of photographs in which women appear cross-dressed in "men's clothes" in places such as Egypt, Palestine, and Lebanon.[1] These images come from private collections dating to the 1920s and 1930s and would not have been produced for public circulation. Yet, in the same period, images of women

Arabic words and names have been transliterated according to a simplified system based on the *International Journal of Middle East Studies*. I have not changed the transliterations of names adopted by authors who write in either English or French.

cross-dressed did appear in the Arab press of the time.[2] To explore what these images—made for and seen by private and public audiences respectively—reveal about issues of gender, nation, and modernity I have selected two photographs from private collections (Figures 8.1 and 8.2) to analyze in comparison with images printed for public eyes. In most cases, private images were preserved in personal archives within the private confines of families. Few historical sources and solid extant records about cross-dressed women in the Near East of that period exist. I read these photographs as an attempt by women to construct themselves through their performance and masquerade while transforming themselves into *images*.[3]

The Garçonne, the Female Dandy, and the Dissident Rebel

Despite the fact that information about them is limited, the photos open up a discourse within the colonial context of Egypt, Palestine, and Lebanon, on cultural models within a diverse cultural landscape of these different countries. In a period when regional definitions of gender and identity roles were a topic of debate, these definitions were not necessarily associated with particular ideologies or traditional practices. For

Figure 8.1 Woman dressed up as a man, photographer unknown, Egypt, undated. Amgad Neguib Collection, courtesy of the Arab Image Foundation.

Figure 8.2 Marguerite dressed up as a man, photographer unknown, Palestine/Jerusalem, 1935. Alice Agazarian Collection, courtesy of the Arab Image Foundation.

example, in Mount Lebanon in the mid-nineteenth century, female peasants broke gendered honor codes by working in silk mills for a little extra income.[4] By breaking with regional definitions of gender identity roles, the photographs (Figures 8.1 and 8.2) display a state of tension and uneasiness. I read this along similar lines to how Judith Butler argues that performativity produces gender as an "essential" component of one's identity.[5] Thus, the act of performing gender, as seen in the photographs, has the potential to displace categories of normative gender construction. The photographs offer us the possibility of a number of readings of the women within them, ranging from interpreting them in roles such as the *garçonne*, the female dandy, the *Za'īmāt* (leader), and the dissident rebel.[6]

Performativity, as articulated by Butler, serves to define identitie(s).[7] Behaviors, gestures, and attire are not only the result of an individual's identity but they contribute to the formation of one's identity which is continuously being redefined through the body. Hence, gender is a continual social process of doing masculinity and femininity as performative.[8] Following this notion of gender as a continuous process, this chapter is premised on the concept that gender does not precede but rather follows from social and cultural practices. I will explore the photographs and their implication in doing masculinity and—as a mode of self-making through which subjects become socially intelligible—within the post-Ottoman period in which Lebanon, Palestine, and Egypt were taking shape as independent modern nations.

In this context, the staging and documenting of gender performances as the dissident rebel, the garçonne, and the za'īmāt can be thought of as a form of social action. Masquerading in front of the camera for a private audience is different than masquerading for commercial purposes—marketing cross-gender presentation and fashion for public audience. Both cross-gender dressing and making photographs are forms of masquerade, however. When staged in private domestic spaces, I argue, the processes of self-fashioning by staging photographs and masquerading in men's attire in front of the camera are active processes of social transformation that simultaneously assert women's agency over the production of their own selves as modern subjects. These representations can be understood as manifestations of losing their womanness or femininity which could trouble social conventions and gender hierarchies. Similar to the French garçonne, the Arab garçonne can be aligned with frivolous pursuits of happiness, romance, and fashion through consumption.[9] However, this definition is limiting in scope. In this chapter, I will explore nuanced identities of what I call the Arab garçonne expanding the stylistic fashioning of the body to reach a more complex articulation, that of a dissident rebel associated with political and social activism.

Gender Instability in the Photograph

"Man Hwa?" (Who is he?) reads the title of an image in *Rūz al Yūsuf* in 1927 with a photograph of a person sporting a tarbush, suit, and necktie, holding a stick and standing in a "masculine" pose (Figure 8.3).[10] The caption reads: "This is Miss Malak Muhammad, the prominent singer of the Bosporus who appears in this photograph sporting a *dallū'a* [coquettish] officer uniform."[11] Dallū'a, or coyness, is contradictory to our expectations of an army officer's gender and behavior in this time and place. The incompatible attire—masculine—and behavior—feminine—underlines the dissonance—is it a man? Is it a woman? This ambiguous photograph stands out as evidence of the existence of the figure of the garçonne in Egypt and, as I will show, extends to Palestine, Lebanon, and beyond. What can we make of the apparent disjuncture between a metaphoric man in the photograph and its referent in the person of a *garçonne*? What of the gender instability of this female subject that appears in the circulating press during a period in which women were debated as "symbols of identity and visions of society and the nation?"[12] Was the sartorial dress perceived as a marker for modernity during this period? Was dressing up as a man seen as a European practice and what does this mean in the context in which women's appearance management is part of an ideological terrain where notions of cultural authenticities and integrity are debated?

It is as if Miss Malak Muhammad's full-page photograph in *Rūz al Yūsuf*'s November 1927 issue is announcing a shift or a transition in history not just for women but for the whole nation. Qāsim Amīn, a jurist, a reformer, and a central figure of the *al-Nahda* (the Arab Renaissance) movement, in his *Tahrīr al-Mar'a* (The Liberation of Women), more than two decades earlier in 1899, recognized the important role of women in building a nation, yet he limited this role to the upbringing and education of the sons of the nation.[13] Qāsim's view has been challenged by a number of feminist scholars, among them Leila Ahmed who pointed out that Amīn's Egyptian woman does not have control over her body. Her body is used to build the nation.[14]

This photograph (Figure 8.3) can be read as a woman's claim of her place as sisters-in-the-nation at a time when " … nation was largely conceived and visualized as a brotherhood, and homeland as female, a beloved, and a mother."[15] In Lebanon, it was Ahmed Fāris Al-Shidyāq, in the 1840s, nearly fifty years before Qāsim Amīn's *Tahrīr al-Mar'a* who advocated for women's rights and the value of equality between genders. Unlike many of his contemporary reformers and those who came after him, he did not engage in the discourse of the idealized woman whose education was in the service of better performance of her domestic duties that are limited to the upbringing and education of a new generation of citizens. In his book, women are seen not as perfect wives but as full and equal participants in society who have the right to work and take part in the building of the nation as equal citizens.[16] Al-Shidyāq claims "there can be no Nahda in the East without a Nahda of women."[17] Al-Shidyāq was more progressive than Amīn, however, his ideas were later replaced by more gender conformist progressives.

من هو؟

(هذه هى الآنسة ملك محمد مطربة البوسفور)
(ونرى هنا فى ملابس ضابط دلوعة)

Figure 8.3 Miss Malak Muhammad, photographer unknown. Published with the caption "Man Hwa?" (Who is he?), in *Rūz al Yūsuf*, November 17, 1927, p. 17.

Performing Masculinity as a Counter Act of Dissidence

Similar to the photograph of Miss Malak Muhammad (Figure 8.3), the two women in Figures 8.1 and 8.2 are dressed as men, yet unlike Miss Malak, they stand or sit in an outdoor space, a public space.[18] The public/private divide has for many scholars of the Middle East prompted debates on the notion of boundaries in relation to class, gender, and race.[19] The porousness and shape of the public/private divide varies depending on the country and the time.[20] However, the configurations of public/private space are impacted upon by institutions. For example, Suad Joseph argues that "in Lebanon the boundaries have been porous and fluid, in part, because of the centrality of patriarchal kinship structures, modes of operation, and idioms in all spheres of social life."[21] The public/private has been the ground for critiques of domestic patriarchy and liberal feminists' efforts to transgress boundaries of the private and to create equitable public spaces. A woman has to abide by the regulations seeking to govern women's behavior in public, she does not behave similarly in a private as in a public space. In public, she is expected to conform to society's expectations. According to Huda Lutfi, prominent religious scholars during 1920s in Egypt sought to "prevent social anarchy" by urging the community to maintain a "clear division between the public domain of men and the private domain of women."[22] The woman sitting on the pavement—an outdoor space—and the one standing on the roof—an outdoor space too—are not only transgressing the boundaries by challenging the norms and dressing up like men but they are also breaking the boundaries of confined gendered spaces by using "public" spaces as a background stage for their photographs as if they are saying "we want to be seen cross-dressed in public." Cross-dressing does not seem to be a secret practice that occurs in intimate spaces such as their bedrooms. In this case, it is not just the gender non-conformity of their poses and sartorial practices in relation to the conventional array of poses and dress seen on female bodies but also their presence in a "public" space—in photographs—that constitutes their political activism.

While all three are dressed up in a fashion that connotes masculinity, their poses suggest degrees of variations within the gender binary as addressed in the articles that appeared in the circulating press of the time.[23] The pose in Figure 8.1 could easily be achieved in a fashionable dress; however, in Figure 8.2, it is the slouching on one hip that seems to be more of an assertive—masculine—attitude. Whether they are standing or sitting, I presume both Marguerite (Figure 8.2) and her counterpart in Egypt (Figure 8.1) are posing as if demanding to be seen as masculine women. Their sartorial choices, pose, and behavior are not to be understood as a representation of same-sex desire, rather an aspiration for 'adālah (equality). To assume that the representation of 1920s Arab cross-dressed women is an expression of same-sex desire is reductive and short sighted. These ubiquitous sartorial choices need a nuanced probing in regard to the particular gender and cultural context that I will unfold below. The appropriation of male attire and behavior in public space reclaims female homosociality within that space. Female homosociality was seen as a threat to the orderly management of the household.[24] According to Afsaneh Najmabadi, women, in the context of 1920's Iran, in order to preserve their chastity were expected to behave in a feminine way.[25] But what does "feminine way" entail? She describes the desirable and undesirable traits as demonstrated in Iranian children's books in the late nineteenth century—which shares common ideas to a large extent with Arabic children's books as well. Being frivolous, "undisciplined and shameless, laughs a great deal for no reason, opens her mouth in front of people and makes awful noises, runs around and pays no attention to others … talks nonsense"—all accepted behavior for boys—and so forth are all disliked behaviors for girls in contrast to being "impeccably obedient and well-mannered."[26] A respectable women's *passe-temps*, as described in most of the articles in *Rūz al Yūsuf* around the 1920s, include tidiness, being obedient to their husbands, lack of arrogance, hard work, and learning womanly crafts including knitting, sewing, and embroidery. Amusing themselves by masquerading in front of the camera as men is not on this list.

There is almost no information available about these photographs aside from the limited information in their captions. Many captions were written by the archivist at the Arab Image Foundation retrospectively. Those produced coterminously seem rarely to have been written by the photographer or the subject; rather the coterminous captions are limited to the collector's knowledge of the material or members of the family or original owners of the photographs. All suggest multiple possible layers of readings. Unlike Miss Malak's photo that was meant to circulate in the press, these are personal photos that were part of private family albums before joining the Arab Image Foundation collection.

Figures 8.1 and 8.2 appear more candid than the highly curated photo of Miss Malak that was taken for the purpose of being published in the popular Egyptian magazine, *Rūz al Yūsuf*. In Figure 8.1, c. 1930s, the woman who is sitting with her leg crossed over appears as if she tied back her hair and carefully tucked it under the *tarbush* in order to reinforce signs of confidence, knowledge, and education. The tarbush not only signifies masculinity, it also symbolizes a higher social status among the educated members of the elite during the Ottoman period in Egypt.[27] She has matched the fabric of her handkerchief, carefully placed inside her suit's upper left-side pocket, with that of her necktie. In the carefully staged photograph, she is posing next to a plant that was perhaps placed next to her for the purpose of taking this photo. When probing the photograph, one recognizes that she is not alone in the space of the photograph. In the background, a dark-skinned man is leaning on the balustrade while staring at her from the back. He's dressed casually with his sleeves rolled up. Perhaps a servant who just completed his chores standing in the back anonymously watching the photo shoot? His presence or non-presence in the space—and consequently the photograph—is almost invisible.[28] The woman, turning her back to him seems indifferent to his gaze. The position of the woman in the forefront, her tarbush and her bold, relaxed pose in contrast to his position in the back, attire and standby pose, suggest a social gap or hierarchy. Assuming that he is her servant, he conveniently disappears into the background.[29] While the confrontational gaze of the cross-dressed woman is referenced as the pinnacle of defiance toward patriarchy, the "oppositional gaze" of the man in the background is ignored. He is part of the background with little to no attention given to the critical role of his presence.[30]

Wearing a man's suit that hides all signs of femininity such as the breasts and hips, the *garçonne* in Figures 8.1 and 8.2—as well as Figure 8.3, discussed above—can be perceived as the object of a complex and pervasive discourse, central to which are interrelated deliberations on urbanization, cosmopolitanism, and modernization. In Figure 8.2, Marguerite's attire not only exudes masculinity, but so does her behavior in the photographs. She "smokes" or pretends to smoke in the photo. A sign predominantly associated with freedom, the cigarette—a common prop for the garçonne, the female dandy, and the dissident rebel—appears not to be lit. In taking on a masculine look, the female subjects in these photographs performed a ritual not only of gender, but also of declaring their class, education, and belonging. The *tarbush* connotes signs of authority and education, the cigarette is associated with liberation and dissidence, and the background suggests the geographical context. In other words, photographs of this kind function as evidence of the dynamic social changes of the time.

Another noticeable element of their appearance is that these women are sporting trousers. Bifurcated dress in the form of baggy pants were part of the female wardrobe of peasant women in rural areas of Egypt, Palestine, and Lebanon in the early nineteenth century, for they were comfortable clothes worn for harvesting and doing other chores. They were also historically worn as traditional dress by Arabian princesses. Lebanese novelist Emily Nasrallah recalls of her childhood in South Lebanon, "I grew up in the countryside. My grandmother used to wear sirwal [şalvar], the traditional baggy-style pants commonly worn by peasants […].

The veil was still worn by most local women during the 1920's and 1930's. During this period, women started rebelling by removing the veil and, when they did, their names were written all over the walls of the village […]."[31] Despite recalling the traditional *şalvar*-style pants of their foremothers, neither Nasrallah nor Anīsa Najjār—also a Lebanese novelist who similarly has written extensively about pioneering women in the region and their social and intellectual challenges—recall their mothers and grandmothers ever wearing European-style pants in public. It is this style of trousers that was associated with male dress and symbolized cross-dressing.

Condemning Masculine Women

We have no clear indication of the date when women started cross-dressing in public in the streets of Beirut, Jerusalem, and Cairo. The practice must have been prominent at the turn of the century, however, because practices of cross-dressing increasingly appeared in the press in the late 1920s. Most of the women who cross-dressed in circulating photos of the press were prominent figures of the entertainment industry in Cairo and Alexandria at the height of the growing Egyptian movie industry. For the "artiste" or the glamorous diva—including singers, actors, and dancers—cross-dressing was relatively permissible.[32] While we have no evidence that these women did so offstage, their cross-dressing onstage and in public shots was contested and the women were condemned as failing mothers, Europhiles, and traitors to the nation. They did not conform to what constituted the good wife as described in predominantly male-authored instructions that assigned gender roles as part of the project of constructing a modern nation.

The critique of women who acted like men is expressed in a speech delivered by Gergi Nqūla Bāz at an Orthodox Christian charity event in Tripoli in 1910.[33] In his speech, the orator addressed the audience, condemning gender blurred behavior that had been on the rise in Beirut.[34] In Beirut, according to the eloquent orator's complaint, "men are no longer powerful and authoritarian, but rather women are in power."[35] He continues his speech by lamenting this "anomaly" as social disruption and calling on his audience to resist this new phenomenon before it is too late.[36] He adds, "Watching men becoming feminized and women masculinized is repulsive and socially degrading."[37] He tells the story of a woman who enters a public space walking brazenly, "mutarajjila" (masculinized), in a way that is bold, shameless, and without chastity, like the "ʾabadayāt" or wrestlers proudly marching in a battleground.[38] For him, women are expected to be modest in public, this "disturbing" female behavior is against social principles and nature.[39]

Bāz's speech is just one example of the discourse circulating in the press of the 1920s Arab world that reveals the tension generated in writing about gender roles, the divisions and distribution of obligations and responsibilities according to gendered norms and traditions, and the controversies these discourses raised. The fact that the orator is a man who is affiliated to Christianity indicates that the resistance to women's emancipation was not only directed by the Muslim communities. It should rather be understood as a general social and cultural resistance to change.

During the 1920s, new genre and rules of etiquette texts in the press, *Rūz al Yūsuf* being one of them, instructed women on how to behave properly in public in order to prepare them to step into a heterosocial space without undermining the social and cultural order. Conflicting disciplinary and emancipatory notions are addressed in these texts.

Whereas cross-dressing is predominantly indexed as an expression of homosexual desire in the Western context, it is important to note that when it is practiced in the context of particular cultures, as in this case, it generates different meanings; here, it manifests an aspiration for adala with men. Articles in *Rūz al Yūsuf* deliberately invited contradictory and controversial opinions, whether for creating sensationalist reactions or to offer its readers a fairly objective and "balanced" reaction in an educative manner, they nevertheless rarely addressed effeminate men, and predominantly condemned any fracture of femininity into maleness in the text. Sporadic photos of cross-dressed women, mostly actresses, appear in the journals with awkward titles followed by exclamation marks and often with a brief paragraph that also ends with exclamation marks to imply the embarrassment and discomfort produced by these "strange" gender blurred images.

Figure 8.4 Florence Fawaz—also known as Florence Austral—unknown photographer. Published with the article "The Work of Women," *Al Mar`a al Jadīda*, 1921.

In most cases, *Rūz al Yūsuf*'s editorial board made it a point to invite conservative contributors to address their concerns and condemn cross-dressing practices while women were depicted in the circulating press as female heroes (Figure 8.4), male heroes (Figure 8.5), cross-dressed (Figures 8.3, 8.6 and 8.8) and smoking cigarettes (Figure 8.7).

السيدة عزيزه أمير فى رواية بنت نابليون

Figure 8.5 *"Al-Saiyyda ʿAzīza Amīr fī Riwayāt bint Napoleon"* (Miss ʿAzīza Amīr in the Tale of the Daughter of Napoleon), *Rūz al Yūsuf*, no. 107, November 17, 1927, p. 7.

162

Figure 8.6 *"Munīra Bek Al-Mahdiyya?!,"* on the cover of a 1927 issue of *Rūz al Yūsuf*, January 6, 1927, no. 62.

Figure 8.7 *"Al-Sigāra!! Dala' wa Keyf wa Taqlīd"* (The Cigarette!! Flirt, Pleasure and Imitation), a spread from *Rūz al Yūsuf*, December 22, 1926, pp. 6–7.

Figure 8.8 *"Mughālatāt!!"* (Eccentrics!!), a spread from *Rūz al Yūsuf*, December 15, 1926, pp. 6–7.

The Garçonne and the Rising Film Industry in Egypt

The 1940s are generally considered the beginning of Egyptian cinema's golden age.[40] From its beginnings, the Egyptian film industry served not only the national market, but with its musical stars, among them Umm Kulthūm, Layla Murad, Farīd al-Atrash, and Abd al-Wahāb, it was able to attract audiences all over the Arab world. The formation and consolidation of the Egyptian film industry was highly dependent on the exploitation of already existing theater and music stars. With the opening of early cinema and, later in 1906, the Pathé movie theaters in Alexandria and Cairo, the number of theaters in Egypt rapidly increased.[41] During a period of rapid industrialization of Egyptian cinema in the 1930s, stars gradually appeared in the circulating press. Both garçonne and dandy were figures mostly adopted by entertaining stars such as actresses, singers, and dancers who were on the rise at the height of the entertainment industry in Cairo and Alexandria.

Looking at *Rūz al Yūsuf*'s periodicals published in the late 1920s, we realize that women have often appeared in men's attire in photographs featured in the Arabic circulating press of this period. In Figure 8.6, a frontal portrait of Munīra al-Mahdiyya, placed between two pedestals holding Renaissance-style sculptures of nude male bodies, each holding a disk with a Hellenistic woman engraved on their surfaces graces the cover of a 1927 issue of *Rūz al Yūsuf* (no. 62, January 6, 1927). Looking closer, we see that the woman is sporting a three-piece man's suit, with a striped necktie in a dandy style. At the bottom of the image, the caption reads, "Munīra Bek Al-Mahdiyya?!" Here, the words again indicate a contradiction. The obviously feminine name Munīra al-Mahdiyya, is used with the additional term "Bek," a title commonly used to connote a man with authority. The publisher provides additional explanation for publishing such a photograph of a woman on the cover of the magazine in this particular issue during this specific period in time by mockingly stating "We are publishing such a photograph for the first time to show what the women's movement has achieved within the last few years."[42] This last statement demonstrates *Rūz al Yūsuf* and presumably its readers' position to the women's movement in showing that women are being ruined, becoming unnatural, and masculinized by feminism.

To contextualize cross-dressing further in relation to the figure of the garçonne, it is relevant to note that the Arab garçonne appears in the local press at a roughly similar time that this figure appears in the French press. This complicates widely accepted histories of capitalism, consumption, and visual culture that presume that "modernity" is disseminated from Europe and North America to the rest of the world in a one-way process that happens at the second half of the twentieth century. A closer analysis of the figure of the garçonne used as a heuristic device to examine women's sartorial practices and how they relate to the rise of the film industry in Egypt is a study that challenges such presumptions on the provenance of modernity in relation to consumer culture.[43] Singers, actresses, and predominantly male movie producers appeared in the press at the same time, often flashy and always fashionable (Figure 8.8). Photographs of the singers and actresses were often used to promote plays, concerts, and films; they presented these women in an appealing and provocative way to their potential fans. However, these cross-dressed women can also be considered agents for social change as they are not compatible with the prescribed roles for women as described by the literature of the press circulating a decade earlier that describe the woman's responsibilities as follows:

[T]he wife must submit to her husband and give him legally sanctioned obedience, in service to him and his sons, concerning herself with the arrangement of the house, administration of meals, cleaning, and economy, as well as the upbringing of [their] sons and daughters.[44]

According to the gender dynamics set by this author who clearly condemns the garçonne, women are not to waste their time in amusement outside the home; they must perform their domestic duties accordingly.

Slightly more than a decade after the issue raised above, *Rūz al Yūsuf* continued to promote prominent Egyptian singers, dancers, and actresses such as Badīʿa Masābni, ʿAzīza Amīr, Zaynab Sidqi, Fātima Rushdi, Amīna Muhammad, Fatḥiyya Ahmad, Firdaus Hasan, even Rūz al Yūsuf herself appears in the photograph sporting masculine attire (in Figure 8.8).[45] Egyptian actresses played a major role in founding the Egyptian national cinema. They not only acted in plays and on the screen but they also contributed to the growth of the entertainment industry as independent founding directors and producers. Many of them founded their own production houses in the late 1920s and early 1930s Cairo and Alexandria, including ʿAzīza Amīr who launched her "Isis Film," while Assia Dagher established the "Arab Film Company"—later called "Lotus Film"—and Bahija Hafez founded the "Fanar Film Company."[46]

The article that featured these photos of cross-dressed stars did not circulate without some apprehension (Figure 8.8). Its title, *Mughālatāt!!* (Eccentrics!!), in Arabic refers to the unconventional and "strange" look of the women in the photographs. After listing the names of the Egyptian actresses, producers, and singers, the author writes,

> None of them looks like a woman! They are all men … You will be surprised to learn the reason for a woman to appropriate men's clothing in her attempt to imitate a man in appropriating all his deeds. All actresses with no exception appear in a photograph enacting a masculine look. If she could not find an occasion to do so, than she would just do it to enact a masculine role, on stage, in a play, while sporting a tarbush, an ʿammama (turban), or a hat, or any other masculine prop … and sometimes with no particular occasion? Why? … To voice her determination in liberating herself and being at par with men.[47]

In Figure 8.8, Badīʿa Masābni appears sporting a tarbush, ʿAzīza Amīr appears in an Amazonian attire, Amina Muhammad is sporting boyish clothes perhaps for casting a role of a young man in a play, Firdaus Hasan is wearing Hanna Effendi Wehbi's European dandy-style suit and necktie, and Rūz al Yūsuf is wearing a David Copperfield suit as the caption of the image indicates.[48] The two female "shuyukh," Zeinab Sidqi and Fātima Rushdi, appear in separate photographs armed and wearing the traditional Arab male *ʿigal*.[49] It is interesting to note that Fātima Sirri appears sporting a masculine white shirt, both hands in her pockets. This is a photo that was taken in the garden of one of the private palaces two years before, and she did not agree to publish her photograph until the editors strongly insisted on publishing it as part of this article.[50] These cross-dressing practices were perceived as acts of dissidence and rebellion by *Rūz al Yūsuf's* editors and consequently, its readers. Women, actresses, singers, and belly dancers masqueraded in male attire as an aspiration to free themselves from social restrictions and for the sake of "musauat al-rajul," that is, to be equal to men.[51] The article ends with the following bold statement: "No man appears dressed as women because no man desires to be equal to *al-jins al-latif or* the gentle sex."[52]

In the context of Cairo, political and social changes were another cause for the rise of the garçonne culture. Through making decisions about what to wear and how to dress differently, women began to show that they resented restrictions on their dress, behavior, and movement.

Another article titled *"Al-Sigāra!! Dala' wa Keyf wa Taqlīd"* (The Cigarette!! Flirt, Pleasure and Imitation) appeared in *Rūz al Yūsuf* on December 22, 1926 (Figure 8.7).[53] In the middle of this spread, Miss Angel, a prominent Lebanese dancer and singer in Beirut and in Alexandria, appears in a white jumpsuit standing proudly one foot on a chair, one hand on her waist and the other holding a cigarette, smiling and confidently confronting us (Figure 8.7). The author explains that this photo was sent to *Rūz al Yūsuf* by Ismaʿīl, Fathia Ahmad's husband. Both Fathia and Ismail are close friends of Miss Angel. The author claims that when men smoke, they are not criticized for doing so, however, when women smoke in public, it is seen as shameful and disrespectful. The article (Figure 8.7) is accompanied by a photo in which Muhammad Effendi Karim—

known as Ramsis—is portrayed holding his chin in a deep pensive pose. In another photo, Hasan Effendi al-Bārūdi, another man, is mindfully lighting up his cigarette in a relaxed manner.

Men smoking cigarettes is presented as a "natural" practice whereas women smoking cigarettes is presented as an act of provocation. Women have been smoking for a long time in Egypt—smoking the *nargīleh* as mostly seen in nineteenth-century Orientalist paintings.[54] However, they did not smoke in front of non-familial men. In 1920s Cairo, Alexandria, and other Egyptian urban contexts, upper-class women not only smoked but they smoked with attitude—with pride and confidence. As the article (Figure 8.7) states, "they stand in front of the photographer, cigarette in their hands puffing smoke … "[55] This article features six photographs of actresses who work in Egypt and one Syrian singer and dancer, all of them smoking. The women in these photos do not appear as relaxed or pensive as the men in the two photographs discussed above. They instead appear sensually acting out. According to the author, Henriette and Angel appear to be enjoying the influence of nicotine, whereas Mary Manswr is smiling back at us with a sensuous gaze. For a long time, women have been objectified by the male gaze, however, here, it seems that women are defying such representations by willfully acting the role of the Arab garçonne who is brazenly holding her cigarette and puffing smoke.

Womanliness as a Masquerade

In relation to this tension around gender norms and breaking them, analyzing theatricality in the photos of cross-dressed women works to shatter fixed identities. Women in these photographs not only explore gender expressions but also experiment with identities from different social classes and geographic places to transform themselves into different dramatic personae, casting heroic roles and charismatic personalities. For example, images of women casting roles such as Joan of Arc circulated in *al Mar'a al Jadīda*.[56] In one of the journal's 1921 issues, Florence Fawaz appears in a photograph in full armor and armed with a a spear (Figure 8.4).[57] In this image, she stands like a Greek historical heroine, wearing a traditional costume including a helmet decorated with wings and holding an amulet in one hand and a shield in the other as if leading troops into battle. This recalls the way in which heroines were cited in Arab women's writings at the time, calling on other women to identify with heroines such as Joan of Arc, the national heroine of France who was an inspirational figure for many women and men. Joan of Arc was the most common subject before 1940 according to Marilyn Booth's nuanced analysis of female biographies published in Egypt from the late-nineteenth century until the middle of the twentieth century.[58] She describes how Joan of Arc often appears in Egyptian women's writing on Egyptian women biographies as a historical figure that could project a whole range of social values. Joan of Arc could serve as an exemplar of religious belief, peasant authenticity, nationalist feeling; indeed, even as an anti-imperialist resisting the British colonizers.[59]

Florence Fawaz's theatrical masquerading as Joan of Arc is different from the previous cross-dressing practices in Figures 8.3, 8.5, 8.6, and 8.7. However, both practices, cross-dressing and casting heroic persona, call for further interpretations that subvert social and political ideologies that limit women's role to the domestic sphere. Women's presence and performance in such photographs can be seen as activism, challenging the stereotype of the Ottoman Arab women as silent and passive.[60] Moreover, these photographs resist the portrayal of the Arab woman as a pawn of Arab men who is usurped by her own culture.

Whether the performance is about a dramatic persona such as Joan of Arc or a performance of masculine contemporaneity, it voices concerns over identity, agency, and aspiration for change. Performance can be understood as an act of presenting a form of entertainment. In *He Who Is Photographed*, Roland Barthes writes about the effort to perform another self in the image:

… Once I feel myself observed by the lens, everything changes: I constitute myself in the process of "posing," I instantaneously make another body for myself, I transform myself in advance into an image.[61]

For Barthes, being in the photograph is an act of performance itself. However, masquerading entails an act of mimicry, in which one pretends to be someone else. Masquerading implies being disguised or impersonating someone else. The psychoanalyst theorist Joan Rivière, and later Luce Irigaray, theorized femininity as an operation of masquerade. They both claim that womanliness is assumed and worn as a mask to hide the possession of masculinity and to avert the reprisals expected if found guilty of the crime.[62] For Rivière, women who present themselves as feminine—donning a dress and having long hair—are also masquerading. This approach raises the question of the essential nature of femininity.[63] What does it signify to be a masculine woman in 1920s Cairo, Palestine, or Lebanon?

In March 1919, Zaynab Sidqi donned a combination of Pharaonic and Arab props to lead a group of playwrights, actresses, singers, belly dancers, and other popular stars on a long procession erupting throughout the city. They joined a massive anti-British street protest and marched alongside the prominent feminists Huda Sha'rawi and Saiza Nabrāwi who wore the yashmak whereas the actresses marching side by side were cross-dressed cast as Napoleon Bonaparte, Hārūn al-Rashīd, and Othello, a combination of real and fictional military political leaders.[64] The sartorial dress here transcended gender binary: the women were not imitating men in their attire; what they identified with were the traits of leadership, authority, and control.

In borrowing the Greek hero's spear and shield (Figure 8.4) and Napoleon's bicorn hat, his dark tailcoat with double-rank gold oak leaf embroidery, over white breeches tucked into riding boots (Figure 8.5), both disguised women in the photos destabilize aspects of the feminine as *al-jins al-latif*: they wanted to assert themselves as heroines.

Manifestations of Arab Feminism?

Photos of actresses masquerading as heroes such as in Figures 8.4 and 8.5 and others cross-dressing circulated in the press during the 1920s and 1930s at the same time as the photo of Nabawiyya Mūsa, Huda Sha'rawi, and Saiza Nabrāwi staging a scene in which they removed their face veils to reveal their features at a Cairo railway station was made public through the press.[65] This photo became an icon of the complexity of Arab feminism history since it is intertwined with Islam, nationalism, and post-colonialism. However, this initiative brought many women and their voices out of their homes and into public places for the first time, as well as opening new discourses. The response to this was mixed: some women were shocked, and others removed their veils. Following this event that took place in 1923, Sha'rawi founded and became the first president of the Egyptian Feminist Union. She was also the president of the Wafdist Women's Central Committee. She launched the journal *L'Egyptienne* in 1925, in order to publicize the feminist cause for upper-class women in Egypt.[66]

This staging of the photograph that took place at the Cairo railway station encouraged women to think independently about their sartorial practices, careers, and social activities.

Arab Women as *Za'īmāt*

The cover of *Rūz al Yūsuf* often displayed images of women as *za'īmāt*, or leaders/chiefs (Figure 8.9). A group of short-haired women are playing soccer on the illustrated cover of *Rūz al Yūsuf* (no. 107). Three of them appear in the foreground courageously kicking the ball. They are all wearing short pants and T-shirts, showing their strong and muscular bodies, suggestive of their physical fitness. The caption explains: "A few years ago, a group of women established a tennis club." Women of the upper bourgeoisie were introduced to tennis which can be understood as part of a regional campaign to "modernize" the nation by introducing women to sport.[67] However, the caption continues with a mocking tone followed by three exclamation marks: " … We were recently informed that a number of za'īmāt of the women's movement are planning to form a soccer team and others are planning a wrestling team!!!"[68] This last comment using Za'āma as a notion to underline Egyptian women's appropriation of the notion of leadership—that is commonly attributed to men—implies a certain anxiety that Wilson Chacko Jacob explores in depth in his discussion of the consequences of the growing perceived sense of women's "competing identity" with men during the second decade of the twentieth century.[69] This "competing identity" was not only expressed in their physical body management but also disturbed social hierarchies. Seen through this lens, the rhetoric of this caption can be translated as a critique of the feminist movement and the "significant anxieties about men's ability to lead the new nation."[70] In Figure 8.9 it is the soccer-playing garçonnes who are appealing to the upper-class unmarried women sharing their

Figure 8.9 *"Al-Saiyydāt Wa La'ib Kwrat Al Qadam"* (The Ladies in a Soccer Game), cover of *Rūz al Yūsuf*, no. 107, November 17, 1927.

interest in sport activities, competing and winning games rather than devoting their lives to socially expected responsibilities associated with women such as domestic chores and home economics.

When appropriated by women, playing soccer aligns women's social status with their appearance as rebellious and dissident. Strong-mindedness, when attributed to women, was neither appreciated nor accepted by local Arab cultures. An example of this is that when a woman diverges from socialized gender norms, she is marginalized and called in Arabic *ikht al-rijāl* (tomboy). Activating Arab women's bodies was not accepted without controversy, Arab women faced many challenges before asserting themselves as agents for change in resisting the fixity of their image.

Another Trial of Arab Modernity?[71]

The women dressed like men in the photographs (Figures 8.1 and 8.2) are seen today as confident and self-determined women. By adopting male attire and behavior in the photographs—a representation that is inconsistent with, and not culturally associated with, their assigned gender—they diluted the patriarchal values deeply rooted in institutional ideologies. They embody masculine symbols to project a gender with its own cultural history rather than one that is exclusively derived from masculinity. They sought to be identified with their male counterparts to acquire the freedom, control, and power enjoyed by men. This complex gender reconfiguration creates a space for negotiation. Thinking through the categories and frameworks developed in this chapter, an interesting approach would be to examine the ways these women challenged social norms both in Europe and in the Arab world. Tarek el-Ariss discusses queer expressions of sexuality that take shape at the intersection of Arab-Islamic literature and language and how these can be interpreted as "trials of Arab modernity." In this chapter, I rather examine a visual language articulated through cross-dressed colonial bodies who are trying out their version of modernity throughout, expressing not only their sexuality but also national identity, social class, and women's rights within the context of colonial Egypt, Palestine, and Lebanon.

However, it is important to note here that cross-dressing is central to global culture, to the definition of human identity, in a world where the individual exists in a multicultural and multi-temporal environment. This complicates the assumption of cross-dressing as a Western practice and establishes the practice in the context of Lebanon, Palestine, and Egypt as a modality of feminine freedom. Contested as it may be, cross-dressing as practiced in Figures 8.1 and 8.2 offers a chance for terms of ambiguity and contingent performances of self as other. It is evidence of a subversive movement in parallel with the rising feminist movement in Cairo that expresses discontent and political activism through unexpected sartorial choices. While breaking with tradition, through novel styles of dressing, these women distinguished themselves from their mothers and grandmothers. By challenging the dress code assigned to women, they presented an alternative history in staging scenes that resisted their fixed body management. Hence, they are to be seen as counterhegemonic. Their attire and behavior invoke a complex, ambiguous narrative that implies another "trial of Arab modernity."

Notes

1   The Arab Image Foundation, as is indicated on the website (http://arabimagefoundation.com access January 11, 2021) is an organization established in Beirut in 1997 to collect and preserve photographs from the Middle East, North Africa, and the Arab diaspora. Its collection dates from the 1860s to the present day, and contains more than 500,000 photographs. These include family photos, snapshots, and institutional group portraits, among other photographic genres. It contains the work of over 250 amateur photographers and 700 professional photographers.

2 These are two different types of photographs belonging to separate family collections that joined the Arab Image Foundation collection whereas most of the photos published in the press are extracted from issues of the circulating *Rūz al Yūsuf* periodical in 1926–27. *Rūz al Yūsuf* was founded by Fatma al Yūsuf, also known as *Rūz al Yūsuf,* a Lebanese-born Egyptian actress and journalist. In October 1925 she founded the eponymous news magazine. *Rūz al Yūsuf* was published in Arabic in Cairo and distributed in the Arab world. The magazine started as a cultural and literary publication and later in 1928 became a political journal while it continued publishing entertainment news, photos of celebrities, and public figures who were famous during the rising film entertainment industry in Cairo and Alexandria during the 1920s and 1930s.
   The author wishes to thank Khaled Rajeh for his extensive search and for locating visual supporting documents for this study.

3 Roland Barthes expands on the notion of performing himself in the photograph in Rolande Barthes, *Camera Lucida: Reflections on Photography* (New York: Hill and Wang, 1981), 10–15. I will return to this notion later in this chapter.

4 Akram Khater, *Inventing Home: Emigration, Gender, and the Middle Class in Lebanon, 1870–1920* (Berkeley: University of California Press, 2001).

5 Judith Butler, *Gender Trouble: Feminism and the Subversion of Identity* (New York: Routledge, 1990), 37.

6 *Za'īmāt* is female plural of *za'īm*. In Arabic *za'īm* means leader or chief. The term is commonly used to designate a male leader but the term is used to underline the leadership spirit of the women.

7 Butler, *Gender Trouble*, 37.

8 Ibid.

9 *Journal of Middle East Women's Studies* 6, No. 3, Special Issue: Marketing Muslim Women (Fall 2010), 19–57.

10 *Rūz al Yūsuf* is generally addressed to the local bourgeoisie including *effendis*, *khawajat*, and Arab *shuyukh* who strove to follow the latest news on their fans and watch their latest dancing performances, concerts, and movies. An *effendi* (plural *effendis* or *effendiyya*) is an educated and well-respected man in an Arab country. The *khawaja* or *khawaga* (plural *khawajāt* or *khawagāt*), in Egypt, is the local Egyptian who dresses in a Western attire in contrast to "*awlād al-balad*" or the locals whose attire is traditional. *Shuyukh* is the plural of *sheykh*, a male leader of an Arab family or village.

11 *Rūz al Yūsuf,* November 17, 1927, 17.

12 As expressed by Lila Abu-Lughod in *Remaking Women: Feminism and Modernity in the Middle East* (Princeton, New Jersey: Princeton University Press, 1998), 3. The representation of the woman as a nation is also theorized at length by Afsaneh Najmabadi in the context of Iran in *Women with Mustaches and Men without Beards: Gender and Sexual Anxieties of Iranian Modernity* (Berkeley: University of California Press, 2005) and by Beth Baron in the context of Egypt in *Egypt as a Woman: Nationalism, Gender, and Politics* (Berkeley: University of California Press, 2007).

13 Qāsim Amin's *The Liberation of Women* was originally published in 1899. Qāsim Amin, *The Liberation of Women and The New Woman: Two Documents in the History of Egyptian Feminism*, trans. S. Sidhom Peterson (Cairo: The American University in Cairo Press, 2000 [1899]).

14 Leila Ahmed, *Women and Gender in Islam: Historical Roots of a Modern Debate* (New Haven: Yale University Press).

15 This view was addressed by Afsaneh Najmabadi in her discussion of the development of the notion of a maleness seen as a nation and a femaleness as a homeland that is closely linked to the concept of honor and chastity. Afsaneh Najmabadi, *Women with Mustaches and Men Without Beards* (Berkeley: University of California, 2005), 1.

16 Rebecca C. Johnson, "Foreword," in *Leg over Leg*, vols. 1 and 2, Ahmed Fāris Al-Shidyāq (New York: New York University Press, 2015 [1855]), xxxxiv.

17 Ibid.

18 A public space in Islamo-Arab architecture is a space that is accessible to the public or visitors. For example, the reception area or the salon and the entrance of the domestic space are considered public spaces.

19 For more on the gendering of spaces during the colonial order in Lebanon and Egypt, see Elizabeth Thompson, *Colonial Citizens: Republican Rights, Paternal Privilege, and Gender in French Syria and Lebanon* (New York: Columbia University Press, 2000), 171–211, and Joseph Suad, "The Public/Private: The Imagined Boundary in the Imagined Nation/State/Community: The Lebanese Case," *Feminist Review*, no. 57 (Autumn 1997): 73–92. Beth Baron, *The Women's Awakening in Egypt: Culture, Society, and the Press* (New Haven, Conn: Yale University Press, 1994).

20 Joseph, "The Public/Private," 74.

21 Ibid.

22 Huda Lutfi "Manners and Customs of Fourteenth-Century Cairene Women: Female Anarchy versus Male Shar'i Order in Muslim Prescriptive Treatises," in *Women in Middle Eastern History: Shifting Boundaries in Sex and Gender*, eds. Nikki R. Keddie and Beth Baron (London and New Haven: Yale University Press, 1991), 99–121.

23 Articles that provided instructions on how to behave in public as a respectable woman in society were prominent in the Egyptian popular press of the 1920s.

24 Najmabadi, *Women with Mustaches*, 103.

25 Ibid., 94.

26 Ibid.

27 The tarbush (plural *tarabish*) better known in European sources as the fez, is a red cap shaped like a truncated cone commonly worn by the *effendiyya* in Egypt to symbolize the modernized Ottoman elite. For more on the notion of how the tarbush symbolizes the modernized Ottoman elite, refer to Wilson Chacko Jacob, *Working out Egypt: Effendi Masculinity and Subject Formation in Colonial Modernity, 1870–1940* (Durham: Duke University Press, 2011), and Lucie Ryzova's *The Age of the Efendiyya: Passage to Modernity in National-Colonial Egypt* (Oxford: Oxford Historical Monographs, Oxford University Press, 2014). For other women who sported a tarbush in the photograph refer to Yasmine Nachabe Taan, *Marie al-Khazen's Photographs: Gender, Photography, Mandate Lebanon* (Bloomsbury, London, 2020) and Mary Roberts, "Nazlı's Photographic Games: Said and Art History in a Contrapuntal Mode," *Patterns of Prejudice* 48, no. 5 (2014): 460–478.

28 I thank Reina Lewis for drawing my attention to this significant detail in the photographs.

29 Gender hierarchy collapses when it intersects with class in the way women as the managers of the household affairs managed their servants—men and women. This responsibility, in the context of Iran, was assigned to men according to premodern texts, it shifted to women as stated in the writing of the reformist literature of the nineteenth century. See Najmabadi, *Women With Mustaches,* 96.

30 Gender and feminist scholars have claimed an oppositional gaze to criticize and transform oppressive images of black women such as the representation of the servant in Edward Manet's *Olympia*. See Lorraine O'Grady "Olympia's Maid: Reclaiming Black Female Subjectivity" (1992), in *The Feminism and Visual Cultural Reader*, ed. Amelia Jones (London and New York: Routledge, 2003).

31 Interview with Anīsa Najjār on June 24, 2013, Beirut; interview with Emily Nasrallah on July 2, 2014, Beirut.

32 The figure of the "artiste," a French term that infiltrated Arabic language, was commonly used to indicate a frivolous entertaining figure who was badly regarded because part of her job was to entertain and seduce men, hindering her chastity and consequently her family honor.

33 Gergi Nicolas Bāz delivered his speech on June 3, 1910, during an Orthodox Christian charitable event in Tripoli, Lebanon. The speech was reproduced in a pamphlet entitled *The Agreement Between the Sexes*, 89–131, dated 1910, in which the orator laments the masculinization of women and the feminization of men in Beirut. Even though there are no direct references in the speech to cross-dressing, the speech does point to the emergence of some degree of gender fluidity which might have paved the way for other forms of expression in the 1920s such as cross-dressing.

34 Nicolas Bāz, *The Agreement Between the Sexes*, 89–131.

35 Ibid., 92. My translation.

36 Ibid., 131. My translation.

37 Ibid., 92. My translation.

38 Ibid.

39 Ibid.

40 This period lasted till the 1960s.

41 Viola Shafik, *Popular Egyptian Cinema: Gender, Class, and Nation* (Cairo: American University in Cairo Press, 2007), 282.

42 *Rūz al Yūsuf*, January 6, 1927, no. 62.

43 For more on the introduction of consumer culture and the way it was primarily addressed to women in Egypt, see Mona Russell, "Modernity, National Identity, and Consumerism: Visions of the Egyptian Home, 1805–1922," in *Transitions in Domestic Consumption and Family Life in the Modern Middle East*, ed. R. Shechter (Houses in Motion Conference Proceeding) (London: Palgrave Macmillan, 2003).

44 As quoted in Russell on page 47. This quote is an excerpt from Francis Mikha'il, *al-Tadbīr al-manzili al-hadīth*, Part 2 (Cairo: Matba'at al-Ma'ārif, 1910), 168.

45 For example, Badī'a Masābni (1892–1974) born to a Lebanese father and a Syrian mother, was a singer, a belly dancer, and an actress; she also owned a number of cabarets in Cairo in the 1920s. 'Azīza Amīr (1901–52) is the theater actress

who enacted *Napoleon's Daughter* onstage in the 1920s Cairene theaters. Fāṭima Rushdi (1908–96) was an Egyptian actress and producer who started her own theatrical troupe in 1926; she was known as the "Sarah Bernhardt of the Orient." Fatḥiyya Ahmad (1898–1975) began her career in musical theaters as a young girl in 1910, she later joined the well-known theater companies of Najīb al-Rīhāni and Amīn Sidqi, with the actress and belly dancer, Amīna Muhammad. *Rūz al Yūsuf*, December 15, 1926, 6.

46 Wesley D. Buskirk, "Egyptian Film and Feminism: Egypt's View of Women Through Cinema," *Cinesthesia* 4, no. 2. Available online: https://scholarworks.gvsu.edu/cgi/viewcontent.cgi?article=1079&context=cineon (accessed September 17, 2019).

For more on the rise of the entertainment industry in Cairo in the 1920s and 1930s, see Carmen M. K. Gitre, *Acting Egyptian: Theater, Identity, and Political Culture in Cairo, 1869–1930* (Austin: University of Texas Press, 2019), 94; Andrew Hammond, *Popular Culture in the Arab World: Arts, Politics, and the Media* (Cairo and New York: The American University in Cairo Press, 2009), 192; Viola Shafik, *Popular Egyptian cinema: Gender, Class, and Nation* (Cairo: The American University in Cairo Press, 2007); Oliver Leaman, ed., *Companion Encyclopedia of Middle Eastern and North African Film* (London: Routledge, 2001), 36; Virginia Danielson, *The Voice of Egypt: Umm kulthum, Arabic song, and Egyptian Society in the Twentieth Century* (Chicago: The University of Chicago Press, 1997), 48. Margot Badran, *Feminists, Islam, and Nation: Gender and the Making of Modern Egypt* (Princeton, New Jersey: Princeton University Press, 1994), 190.

47 *Rūz al Yūsuf*, December 15, 1926, 7. This claim is stated in the article, ibid.

48 Hanna Effendi Wehbi's was a prominent Egyptian actor during the 1920s–1930s in Cairo.

49 Here the term "*shuyukh*" that is commonly used as a form of address for men is used for women to allude to the masculine attire and behavior of the women in the photograph. '*Igal* is an accessory usually worn by Arab men. It is a black cord, worn doubled, used to keep the *ghutrah* or headwear in place on the wearer's head.

50 *Rūz al Yūsuf*, December 15, 1926, 7.

51 Ibid.

52 Ibid.

53 Ibid., 6

54 The *nargīleh* or hookah is an oriental water pipe with a long flexible tube connected to a container where the smoke is cooled by passing through water.

55 *Rūz al Yūsuf*, December 15, 1926, 6

56 *Al Mar'a al Jadīda* (The New Woman) is the title of a woman's journal launched by Julia Dimashqiyya (1882–1954).

57 Florence Fawaz—also known as Florence Austral—was a Lebanese-Syrian actress. In "The Work of Women," *Al Mar'a al Jadīda*, 1921.

58 Marilyn Booth, *May Her Likes Be Multiplied* (Berkeley: University of California Press, 2001), 233–69.

59 Ibid.

60 Mary Roberts in her fascinating analysis of the Ottoman-Egyptian Princess Nazlı Hanım's cross-dressing in the photograph (c. 1880s) describes Nazlı's cross-dressing as an Ottoman gentleman as confrontational. "[She] posed as though part of Nazlı's imaginary harem in a parodic restaging of the western harem stereotype … challenging notions of silence and passivity of Ottoman-Egyptian women that is implied in the more familiar image of harem women that was so popular in Europe" (474–75); see Mary Roberts, "Nazlı's Photographic Games: Said and Art History in a Contrapuntal Mode," *Patterns of Prejudice* 48, no. 5 (2014): 460–78.

61 Roland Barthes, "He Who Is Photographed," in *Camera Lucida: Reflections on Photography*, Roland Barthes, trans. Richard Howard (New York: Hill and Wang, 1981), 10.

62 Joan Rivière, "Womanliness as a Masquerade," in Russell Grigg, *Female Sexuality: The Early Psychoanalytic Controversies* (London: Karnac Books, 2018), 172. Originally published in *International Journal of Psycho-Analysis* 9 (1929): 303–13. Luce Irigaray, *This Sex Which is Not One*, trans. Catherine Porter (New York: Cornell University, 1996).

63 Rivière, "Womanliness as a Masquerade," 172.

64 Gitre, *Acting Egyptian*, 94.

65 In 1922, after returning from the International Woman Suffrage Alliance Congress in Rome, Sha'rawi and her upper-class Egyptian feminist peers staged a photo, which was widely circulated in the press. Their faces were uncovered but the hair remained covered.

66 Sania Sha'rawi Lanfranchi, *Casting off the Veil: The Life of Huda Shaarawi, Egypt's First Feminist* (London: I.B. Tauris, 2012).

67 For regional campaigns to circulate institutional photographs of women doing sport activities in contrast with the "indolent" harem women, refer to the article by William Allen, "The Abdul Hamid II Collection," *History of Photography* viii, no. 2 (April–June 1984): 119–45, in which the Sultan's efforts toward modernizing his Empire, through revealing photographs of active women, are surveyed.

68 In Figure 8.9, on the cover of *Rūz al Yūsuf*, no. 107, "*Al-Saiyydāt Wa La'ib Kwrat Al Qadam*" (The Ladies in a Soccer Game), November 17, 1927.

69 Wilson Chacko Jacob, *Working out Egypt: Effendi Masculinity and Subject Formation in Colonial Modernity, 1870– 1940* (Durham: Duke University Press, 2011), 171.

70 Ibid., 178.

71 I borrow this term from the title of Tarek el-Ariss's book, *Trials of Arab Modernity: Literary Affects and the New Political* (New York: Fordham University Press, 2013).

CHAPTER 9

THE PHOTOGRAPH, THE DRESS, AND THE CONJUGALIZATION OF THE FAMILY

Afsaneh Najmabadi

Historians have mapped out the sweep of "the conjugal couple" as the ideal of family over vast, initially urban, areas of the Ottoman Empire and Qajar Iran, starting in the last decades of the nineteenth century. This chapter focuses on three objects of life—the family photograph, the wedding outfit, and the studio wedding photograph—as significant objects through which, among other things, this conjugalization took shape. The idea of what constitutes, or ideally ought to constitute, the family, and linked with it the meaning of marriage, changed dramatically over a relatively short time. Initially affecting a smaller segment of the cultural elite of social and political reformers, these changes began to spread rapidly to a growing layer of the population, especially in large urban centers. New ideas about personal, family, and societal life spread across a region that is now divided into many nation-states, but that was, until the late-nineteenth and early-twentieth century, part of the Ottoman domain and Qajar Iran. As many scholars have shown, two critical changes were entwined: first, the ideal of family shifted from a generationally expansive and at times polygynous structure to become a *conjugally centered* family, and second, the ideal marriage became a *companionate* and preferably monogamous marriage chosen by the partners, rather than arranged by families, and based on deep affection (*muhibbat*), if not love (*'ishq*).[1]

Conjugality, Affection, and the Modern Family

The ideas of conjugal couple and affection-centered families were, from the start, intimately linked with notions of the nation, patriotic aspirations, what constituted the modern, and the changing structure of governance that was to shift from elite household-integrated patterns of personalized and family patronage toward centralized, civil bureaucracies operating on an ideal of impersonal management of government. But how do we understand the hold of these ideas not simply on the political and intellectual elite discourses, but on the imagination of the growing urban middle class, in particular among a growing layer of urban women? How did the ideas of the companionate—monogamous—marriage and the conjugal couple as family gain their near imperial hegemony, to borrow Elizabeth Povinelli's term?[2]

Povinelli works with the idea of the near imperial hegemony of love in the context of liberal settler colonies—and progressive queers in the United States—in comparison to a small community of men and women in

Large portions of this essay are extracted from a manuscript in progress, *Familial Undercurrents: Kin Who Count and Those in Their Shadow* .... I would like to thank Yasmine Nachabe Taan and Reina Lewis for their generative and generous feedback on an earlier version of this paper. The larger project is accumulating gratitude, over the past five years, to a huge number of people; however, I do want to mention a few persons—who have kept faith in my project even as I lost mine in its viability—Azadeh Tajpour, Roya Amigh, Naghmeh Sohrabi, Kanan Makiya, and Michael M. J. Fischer, to whom I owe not just many insights, but also the title of the manuscript.
Transliteration in this chapter is a simplified version of the system recommended by the *International Journal of Middle East Studies* with no diacritics.

the Northern Territory of Australia, over the course of the late nineteenth century into the twentieth.[3] She analyzes "how discourses of individual freedom and social constraint – what I refer to as *autological* and *genealogical* imaginaries – animate and enflesh love, sociality, and bodies; how they operate as strategic maneuvers of power whose purpose – or result – is to distribute life, goods, and values across social spaces; and how they contribute to the hardiness of liberalism as a normative horizon."[4] Povinelli further claims that "the intimate couple is a key transfer point between, on the one hand, liberal imaginaries of contractual economies, politics, and sociality and, on the other, liberal forms of power in the contemporary world. Love, as an intimate event, secures the self-evident goodness of social institutions, social distributions of life and death, and social responsibilities for these institutions and distributions."[5] She pursues the question of "the intimate event," as "related to the sovereign subject, and how it secures its legitimacy vis-à-vis the negative image of the genealogical society."[6] It is in this context that she asks,

> How, then, do these discourses deepen their grip on social life though they are internally unstable and referentially untrue? The maintenance of intimate sovereignty as a truth of liberal empire depends on a method of constituting three kinds of truth about the subjects and objects of empire: the truth of intimacy's proper domain, the truth of its normative ideals, and the truth of contrasting evils that surround it.[7]

My line of argument in this paper is inspired by Povinelli's arguments, with a difference: I am looking at the fractures and lines of differentiation *within* Iranian society that had begun to take shape since at least the mid-nineteenth century, between a modernist desire for an imagined future *autological* society and its demarcation from a present/past imaginary of the *genealogical* society that was constricting the choices to which the modernists aspired. In that context, "the intimate couple is a key transfer point."[8] In the context of early twentieth-century Iran, the power of the concept of love-based marriage—which women presumed would be monogamous—and of a conjugally centered household—the truth of its normative ideal—depended (and continues to depend) on the co-emergent self-evident evilness of arranged marriage and polygyny and the desire for a preferably not-generationally expansive household.[9] In Ottoman domains, polygyny was often configured in relation to slavery and concubinage;[10] in Iran part of the foil against which monogamy developed its ideational power was *mut'a* marriages—fixed-time marriages for sexual pleasure, often considered in modernist discourse to be a veneer for prostitution. The love-based companionate marriage was to be monogamous *and* for life.

As scholars writing about similar developments in Ottoman Turkey and Egypt have noted, polygyny was statistically insignificant—though the possibility of it hung over one's marriage. Additionally, there is no evidence-based study to demonstrate that arranged marriages were necessarily or largely experienced as forced—even when resented, it could possibly be experienced or at least expressed as fate (*qismat*)—nor that most households were indeed multi-generational over much of one's life cycle.[11] Following Povinelli, I suggest that the emerging and sustained notion of polygyny and arranged marriage as evidently evil has intimately depended on the life of the co-emergent idea of the self-evident goodness of the monogamous companionate marriage. The lives of these ideas have mutually regenerated and sustained each other. Who could be against love? Who could advocate arranged marriage—now experienced, at least by educated urban women, as forced familial imposition? Who could possibly desire to share her husband with another wife?

While inspired by Povinelli's propositions, I do want to note an important qualification. Her propositions work well on the *broad* level of societal changes and teleological observations, looking from where the historian or theorist writes today at actors in the past. What works for the level of the *individual's* desire for a companionate marriage, or the hope of something better, in their specific time, is examining what they saw around them, how they processed their own experiences and the experiences of others in their life. That is what historians need to do; to explain people's past experiences to today's readers, rather than presume that we can understand people in the past, their choices and practices, better than they did.

To offer an example I know well, my mother, Fari, born in 1911, was—along with her sisters—among the first generation of Iranian women going into higher education and working in various professions—in her case and those of her sisters, almost all went into teaching. She married my father when she was thirty years old—a rather late first marriage for her generation, perhaps even now. She successfully warded off several familially arranged marriage proposals. She was determined, she said again and again, to marry for love. Yet, Fari's decision to marry for love was not simply living an emerging dominating idea, obtained from reading novels and watching silent movies of the 1930s. She witnessed varying practices of marriage all around her. In later years, she recounted many of those marriages as failures—including two of her older sisters—others she remembered in more positive terms. In her narrative, every instance was directly linked to whether the marriage had been arranged by "the elders" or entered into by partners who had come to know each other and liked each other before getting married. Fari's eldest sister's marriage, for example, had been arranged by the two families. Her husband turned out to be more inclined to young male adolescents than to women. She spent many years in a terribly unhappy marriage before she finally obtained a divorce. Fari's third sister's marriage had been arranged through a friend recommending her sister to the groom's family. That too ended in divorce. Not only had she witnessed the terrible marriages of these two sisters, she also had the example of another older sister, 'Iffat, who, like her, resisted arranged marriage. Only at the age of thirty-six did 'Iffat finally meet someone at work who she liked and eventually married. Being working women, with their own income and a career, offered alternative visions of a desired life for 'Iffat and Fari, including a desired marriage.

Fari's resistance against familially-arranged marriage and the desire for a marriage of her choice based on knowing and socializing with her future husband, a desire for a marriage of mutual affection and love, was not unique to her. By the 1930s, modern education and professional careers in Iran had enabled a layer of urban middle-class women to think of marriage as something to do with their individual lives, as a choice by a woman and a man, rather than as a familial affair—an alliance based on negotiation between two families. This by no means implies that marriages in Iran, even today, are no longer "family affairs." The embeddedness of individuals in family life continues to inform marriage decisions and practices. The two families' being of a similar sociocultural status (*kufu*) weighs on all marriage choices. In practice, even couples who meet at work or educational establishments and who socialize for sustained periods of time before making a marriage decision go through the same practices: sending the man's family to the woman's family to ask for her hand, etc.

What this chapter—and my larger manuscript—is concerned with is how the dominance of this idea—the conjugalization of the family—to use Kenneth Cuno's apt expression—shaped the actual living practices of everyday familial life. Here, I focus on one aspect of this process: what were some of the everyday objects that affected this transformation? In particular, I take up the emergent popularity and ubiquity of family photographs, the changes in wedding outfits, and the taking of a studio wedding photograph.

As Alan Duben and Cem Behar have argued, the entry of European objects of daily use—such as cutlery, furnishings, etc.—into Ottoman homes, bringing with them new manners of doing things, distanced people from the ways their parents did things, setting in motion "a complex symbolic act laden with various layers of meaning."[12] Often, social histories discuss at length seemingly more important grand changes, under the rubric of modernity, modernization, and the modern individuated self, but tend to ignore the very ordinary processes through which changes in concepts and practices of daily life take shape. Thomas Levin quotes Siegfried Kracauer on "quotidian micrologies," beyond the latter's micro-catastrophes, that could be useful to think with: "One must rid oneself of the delusion that it is the major events which have the most decisive influence on people. They are much more deeply and continuously influenced by the tiny catastrophes which make up daily life."[13]

The tiny changes in daily life, and their almost ordinariness, also contribute to the unfinished character of "achieving modernity"—it is never smooth, nor evenly and homogeneously spread. Modernity is never achieved. As Bruno Latour famously put it: we have never been modern.[14]

Because of the ordinary ways in which, for instance, people begin to use individual eating utensils on individual plates—in place of using one's fingers and eating from a common platter—and because even people who have for several generations eaten with knives and forks still continue at times to eat from a common platter and with their fingers, the very ordinariness of the shaping of modern individual through these life habits continues to regenerate totally un-modern or, better yet in Svetlana Boym's expression, "off-modern" practices as well.[15] Here, I focus on the work of material objects in the reconfiguration of family toward a dominant conjugally centered ideal in Iran.

Family Photographs

The changes in familial concepts and practices of everyday life coincided with the arrival of photography in the Middle East. Photography came to some of the urban centers of the Ottoman domains and to Qajar Iran shortly after its invention in 1841.[16] Both the camera and the family photograph were among those objects of everyday life that generatively contributed to the changes in concepts and practices that they were to record and archive. Photographs, and in particular family photographs, are "evocative objects," to use Sherry Turkle's idea, "underscoring the inseparability of thought and feeling in our relationship to things. We think with the objects we love; we love the objects we think with."[17] At times, they render, as Arunima has put it, "certain modern familial moments—for example, birthdays or weddings—into events."[18]

Historians and cultural analysts have done vastly different things with family photographs and albums. One example is Annette Kuhn, *Family Secrets: Acts of Memory and Imagination*. Working with photographs from her own childhood—some alone, one with her mother, as early as four months of age—two copies, hers, and another with her mother's notes on verso—one at the time of Queen Elizabeth II's coronation—and other photographs and film stills, Kuhn narrates stories of her relations to her mother and father, and her mother's relations with her father, and others.[19] Her stories and her readings of the photographs are deeply informed by psychoanalytic approaches to memory and ways of seeing.

I take a different approach, more inspired by material object historians, such as Laura Ulrich and Janet Hoskins.[20] I take up the materiality of the photograph and its circulation, and include photographs and family albums among those "domestic objects – ordinary household possessions that might be given an extraordinary significance by becoming entangled in the events of a person's life and used as a vehicle for a sense of selfhood," as Hoskins points out, perhaps a more appropriate approach toward biographical objects "in a society that has not been 'psychologized' in a confessional tradition."[21]

Family photographs and albums come to life through oral tales about them or other stories they evoke, which bring layers of meaning out of the flat surface of the photograph.[22] In a way, similar to Sharon Marcus's "just reading," I wonder if we have enacted an injustice to reading of family photographs by at times single-mindedly trying to excavate through them layers of psychoanalytical insight for family relations between mother and daughter, father and daughter, oedipal and pre-oedipal, etc.[23] What if, instead of engaging in reading practices that attempt to "pierce through the photograph's flat surface," we read superficially, staying on the surface, and instead of employing psychoanalytically informed reading practices, we tuned into oral stories about the photograph and listened to multiple stories?[24]

This reading of photographs becomes possible with increasing access to multi-genre archives. My work, for example, has been enabled by the *Women's Worlds in Qajar Iran Digital Archive and Website*. Since 2009, along with a large group of scholars, editors, photographers, and project managers, I have worked on this archive. We visit families to photograph and digitize their relevant documents, photographs, and objects of daily life. Within that context, we have heard numerous stories of lives. A photograph brings out a memory, an object becomes the occasion for recalling a relative's wedding—yet another family story. Seeing photographs together with hearing family stories thus informs my understanding of what family photographs and albums have done for our concepts and practices of understanding the family.

Like the change in wedding outfits, as I will discuss further below, taking a photograph of the bride and groom in novel outfits became a practice that distinguished people from their parents' generation. Bride and groom studio photographs were not necessarily taken on the wedding day. This was its own ceremonial occasion that became part and parcel of performing conjugality of the new family. Malek Alloula, in a chapter titled "Couple," discusses the couple as a misreading of the European camera, "an aberration, a historical error, an unthinkable possibility in Algerian society."[25] But by the early decades of the twentieth century, the couple photograph had become a "nativized" performance of marriages in many Middle Eastern countries, including Egypt, Iran, and Turkey—itself an indication of the conjugalization of the ideal family. Numerous "husband and wife" photographs on *Women's Worlds in Qajar Iran* attest to the performance of conjugality as family.[26] Figures 9.1 and 9.2 are two photographs of a husband and wife as an invitation for readers to browse the collection.

Figure 9.1 Rahil and David Aminuf, matriarch and patriarch of the Aminuf family, photographer unknown, 1870. Center for Iranian Jewish Oral History (977-P-2000), no. 1025A125. Available online: qajarwomen.org. Source: http://www.qajarwomen.org/en/items/1025A125.html.

Figure 9.2 Heripsima and her husband, photographer unknown, *c.* 1915. Shahin and Arsineh Basil, no. 1144A91. Available online: qajarwomen.org. Source: http://www.qajarwomen.org/en/items/1144A91.html.

Some photographs, at times printed as postcards, were sent to other kin and friends, thus further contributing to the crafting of the conjugal couple as family through circulation within a larger social network.

But the studio wedding photograph was not the only scene of photographic familiality. Taking occasional family photographs, often at particular celebratory moments when the whole family got together, produced other performances of the familial. These presentations were not necessarily conjugally centered; generally, they marked the sense of the familial formed around the most senior members of the group. The latter could be the most senior conjugal couple, or other familial elders, especially in households that continued to live as generationally combined. This occurred in some cities well into the middle decades of the twentieth century, before increasing urban populations and changing residential patterns dramatically strengthened the spatial

Figure 9.3 Muhammad 'Ali Nik Bin and his wife, photographer unknown, February 4, 1929. Khan Nakhjavani Collection, no. 14146A21. Available online: qajarwomen.org. Source: http://www.qajarwomen.org/en/items/14146A21. html.

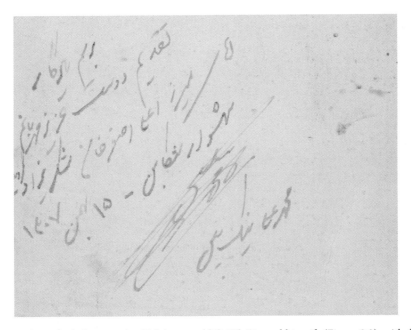

Figure 9.4 Verso of postcard photograph of Muhammad 'Ali Nik Bin and his wife (Figure 9.3), with dedication of the photo by the husband to his dear friend Mirza 'Ali Asghar Khan Shukrizad, February 4, 1929. Khan Nakhjavani Collection, no. 14146A21. Available online: qajarwomen.org. Source: http://www.qajarwomen.org/en/items/14146A21.html.

conjugalization of the family. Although, as several urban ethnographers have shown, even with increased urbanization, dispersion of large upper- and middle-class families, and the reduction in the size of residential spaces, at times smaller familial units would move into the same apartment block, each occupying one floor, thus preserving in vertical architectural layout its multi-generational, previously horizontally connected, character.

Family photographs and albums worked as important cultural objects, and photography functioned as one of the technologies that generated who counted as kin. Different inclusions and exclusions continue to this day, indicating that practices, despite the ideational power of the concept of the conjugal couple as family, are varied in important ways. Indeed, photography has also been used to generate a sense of the familial that at times worked against its conjugalization. Several photographs of one family, the Mallahs/Vaziris, indicate a purposeful, insistent inclusion of children from different wives. For example, at times, collages of photographs were made to clearly and decidedly make visible which persons should be included as family. In the collage represented in Figure 9.5, conjugal centeredness is fully on display, as the writing in the center of the collage also insists: "The Mallah Family." At the same time, children and grandchildren from other marriages have been folded into "the family."

The collage (Figure 9.5) possibly dates to the 1960s, though the individual photos are from various dates. The writing at the center of the collage reads: "The Mallah Family." The conjugal couple—Khadijeh Afzal Vaziri (1890–1980) and her husband, Aqa Buzurg Mallah (1884–1964)—constitute the nodal point of the collage that captures the eye on first glance. Khadijeh Khanum was Aqa Buzurg's second wife. Also included in the collage, moving from the top left corner counterclockwise, are:

Figure 9.5 Collage representing the family of Khadijah Afzal Vaziri and Aqa Buzurg Mallah, undated. Mahlaqa Mallah Collection, no. 14129A17. Available online: qajarwomen.org. Source: http://www.qajarwomen.org/en/items/14129A17.html.

Zubayadeh Mallah (daughter of Aqa Buzurg Mallah from his first wife), Mahlaqa Mallah (1917–), Amir Hushang Mallah (1919–), Husayn'ali Mallah (1921–92), Nusrat Allah Changizi (the son of Zubayadeh, thus Aqa Buzurg's grandson), Behrouz Bayat (son of Mahlaqa Mallah and her first husband Muhammad Zaman Bayat), Guli Mallah (daughter of Nusrat Zaman, Aqa Buzurg's third wife—co-wife with Khadijeh Khanum), Khusraw Mallah (1927–), and Mihrangiz Mallah (1923–2013).

Significantly, Khanum Afzal is shown at a table, in the gesture of writing. Like her mother, Bibi Khanum Astarabadi, and her sister Maulud A`lam al-Saltaneh, Khanum Afzal was among the early pioneers of women's education and wrote about women's rights in the press.[27] Her children, in particular her two daughters, Mahlaqa and Mihrangiz, were proud of their mother's achievements. In this central photograph, she is wearing the outer garment that she had designed to show that women could go to work in decent clothes without needing to wear a traditional chador and face cover (Figure 9.6).

Furthermore, the table behind which she is positioned is the same table she used to tutor her two daughters (Figure 9.7).

Figure 9.6 Khanum Afzal in outer garment and headcover for going to work, photographer unknown, 1930 or 1931. Mahlaqa Mallah Collection, no. 14129A57. Available online: qajarwomen.org. Source: http://www.qajarwomen.org/en/items/14129A57.html.

The collage (Figure 9.5) thus not only insistently constructs an expansive sense of the conjugally centered Mallah family, it also insistently emphasizes the modernness of the family and the pride of the daughters in their mother as a modern woman, a writer, and an educator.

Photographs, like texts, do not have a singular intrinsic meaning. Reading this collage as the Mallahs' purposeful inclusion of siblings from multiple wives as family is informed by seeing many other family photographs they have cherished and hearing the stories they have told about persons and photographs. The repeated visualization of the generationally expansive and genealogically inclusive Mallah family, along with conjugal photographs or conjugally centered photographs, demonstrate the many complex ways that families

Figure 9.7 Khanum Afzal, tutoring her children, *c.* 1929. Available online: qajarwomen.org. Source: http://www.qajarwomen.org/fa/items/14129A50.html.

in real life created their familyness. In a family photograph that shows a large group of twenty-one members of the Mallahs and Vaziris (Figure 9.8), the center is again occupied by Khadijeh Khanum and Aqa Buzurg. Included are not only the many children and their spouses, grandchildren of the central couple, nieces and nephews, half-siblings, and other relatives—immediate and mediated kin—but also a nanny of one of the children.[28]

As Mahlaqa Mallah once put it, in a nutshell, "we lived tribally [*'ilyati*]; people became integrated into the Mallah family from all kinds of directions."[29]

Despite the near dominance of the idea of love-based—monogamous—marriage and the conjugally centered family in the twentieth century, people have continued to live vastly complex familial lives. Conjugalization seems to have remained an unfinished and unfinishable project. It demanded a rearranging

Figure 9.8 The Mallah/Vaziri Family, photographer unknown, undated (*c.* 1960). Mahlaqa Mallah Collection, no. 14129A36. Available online: qajarwomen.org. Source: http://www.qajarwomen.org/en/items/14129A36.html.

of one's attachments and loyalties within the familial network, putting the loyalty between the conjugal couple above those between parents and child, among siblings, with aunts and cousins, and even with friends. This was neither a smooth nor an achieved process once and for all. Wives continued to travel a great deal with sisters and female friends, rather than with their husbands; they continued to keep close intimate ties to sisters and female friends—at times to the exclusion of their husbands from these intimacies. Mushfiq Kazimi, for instance, expressed dismay that his wife would make decisions over her paternal inheritance in consultation with her mother without seeking his advice, and transferred her share to her mother.[30] The sentiment of belonging to one's maternal family and to the world of one's female friends, more than to one's husband, comes through numerous recently published women's autobiographical writings.

The Wedding Outfit and Studio Photograph

As I have suggested, seemingly ordinary objects of life have acted as generational markers, signaling the changing meaning of family. They have thus contributed to the conjugal centeredness of family.

Along with family photographs, the white bridal wedding gown and the dark formal suit of the groom, replacing colorful and often fancily embroidered clothes brides (Figures 9.10 and 9.11) and grooms (Figure 9.9) used to wear at wedding celebrations, constituted such material objects.[31]

As Sohelia Shahshahani has noted, "Silk and velvet were very pricey, and were considered suitable … for brides. The bride's skirt was densely pleated, using 10–15 meters of fabric … Brides wore pantaloons under the short skirt."[32]

The shift to the white wedding gown of the bride and the tuxedo of the groom made the bride and groom a different couple from their parents. The conjugal couple was now sartorially distinct from the rest of their families within the scene of marital celebration. Previously, brides and grooms wore fancier clothes, but generally not clothes uniquely marked as wedding clothes, nor as necessarily and uniquely distinct from those of their guests.[33]

In Iran, in some aristocratic families, the white European-style wedding dress had made its entry by the second decade of the twentieth century. 'Ayn al-Saltaneh, in his memoir entry of October 5, 1917, notes the novelty of two wedding dresses that had been tailored like those in Europe, "white, with a long train on the back that has to be carried by the bride's maids."[34]

The change was uneven and partial—often class specific. In Mihrmah Farmanfarmayiyan's household, the wedding gown of Ma'sumeh—the daughter of Kal Hadi, the old gardener of their Shimiran garden—was pink silk with a white veil to cover her face. This was around 1925. A decade and a class apart, Mihrmah's own 1935 wedding gown was a full white gown with a long flowing train.[35] Even into the 1940s, at times some aspects of wedding clothes changed, but not others. For instance, some brides would simply add a white lace veil to a colorful dress instead of donning the full white wedding gown.[36]

The change slowly began to inform urban culture more broadly. Yet it is not clear whether for early generations, the wedding outfits were necessarily affectively significant. For my mother, Fari, and her older sister, 'Iffat, the wedding dress as such was not uniquely and individually emotionally invested. From a relatively lower- middle-class economic bracket, it made no sense to get a new dress for Fari. For her wedding, she wore the same dress 'Iffat had worn over a year earlier. The significant event was to be dressed in a white wedding gown and take a studio photograph in it. Fari and 'Iffat had identical studio wedding photographs (Figures 9.12 and Figure 9.13).

From the early 1930s, for many middle-class urban couples, going to a professional studio in wedding clothes, and staging "conjugal coupledom" in front of the photographic lens, became part of the ceremony, as

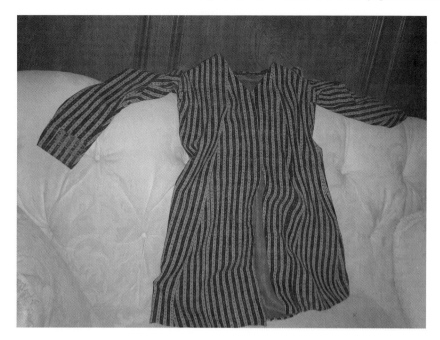

Figure 9.9 Groom's wedding outfit, which belonged to Bahram Sheikholeslami's grandfather, early to mid-nineteenth century. Private collection of Bahram Sheikholeslami, no. 1139A184. Available online: qajarwomen.org. Source: http://www.qajarwomen.org/en/items/1139A184.html.

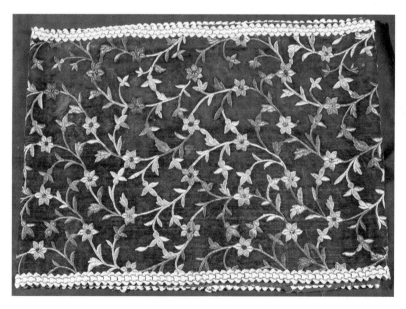

Figure 9.10 Folded embroidered velvet segment of a skirt for Shams al-Muluk Jahanbani's wedding (600 x 43 cm), 1902. Bahman Bayani Collection, no. 42a040. Available online: qajarwomen.org. Source: http://www.qajarwomen.org/en/items/42a040.html.

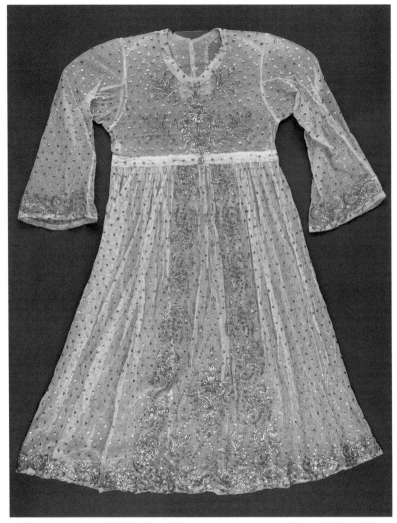

Figure 9.11 Tulle wedding dress embroidered with gold metal thread (naqdah embroidery), (early) twentieth century. Olga Davidson Collection, no. 1024A33. Available online: qajarwomen.org. Source: http://www.qajarwomen.org/en/items/1024A33.html.

Fari's remembrance of her wedding day indicates. In her memoir, Fari describes her wedding in great detail, with much evident pleasure, as a very happy event. She notes that after the marriage contract part of the event (*'aqd*) had been performed in the house of the bride—where she lived with her mother Khanum Jun, 'Iffat, and 'Iffat's husband 'Isa—they went to a studio for a formal wedding picture before going to the evening celebrations held in the house of one of her paternal brothers, Suhrab.

The non-studio wedding festivities photographs were often familial groups; at times the bride and the groom would be photographed with the most important patriarch, as in the photograph of Bihjat al-Muluk Mu`izzi and 'Abd Allah Ashraf with the bride's uncle (Figure 9.14).

As Cuno has argued, "Regardless of whether they lived in a joint or conjugal family household, couples who posed for intimate photos … presented themselves as bourgeois conjugal families."[37] These photographs,

Figure 9.12 Fari and 'Abbas, January 14, 1942. Author's family album.

Figure 9.13 'Iffat and 'Isa, August 1, 1940. Author's family album.

Figure 9.14 A photograph from the wedding day of Bihjat al-Muluk Mu'izzi and 'Abd Allah Ashrafi; *from left to right*: Bihjat al-Muluk, 'Abd al-Baqir Mirza Mu'izzi (paternal uncle of Bihjat), and 'Abd Allah Ashrafi—note the bride's older style dress and the appearance of the groom in his military outfit to mark his social standing—unknown photographer, November 18, 1921. Ashrafi family collection, no. 1138A17. Available online: qajarwomen.org. Source: http://www. qajarwomen.org/en/items/1138A17.html.

framing the couple in their distinct clothes, not only reflected the process of the idealization of the conjugal couple; they in turn incessantly contributed to its power. Photographs were framed and displayed in the home in prominent places: on walls, on cupboards and bookshelves, or over pianos in more prosperous homes.[38] Their ubiquitous visual presence—one saw them every day in most urban middle-class homes—contributed to the crafting of its normative idealness. The studio wedding photograph, along with the visual distinction of the bride and the groom displayed by their outfits, trained the eyes in seeing the conjugal couple as the self-evident meaning of family.

Photographs and wedding outfits are not the only material objects of life that contributed to the conjugal centeredness of the family. Among other such objects, one may note the wedding ring. In the nineteenth century the *mahr* (dowry), as specified in the marriage contract often included jewelry, such as rings. These types of rings were what only a woman would have received. The rings, moreover, were always with precious stones—at times specified, such as turquoise, emerald, etc. The all-gold, usually plain, wedding ring, exchanged between the bride and groom at the time of marriage, came possibly in the 1920s or 1930s, and played a similar role in the consolidation of the conjugal nature of the couple.[39]

This essay has attempted to demonstrate how objects of daily life have been key to the production of conjugal centeredness of the family and its evident naturalness, by their ubiquitous presence in daily life. At the same time, I would also like to emphasize that conjugalization of family has not been an achieved, completed, outcome. In real life, people continue to live more complex family lives that simultaneously reproduce and undercut conjugal centeredness.

Notes

1 The literature on the topic is rich and large; including Kenneth Cuno, *Modernizing Marriage: Family, Ideology, and Law in Nineteenth- and Early Twentieth-Century Egypt* (Syracuse: Syracuse University Press, 2015); Beth Baron, "The Making and Breaking of Marital Bonds in Modern Egypt," in *Women in Middle Eastern History: Shifting Boundaries in Sex and Gender*, eds. Nikki R. Keddie and Beth Baron (New Haven: Yale UP, 1991), 275–91; Beth Baron, *Egypt as a Woman: Nationalism, Gender, and Politics* (Berkeley: University of California Press, 2005), especially chapter 1; Judith E. Tucker, *Women in Nineteenth-Century Egypt* (Cambridge: Cambridge University Press, 1985); Beshara B. Doumani, *Family Life in the Ottoman Mediterranean: A Social History* (Cambridge: Cambridge University Press, 2017); Alan Duben and Cem Behar, *Istanbul Households: Marriage, Family and Fertility, 1880–1940* (Cambridge: Cambridge University Press, 1991); Amy Motlagh, *Burying the Beloved: Marriage, Realism, and Reform in Modern Iran* (Stanford: Stanford University Press, 2012); Hanan Kholoussy, *For Better, For Worse: The Marriage Crisis that Made Modern Egypt* (Stanford: Stanford University Press, 2010); Guity Nashat, "Marriage in the Qajar Period," in *Women in Iran: From 1800 to the Islamic Republic*, eds. Lois Beck and Guity Nashat (Urbana: University of Illinois Press, 2004), 37–62.

2 Elizabeth Povinelli, *The Empire of Love: Toward a Theory of Intimacy, Genealogy, and Carnality* (Durham: Duke University Press, 2006).

3 Ibid., 2–3.

4 Ibid., 3–4.

5 Ibid., 17.

6 Ibid., 183.

7 Ibid., 198.

8 Ibid., 17.

9 I use "generationally expansive household" instead of "extended family." As Naomi Tadmor noted some two decades ago, the concept of "extended family" is misinforming of the familial concepts that would make sense to those whose familial practices we so name. It presumes a nucleated family as a core concept, in relation to which some have extensions beyond the core. Naomi Tadmor, "The Concept of the Household-Family in Eighteenth-Century England," *Past and Present* 151 (May 1996): 111–40. For eighteenth-century England, she suggests the use of household-family, and argues that the notion of extended family "rests on the concept of the nuclear family, and particularly the conjugal unit. Thus, for example, households that include relatives beyond the nuclear core are defined as 'extended', … in the eighteenth century, families could exist quite apart from notions of conjugality. … The concept of the household-family … enables us to question the usefulness of the term 'extended family'" (133).

10 Baron, *Egypt as a Woman*, 22.

11 Cuno, *Modernizing Marriage*; Duben and Behar, *Istanbul Households*.

12 Duben and Behar, *Istanbul Households*, 206.

13 Siegfried Kracauer, trans. Thomas Y. Levin, "Photography," *Critical Inquiry* 19 (Spring 1993): 422.

14 Bruno Latour, *We Have Never Been Modern* (Cambridge: Harvard University Press, 1993).

15 Svetlana Boym, *The Future of Nostalgia* (New York: Basic Books, 2001).

16 Beth Baron, *Egypt as a Woman*; Stephen Sheehi, *The Arab Imago: a Social History of Portrait Photography 1860–1910* (Princeton: Princeton University Press, 2016); David J. Roxburgh and Mary McWilliams, eds., *Technologies of the Image: Art in 19th-Century Iran* (Cambridge: Harvard Art Museums, 2017); Zeynep Çelik and Edhem Eldem, eds., *Camera Ottomana: Photography and Modernity in the Ottoman Empire 1840–1914* (Istanbul: Koç University Publications, 2015); Carmen Pérez González, *Local Portraiture: Through the Lens of the 19th-Century Iranian Photographers* (Leiden: Leiden University Press, 2012). For a brilliant analysis of the significance of photography's generative effects in changes of gender and sexual concepts in Iran, see Staci Gem Scheiwiller, *Liminalities of Gender and Sexuality in Nineteenth-Century Iranian Photography: Desirous Bodies* (New York: Routledge, 2017).

17 Sherry Turkle, ed., *Evocative Objects: Things We Think With* (Cambridge: The MIT Press, 2007), 5.

18 G. Arunima, "Bonds of Love, ties of kinship? Or are there other ways of imagining the family?" *The Indian Economic and Social History Review* 53, no. 3 (2016): 14.

19 Annette Kuhn, *Family Secrets: Acts of Memory and Imagination* (London: Verso, 2002 [1995]).

20 Janet Hoskins, *Biographical Objects: How Things Tell the Stories of People's Lives* (New York: Routledge, 1998). For Laura Ulrich's latest book, see *A House Full of Females: Plural Marriage and Women's Rights in Early Mormonism, 1835–1870* (New York: Alfred A. Knopf, 2017).

21   Hoskins, *Biographical Objects*, 2.

22   See Kracauer, "Photography," 421–36; Meir Wigoder, "History Begins at Home: Photography and Memory in the Writings of Seigfried Kracauer and Roland Barthes," *History and Memory* 13, no. 1 (2001): 19–59.

23   Sharon Marcus, *Between Women: Friendship, Desire, and Marriage in Victorian England* (Princeton: Princeton University Press, 2007).

24   Marianne Hirsch, ed., *The Familial Gaze* (Hanover: Dartmouth College (University Press of New England), 1999), xvi.

25   Malek Alloula, *The Colonial Harem*, trans. Myrna Godzich and Wlad Godzich (Minneapolis: University of Minnesota Press, 1986), 38.

26   See http://search.qajarwomen.com/search?lang=en&filter=genres_en:photographs|subjects_en:husband%2Band%2Bwife
     See, in particular:
     http://www.qajarwomen.org/en/items/1025A129.html 1934 (accessed on December 20, 2020).
     Siyun Rifua and his wife Naomi Muhbir
     http://www.qajarwomen.org/en/items/1394A6.html early twentieth Century (accessed on December 20, 2020).
     Aqdas Gharbi and her husband, Ahmad Rustami
     http://www.qajarwomen.org/en/items/16175A30.html late 1920s (accessed on December 20, 2020).
     Nimtaj and her husband Kushish Safavi
     http://www.qajarwomen.org/en/items/13119A13.html 1935 (accessed on December 20, 2020).
     Arghavan and Rustam Aidun.

27   Narjis Mihrangiz Mallah, *Az zanan-i pishgam-i Irani: Afzal Vaziri, dukhtar-i Bibi Khanum Astarabadi* (Tehran: Shirazeh, 2006).

28   The people in this photograph, according to the numbers marked on the second image of the link, are: 1. Gawhar Khanum (Shirin Mallah's nanny), 2. Rawshan Vaziri (daughter of Shah Zanan 'Alavi and 'Ali Asghar Vaziri), 3. Maryam Vaziri (daughter of Musa Khan Vaziri), 4. Shirin Mallah (daughter of Mahindukht Vaziri and Khusraw Mallah), 5. Khusraw Mallah (son of Khadijah Afzal Vaziri and Aqa Buzurg Mallah), 6. Firishtah Vaziri (daughter of Gawhar al-Saltanah and Fath'ali Vaziri), 7. Asad Allah Tarvirdi (husband of Mihrangiz Mallah), 8. Mihrangiz Mallah (daughter of Khadijah Afzal Vaziri and Aqa Buzurg Mallah), 9. Mahindukht Vaziri (daughter of Ruqiyah Khanum and Hasan'ali Vaziri), 10. Parvanah Vaziri (daughter of Shah Zanan 'Alavi and 'Ali Asghar Vaziri), 11. Aqa Buzurg Mallah, 12. Khadijah Afzal Vaziri, 13. 'Azra Hijazi, 14. Shah Zanan 'Alavi (wife of 'Ali Asghar Vaziri), 15. Unidentified, 16. 'Aliyah Khanum (wife of 'Abd Allah Khan), 17. 'Abd Allah Khan Vaziri (brother of Musa Khan Vaziri), 18. 'Alinaqi Vaziri (Colonel), 19. Shidah Vaziri (daughter of Shah Zanan 'Alavi and 'Ali Asghar Vaziri), 20. Giti Banan (daughter of Maryam Vaziri and Ghulam Husayn Banan), 21. Behrouz Bayat (son of Mahlaqa Mallah and Muhammad Zaman Bayat).
     For another similar twenty-six-person family photograph, see http://www.qajarwomen.org/en/items/14129A53.html—*c.* 1930 (accessed on December 20, 2020).

29   Taped interviews on the Women's Worlds in Qajar Iran Digital Archive: http://www.qajarwomen.org/en/items/14129A1.html, and http://www.qajarwomen.org/en/items/14129A60.html. For other Mallah family photographs, visit http://www.qajarwomen.org/en/collections/14129.html.

30   Mushfiq Kazimi, *Ruzgar va andishah-ha* (Tehran: Ibn Sina, 1971), 1:243. While the first volume was published in 1971, the writing was completed in 1959.

31   For examples of bridal wear, see the following:
     http://www.qajarwomen.org/en/items/1025A209.html (accessed on December 20, 2020).
     http://www.qajarwomen.org/en/items/1025A195.html (accessed on December 20, 2020).
     http://www.qajarwomen.org/en/items/1025A143.html (accessed on December 20, 2020).
     http://www.qajarwomen.org/en/items/1025A172.html (accessed on December 20, 2020).
     http://www.qajarwomen.org/en/items/1391A44.html (accessed on December 20, 2020).
     http://www.qajarwomen.org/en/items/1024A33.html (accessed on December 20, 2020).
     http://www.qajarwomen.org/en/items/42a040.html (accessed on December 20, 2020).

32   Sohelia Shahshahani, *Persian Clothing During the Qajar Reign* (Tehran: Farhangsara-yi Mirdashti, 2008), 148. I do not have much information about wedding outfits in other cases.

33 A tour of wedding photographs on *Women's Worlds in Qajar Iran Digital Archive* visually maps these differences: http://search.qajarwomen.com/search?lang=en&query=wedding&filter=genres_en:photographs (accessed on December 20, 2020).

34 'Ayn al-Saltanah, *Ruznamah-i khatirat-i 'Ayn al-Saltanah*, vol. 6 of 10 (Tehran: Asatir, 1995–99), 4896.

35 Mihrmah Farmanfarmayiyan, *Zir-i nigah-i pidar: khatirat-i Mirmah Farmanfarmayiyan az andaruni* (Tehran: Kavir, 2004), 280 and 330.

36 For an example, see http://www.qajarwomen.org/en/items/1274A23.html—1944 (accessed on December 20, 2020).

37 Cuno, *Modernizing Marriage*, 55.

38 In connection with the significance of domestic objects in general and photographs in particular for shaping the meaning of domesticity and home, see Toufoul Abou-Hodeib, *A Taste for Home: The Modern Middle Class in Ottoman Beirut* (Stanford: Stanford University Press, 2017), especially chapter 4.

39 At this point, however, I have not been able to collect the necessary archival material to trace its entry into modern marriages.

BIBLIOGRAPHY

Abou-Hodeib, Toufoul. *A Taste for Home: The Modern Middle Class in Ottoman Beirut*. Stanford: Stanford University Press, 2017.

AbuKhalil, As'ad, "Gender Boundaries and Sexual Categories in the Arab World." *Feminist Issues* 15, nos. 1–2 (1997): 91–104.

Abu-Lughod, Janet L. "The Islamic City – Historic Myth, Islamic Essence, and Contemporary Relevance." *International Journal of Middle East Studies* 19 (1987): 155–76.

Abu-Lughod, Lila, ed. *Remaking Women: Feminism and Modernity in the Middle East*. Princeton: Princeton University Press, 1998.

Ağca, Sevgi. "Organizational Structure of Topkapı Harem." In *Topkapı Palace: The Imperial Harem: House of the Sultan*, edited by Gül İrepoğlu, 12–17. Istanbul: Topkapı Palace Museum, 2012.

Ahmed, Leila. *Women and Gender in Islam: Historical Roots of a Modern Debate*. New Haven: Yale University Press, 1992.

Akçam, Taner. *The Young Turks' Crime Against Humanity: The Armenian Genocide and Ethnic Cleansing in the Ottoman Empire*. Princeton: Princeton University Press, 2012.

Allen, William. "Sixty-five Istanbul Photographers, 1887–1914." In *Shadow and Substance: Essays in the History of Photography*, edited by Kathleen Collins, 127–36. Bloomfield Hills: The Amorphous Institute Press, 1990.

Allen, William. "The Abdul Hamid II Collection." *History of Photography* 8, no. 2 (April–June 1984): 119–45.

Alloula, Malek. *The Colonial Harem*, translated by Myrna Godzich and Wlad Godzich. Minneapolis: University of Minnesota Press, 1986.

Almila, Anna-Mari and David Inglis. "On the Hijab-Gift: Theoretical Considerations on the Ambiguities of Islamic Veiling in a Diasporic Context." *Journal of Cultural Analysis of Social Change* 3, no. 1 (2018).

Al-Shidyāq, Ahmad Fāris. *Leg over Leg: Volumes One and Two*, translated by Humphrey Davies. New York: New York University Press, 2015.

Al-Tahtawi, Rifa'a. *Al-Murshid al-Amin lil babat wa al-banin* (The Trusted Guide for Girls and Boys). Cairo: The Supreme Council for Culture, 2002.

Amin, Ahmad. *Al-Akhlaq*. Cairo: Lajnat al-Ta'lif wa al-Tarjama wa al-Nashr, 1920.

Amin, Qāsim. *The Liberation of Women and The New Woman: Two Documents in the History of Egyptian Feminism*. 1899. This edition translated by Samiha Sidhom Peterson. Cairo: The American University in Cairo Press. Reprinted, 2000.

Anderson, Benedict. *Imagined Communities. Reflections on the Origin and Spread of Nationalism*. Rev. edn. London and New York: Verso, 2006.

Appadurai, Arjun, ed. *The Social Life of Things: Commodities in Cultural Perspective*. Cambridge: Cambridge University Press, 1988.

Aracı, Emre. *Osmanlı Sarayı'ndan Avrupa Müziği/European Music at the Ottoman Court*, London Academy of Ottoman Court Music. Istanbul: Kalan, 2000.

Aracı, Emre. "Giuseppe Donizetti Pasha and the Polyphonic Court Music of the Ottoman Empire." *Court Historian* 7, no. 2 (2002): 135–43.

Armbrust, Walter. *Mass Culture and Modernism in Egypt*. New York: Cambridge University Press, 1996.

Arunima, G. "Bonds of Love, Ties of Kinship? Or are There Other Ways of Imagining the Family?" *The Indian Economic and Social History Review* 53, no. 3 (2016): 1–22.

Asad, Talal. *Secular Translations: Nation State, Modern Self, and Calculative Reason*. New York: Columbia University Press, 2018.

Atabaki, Touraj and Iran Heritage Foundation. *Iran in the 20th Century: Historiography and Political Culture*. London: I.B. Tauris, 2009.

Aubry, Alex. "Beyond Orientalism: A Journey through Two Centuries of Muslim Patronage at the Paris Haute Couture." In *Contemporary Muslim Fashions*, edited by Jill D'Alessandro and Reina Lewis, 64–73. San Francisco: Fine Arts Museums of San Francisco, 2018.

'Ayn al-Saltanah. *Ruznamah-'i khatirat-i 'Ayn al-Saltanah*. 10 vols. Tehran: Asatir, 1995–99 (accessed online September 17, 2019).

Badran, Margot. *Feminists, Islam, and Nation: Gender and the Making of Modern Egypt*. Princeton: Princeton University Press, 1995.

Balaghi, Shiva and Lynn Gumpert, eds. *Picturing Iran: Art, Society, and Revolution*. New York: I.B. Tauris, 2002.

Barchard, David. "'The Imperial Rescript' Bringing Turkey into the Family of European Nations," in *Kırım Savaşı'nın 150nci Yılı (150th Anniversary of the Crimean War)*, edited by Bahattin Öztuncay, 70–73. Istanbul: Sadberk Hanım Müzesi, 2006.

Barko, Ivan. "Georges Biard d'Aunet: the Life and Career of a Consul General," *Australian Journal of French Studies*, Issue 2, vol. 39 (2002).

Baron, Beth. "The Making and Breaking of Marital Bonds in Modern Egypt." In *Women in Middle Eastern History: Shifting Boundaries in Sex and Gender*, edited by Nikki R. Keddie and Beth Baron, 275–91. New Haven: Yale University Press, 1991.

Baron, Beth. *The Women's Awakening in Egypt: Culture, Society and the Press*. New Haven: Yale University Press, 1994.

Baron, Beth. *Egypt as a Woman: Nationalism, Gender, and Politics*. Berkeley: University of California Press, 2005.

Baron, Beth. "Liberated Bodies and Saved Souls: Freed African slave girls and missionaries in Egypt." In *African Communities in Asia and the Mediterranean: Between Integration and Conflict*, edited by E. R. Toledano, 215–36. Halle and Trenton, and Asmara, Eritrea: Max Plank Institute and Africa World Press, 2011.

Barthes, Roland. *Camera Lucida: Reflections on Photography*. New York: Hill and Wang, 1981.

Barzilai-Lumbroso, Ruth. "Turkish Men and the History of Ottoman Women: Studying the History of the Ottoman Dynasty's Private Sphere through Women's Writing." *Journal of Middle East Women's Studies* 5, no. 2 (Spring 2009): 53–82.

Bashkin, Orit. "Harems, Women and Political Tyranny in the Works of Jurji Zaydan." In *Harem Histories: Envisioning Places and Living Spaces*, edited by Marilyn Booth, 290–318. North Carolina: Duke University Press, 2010.

Baudelaire, Charles. *The Painter of Modern Life and Other Essays*, translated and edited by Jonathan Mayne. New York: Da Capo Press, 1986.

Beaulieu, Jill and Mary Roberts. *Orientalism's Interlocutors: Painting, Architecture, Photography*. Durham: Duke University Press, 2002.

Behdad, Ali. *Camera Orientalis: Reflections on Photography of the Middle East*. Chicago: University of Chicago Press, 2016.

Behdad, Ali. "Mediated Visions: Early Photography of the Middle East and Orientalist Network." *History of Photography* 41, no. 4 (2017): 362–75.

Behdad, Ali and Luke Gartlan, eds. *Photography's Orientalism: New Essays on Colonial Representation*. Los Angeles: Getty Research Institute, 2013.

Benson, Susan Porter. *Counter Cultures: Saleswomen, Managers, and Customers in American Department Stores 1890–1940*. Champaign: University of Illinois Press, 1988.

Bernard Yeazell, Ruth. *Harems of the Mind: Passages of Western Art and Literature*. New Haven: Yale University Press, 2000.

Bhachu, Parminder. *Dangerous Design: Asian Women Fashion the Diaspora Economics*. London and New York: Routledge, 2004.

Bizri, Hala. "Introduction." In *Rasul al-`Uri* (The Prophet of the Nude), 2nd edn., edited by Hala Bizri, 10–12. Beirut: Editions Snoubar Bayrout, 2014.

Bizri, Hala. "The Nudism of Sheikh Fouad Hobeiche," translated by Elisabeth Jaquette. In *Art, Awakening, and Modernity in the Middle East: The Arab Nude*, edited by Octavian Esanu, 86–96. London: Routledge, 2018.

Boone, Joseph, *The Homoerotics of Orientalism*. New York: Columbia University Press, 2014.

Booth, Marilyn. *May Her Likes be Multiplied: Biography and Gender Politics in Egypt*. Berkeley: University of California Press, 2001.

Booth, Marilyn. "Un/safe/ly at Home: Narratives of Sexual Coercion in 1920s Egypt." *Gender and History* 16, no. 3 (November 2004): 744–68.

Boyar, Ebru. "An Imagined Moral Community: Ottoman Female Public Presence, Honour and Marginality." In *Ottoman Women in Public Space*, edited by Ebru Boyar and Kate Fleet, 187–229. Leiden: Brill, 2016.

Bibliography

Boyar, Ebru and Kate Fleet. *A Social History of Ottoman Istanbul*. Cambridge: Cambridge University Press, 2010.

Boyar, Ebru and Kate Fleet, eds. *Ottoman Women in Public Space*. Leiden: Brill, 2016.

Boym, Svetlana. *The Future of Nostalgia*. New York: Basic Books, 2001.

Brown, Peter. *The Body and Society: Men, Women and Sexual Renunciation in Early Christianity*. New York: Columbia University Press, 1988.

Brumett, Palmira. "The 'what if' of the Ottoman female: Authority, Ethnography, and Conversation." In *Ottoman Women in Public Space*, edited by Ebru Boyar and Kate Fleet, 18–47. Leiden: Brill, 2016.

Buskirk, Wesley D. "Egyptian Film and Feminism: Egypt's View of Women Through Cinema." *Cinesthesia* 2, vol. 4 (2015). Available online: https://scholarworks.gvsu.edu/cine/vol4/iss2/1/ (accessed on December 20, 2020)

Butler, Judith. *Gender Trouble: Feminism and the Subversion of Identity*. New York: Routledge, 1990.

Butler, Judith. *Bodies That Matter: On the Discursive Limits of "Sex"*. New York: Routledge, 1993.

Butler, Judith. *Notes Toward a Performative Theory of Assembly*. Cambridge: Harvard University Press, 2015.

Bynum, Caroline. "Why All the Fuss about the Body? A Medievalist's Perspective," *Critical Inquiry* 22, no. 1 (1995): 1–33.

Callaço, Gwendolyn. "Dressing a City's Demeanour: Ottoman Costume Albums and the Portrayal of Urban Identity in the Early Seventeenth Century." *Textile History* 48, no. 2 (2017): 248–67.

Catalogue of the Oriental Museum, Great Globe Leicester Square, London: W.J. Golbourn, 1857.

Cazentre, Thomas. "Entre l'album et le livre: Images du bout du monde dans les collections Imbault-Huart et Vossion," *Revue de la Bibliothèque Nationale de France* 44, no. 2 (2013): 25–35.

Çelik, Zeynep. *The Remaking of Istanbul: Portrait of an Ottoman City in the Nineteenth Century*. Berkeley: University of California Press, 1993.

Çelik, Zeynep. "Colonialism, Orientalism, and the Canon." *The Art Bulletin* 78, no. 2 (June 1996): 202–05.

Çelik, Zeynep and Edhem Eldem, eds. *Camera Ottomana: Photography and Modernity in the Ottoman Empire, 1840–1914*. Istanbul: Koç University Press, 2015.

Chacko Jacob, Wilson. *Working Out Egypt: Effendi Masculinity and Subject Formation in Colonial Modernity, 1870–1940*. Durham: Duke University Press, 2011.

Chakrabarty, Dipesh. "Labor History and the Politics of Theory: An Indian Angle on the Middle East." In *Workers and Working Classes in the Middle East: Struggles, Histories, Historiographies*, edited by Zachary Lockman, 321–34. Albany: SUNY Press, 1994.

Chehabi, Houchang E. "Staging the Emperor's New Clothes: Dress Codes and Nation-Building under Reza Shah." *Iranian Studies* 26, nos. 3/4 (Summer/Autumn 1993): 209–29.

Christensen, Peter H. *Germany and the Ottoman Railways: Art, Empire, and Infrastructure*. New Haven: Yale University Press, 2017.

Cizgen, Engin. *Photography in the Ottoman Empire*. Istanbul: Haşet Kitabevi A., 1987.

Codell, Julie and Joan Del Plato, eds. *Orientalism, Eroticism, and Modern Visuality in Global Cultures*. London: Routledge, 2018.

Colonial Egypt. Oxford Historical Monographs Oxford: Oxford University Press, 2014.

Coulthard, Glen. *Red Skin, White Masks: Rejecting the Colonial Politics of Recognition*. Minneapolis: University of Minnesota Press, 2014.

Craik, Jennifer. *Fashion: Key Concepts*. London: Bloomsbury, 2009.

Criss, Nur Bilge. *Istanbul under Allied Occupation, 1918–1923*. Leiden: Brill, 1999.

Cumming, Valerie, C.W. Cunnington, and P. E. Cunnington. *The Dictionary of Fashion History*. Oxford: Berg Publishers, 2010.

Cunningham, Allan. *The Life of Sir David Wilkie; With his Journals, Tours, and Critical Remarks on Works of Art and a Selection from His Correspondence*. London: John Murray, 1843, 3 vols.

Cuno, Kenneth. *The Pasha's Peasants: Land, Society and Economy in Lower Egypt*. New York: Cambridge University Press, 1992.

Cuno, Kenneth. *Modernizing Marriage: Family, Ideology, and Law in Nineteenth- and Early Twentieth-Century Egypt*. Syracuse: Syracuse University Press, 2015.

Curtis, Charles George. *Broken Bits of Byzantium, lithographed with some additions by Mary A. Walker*. Constantinople: Lorentz and Keil, 1887.

Daggett, Cara. "Drone Disorientations." *International Feminist Journal of Politics* 17, no. 3 (2015): 361–79. DOI: 10.1080/14616742.2015.1075317.

Danielson, Virginia. *The Voice of Egypt: Umm Kulthum, Arabic Song, and Egyptian Society in the Twentieth Century*. Chicago: The University of Chicago Press, 1997.

Davis, Fanny. *The Ottoman Lady: A Social History from 1718–1918*. New York, Greenwood Press, 1986.

De la Haye, Amy and Valerie D. Mendes. *The House of Worth 1890–1914: Portrait of an Archive*, London: V&A Publishing, 2014.

Deeb, Marius. "The Socioeconomic Role of the Local Foreign Minorities in Modern Egypt, 1805–1961." *International Journal of Middle East Studies* 9, no. 1 (1978): 11–22.

Del Plato, Joan. *Multiple Wives. Multiple Pleasures: Representing the Harem, 1800–1875*. Madison: Fairleigh Dickinson University Press, 2002.

Delice, Serkan. "The Janissaries and their Bedfellows: Masculinity and Male Homosexuality in Early Modern Ottoman Istanbul, 1500–1826." PhD thesis, University of the Arts London, 2015.

Doumani, Beshara B. *Family Life in the Ottoman Mediterranean: A Social History*. Cambridge: Cambridge University Press, 2017.

Du Gay, Paul, Stuart Hall, Linda Janes, Anders Koed Madsen, Hugh Mackay, and Keith Negus. *Doing Cultural Studies: The Story of the Sony Walkman*. 2nd edn. 1997. Reprinted, Milton Keynes: Open University, 2013.

Duben, Alan and Cem Behar. *Istanbul Households: Marriage, Family and Fertility, 1880–1940*. Cambridge: Cambridge University Press, 1991.

Dueck, Jennifer. "A Muslim Jamboree: Scouting and Youth Culture in Lebanon under the French Mandate." *French Historical Studies* 30, no. 3 (2007): 485–516.

Duflo, Pierre. *Constantin Guys. Fou de Dessin, Grand Reporter, 1802–1892*. Paris: Éditions Arnaud Seydoux, 1988.

Dunne, Bruce. "Sexuality and the 'Civilizing Process' in Modern Egypt." PhD thesis, Georgetown University, Washington D.C., 1996.

Edib, Halide Adivar. *Memoirs of Halidé Edib*. London: John Murray, 1926.

El-Ariss, Tarek. *Trials of Arab Modernity: Literary Affects and the New Political*. New York: Fordham University Press, 2013.

Eldem, Edhem. *Pride and Privilege. A History of Ottoman Orders, Medals and Decorations*. Istanbul: Ottoman Bank Archives and Research Centre, 2004.

Ellison, Grace. *An Englishwoman in a Turkish Harem*. 1915. Reprinted, Piscataway: Giorgias Books, 2007.

Elshakry, Marwa. *Reading Darwin in Arabic, 1860–1950*. Chicago: University of Chicago Press, 2013.

Entwistle, Joanne and Agnès Rocamora. "The Field of Fashion Materialized: A Study of London Fashion Week." *Sociology* 40, no. 4 (2006): 735–51.

Entwistle, Joanne. *The Aesthetic Economy of Fashion: Markets and Value in Clothing and Modelling*. Oxford and New York: Berg, 2009.

Evans, Caroline. *The Mechanical Smile: Modernism and the First Fashion Shows in France and America, 1900–1929*. New Haven: Yale University Press, 2013.

Fahmy, Khaled. *All the Pasha's Men: Mehmed Ali, His Army and the Making of Modern Egypt*. New York: Cambridge University Press, 1997.

Farmanfarmayiyan, Mihrmah. *Zir-i nigah-i pidar: khatirat-i Mirmah Farmanfarmayiyan az andaruni*. Tehran: Kavir, 2004.

Faroqhi, Suraiya. "Introduction, or Why and How One Might Want to Study Ottoman Clothes." In *Ottoman Costumes: From Textile to Identity*, edited by Suraiya Faroqhi and Christof K. Neuman, 15–48. Istanbul: Eren 2004.

Faroqhi, Suraiya and Christof K Neuman, eds. *Ottoman Costumes: From Textile to Identity*. Istanbul: Eren, 2004.

Farrukh, Mustafa. *Tariqi ila al-Fann* (My Road to Art). Beirut: Dar Naufal, 1986.

Fay, Mary Ann. "From Concubines to Capitalists: Women, Property, and Power in Eighteenth-century Cairo." *Journal of Women's History* 10, no. 3 (1988).

Findley, Carter Vaughn. *Turkey, Islam, Nationalism and Modernity, a History, 1789–2007*. London: Yale University Press, 2010.

Fleet, Kate. "The Extremes of Visibility: Slave Women in Ottoman Public Space." In *Ottoman Women in Public Space*, edited by Ebru Boyar and Kate Fleet, 128–49. Leiden: Brill, 2016.

Fleet, Kate. "The Powerful Public Presence of the Ottoman Female Consumer." In *Ottoman Women in Public Space*, edited by Ebru Boyar and Kate Fleet, 91–27. Leiden: Brill, 2016.

Foucault, Michel. *The History of Sexuality: An Introduction*, translated by Robert Hurley. New York: Vintage, 1990.

Frierson, Elizabeth B. "Mirrors Out, Mirrors In: Domestication and Rejection of the Foreign in Late-Ottoman Women's Magazines." In *Women, Patronage, and Self-Representation in Islamic Societies*, edited by Dede Fairchild Ruggles, 177–204. New York: State University of New York Press, 2000.

Bibliography

Gavand, Eugène-Henri. *Chemin de Fer Métropolitain de Constantinople ou Chemin de Fer Souterrain de Galata a Péra Dit Tunnel de Constantinople*. Paris: Typographie Lahure, 1876.

Genell, Aimee. "Empire by Law: Ottoman Sovereignty and the British Occupation of Egypt, 1882–1923". PhD thesis, Columbia University, New York, 2013.

Germaner, Semra and Zeynep İnankur. *Constantinople and the Orientalists*. Istanbul: İşbank, 2002.

Gershoni, Israel and James Jankowski. *Redefining the Egyptian Nation, 1930–45*. New York: Cambridge University Press, 1995.

Ghoussoub, Mai and Emma Sinclair-Webb, eds. *Imagined Masculinities: Male Identity and Culture in the Modern Middle East*. London: Saqi Books, 2000.

Gitre, Carmen M. K. *Acting Egyptian: Theater, Identity, and Political Culture in Cairo, 1869–1930*. Austin: University of Texas Press, 2019.

González, Carmen Pérez. *Local Portraiture: Through the Lens of the 19th-Century Iranian Photographers*. Leiden: Leiden University Press, 2012.

Görünür, Lale, ed. *Osmanlı İmparatorluğu'nun son Döneminden Kadın Giysileri, Sadberk Hanım Müzesi Koleksiyonu/Women's Costume of the late Ottoman Era from the Sadberk Hanım Museum*. Istanbul: Vehbi Koç Vakfı, 2010.

Graham-Brown, Sarah. *Images of Women. The Portrayal of Women in Photography of the Middle East 1860–1950*. London: Quartet, 1988.

Grandidier, G. "Obituary of Roland Bonaparte," *Nature*, vol. 113 (May 24, 1924): 755.

Grigsby, Darcy. "'Whose colour was no black nor white nor grey, But an extraneous mixture, which no pen, Can trace, although perhaps the pencil may': Aspasie and Delacroix's Massacres of Chios," *Art History* 22, no. 5 (December 1999): 676–704.

Grosz, Elizabeth. *Volatile Bodies: Toward a Corporeal Feminism*. Bloomington: Indiana University Press, 1994.

Gülçin Ambros, Edith, Ebru Boyar, Palmira Brummett, Kate Fleet, Svetla Ianeva. "Ottoman Women in Public Space: an Introduction." *Ottoman Women in Public Space*, edited by Ebru Boyar and Kate Fleet. Leiden: Brill, 2016.

Gürsel, Zeynep Devrim. "A Picture of Health: The Search for a Genre to Visualize Care in Late Ottoman Istanbul." *Grey Room* 72, (2018): 36–67.

Haidar, Musbah. *Arabesque*. London: Hutchinson & Co. 1944.

Haj, Samira. *Reconfiguring the Islamic Tradition: Reform, Rationality, and Modernity*. Stanford: Stanford University Press, 2009.

Hammad, Hanan. *Industrial Sexuality: Gender, Urbanization, and Social Transformation in Egypt*. Austin: University of Texas Press, 2016.

Hammond, Andrew. *Popular Culture in the Arab World: Arts, Politics, and the Media*. Cairo and New York: The American University in Cairo Press, 2009.

Hanioğlu, Şükrü. *A Brief History of the Late Ottoman Empire*. Princeton: Princeton University Press, 2008.

Hanssen, Jens. *Fin de Siècle Beirut: The Making of an Ottoman Provincial Capital*. Oxford: Clarendon Press, 2005.

Heffernan, Teresa. *Veiled Figures: Women, Modernity, and the Spectres of Orientalism*. Toronto: University of Toronto Press, 2016.

Hegel, G.W.F. *Reason in History, a general introduction to the Philosophy of History*, translated by Robert S. Hartman. 1953. Indianapolis, Indiana: A Liberal Arts Press Book, The Bobbs-Merrill Company, Inc. Part IV, no. 3. Available online: https://www.marxists.org/reference/archive/hegel/works/hi/introduction.htm (accessed November 9, 2018).

Hegel, Georg Wilhelm Friedrich. *Miscellaneous Writings of G.W.F. Hegel*, edited by Jon Stewart. Evanston: Northwestern University Press, 2002.

Hennessy, Rosemary and Chrys Ingraham, eds. *Materialist Feminism: A Reader in Class, Difference, and Women's Lives*. New York: Routledge, 1997.

Hill, Richard L. *A Biographical Dictionary of the Anglo-Egyptian Sudan*. Oxford: Clarendon Press, 1951.

Hill, Richard L. *A Biographical Dictionary of the Sudan*. 2nd edn. London: Frank Cass & Co Ltd., 1967.

Hirsch, Marianne, ed. *The Familial Gaze*. Hanover: Dartmouth College (University Press of New England), 1999.

Hodgson, Marshal G.S. *The Venture of Islam: Conscience and History in a World Civilization*. vol. 1. Chicago: University of Chicago Press, 1974.

Hoffman, Brian Scott. "Making Private Parts Public: American Nudism and the Politics of Nakedness, 1929–1963." PhD diss., University of Illinois at Urbana-Champaign, 2009.

Hoskins, Janet. *Biographical Objects: How Things Tell the Stories of People's Lives*. New York: Routledge, 1998.

Hourani, Albert. *The Emergence of the Modern Middle East*. London: Macmillan, 1981.

Hubaysh, Fu'ad. *Rasul al-`Uri* (The Prophet of the Nude). Originally published, Beirut: Dar Sader, 1930. Reprinted, Beirut: Editions Snoubar Bayrout, 2014.

İgüs, Esma. "A British Touch on Tanzimat: Architect William James Smith, Tanzimat'a İngiliz Dokunuşu: Mimar William James Smith." *Journal of Ottoman Legacy Studies (JOLS)/Osmanlı Mirası Araştırmaları Dergisi (OMAD)* 2, no. 3 (2015): 66–87.

İnal, Onur. "Women's Fashions in Transition: Ottoman Borderlands and the Anglo-Ottoman Exchange of Costumes." *Journal of World History* 22, no. 2 (June 2011): 243–72.

İnankur, Zeynep. "Mary Adelaide Walker." In *The Poetics and Politics of Place: Ottoman Istanbul and British Orientalism*, edited by Zeynep Inankur, Reina Lewis, and Mary Roberts, 199–209. Seattle: University of Washington Press, 2011.

İpek, Selin. "Fashion in Court Women's Attire of the Eighteenth and Nineteenth Centuries in the Light of Written and Visual Sources kept in the Topkapı Palace Museum [in Turkish]." Unpublished PhD thesis, Mimar Sinan Fine Arts University, Istanbul, 2009.

İpek, Selin. "Festive Finery for the Harem: Seamstress Mademoiselle Kokona's Order Book." In *Topkapi Palace: The Imperial Harem, House of the Sultan*, 56–59. Istanbul: Ministry of Culture and Tourism, 2012.

İrepoğlu, Gül. *Topkapı Palace: The Imperial Harem: House of the Sultan*. Istanbul: Topkapı Palace Museum, 2012.

Irigaray, Luce. *This Sex Which is Not One*, translated by Catherine Porter. New York: Cornell University, 1996.

Jackson, Michael. *The Work of Art: Rethinking the Elementary Forms of Religious Life*. New York: Columbia University Press, 2016.

Jacob, Wilson Chacko. "Overcoming Simply Being: Straight Sex, Masculinity, and Physical Culture in Egypt." *Gender and History* 22, no. 3 (November 2010): 1–19.

Jacob, Wilson Chacko. *Working Out Egypt: Effendi Masculinity and Subject Formation in Colonial Modernity, 1870–1940*. Durham: Duke University Press, 2011.

Jacob, Wilson Chacko. *For God or Empire: Sayyid Fadl and the Indian Ocean World*. Stanford: Stanford University Press, 2019.

Jansen, M. Angela and Jennifer Craik, eds. *Modern Fashion Traditions: Negotiating Tradition and Modernity through Fashion*. London: Bloomsbury, 2016.

Jirousek, Charlotte. "Ottoman Influences in Western Dress." In *Ottoman Costumes: From Textile to Identity*, edited by Suraiya Faroqhi and Christof K Neumann, 231–51. Istanbul: Eren Publishing, 2005.

Johnson, Rebecca C. "Foreword." In *Leg over Leg*, vols. 1 and 2, 1855, by Ahmed Fāris Al-Shidyāq. New York: New York University Press, 2015.

Kaiser, Susan. *Fashion and Cultural Studies*. London: Bloomsbury, 2012.

Kazimi, Mushfiq. *Ruzgar va andishah-ha*. Tehran: Ibn Sina, 1971.

Keddie, Nikki. *Modern Iran: Roots and Results of Revolution*. London: Yale University Press, 2003.

Khater, Akram. *Inventing Home: Emigration, Gender, and the Middle Class in Lebanon, 1870–1920*. Berkeley: University of California Press, 2001.

Kholoussy, Hanan. "Stolen Husbands, Foreign Wives: Mixed Marriage, Identity Formation, and Gender in Colonial Egypt, 1909–1923." *Hawwa* 1, no. 2 (2003): 206–40.

Kholoussy, Hanan. *For Better, For Worse: The Marriage Crisis That Made Modern Egypt, 1898–1936*. Stanford: Stanford University Press, 2010.

Kozma, Liat. *Policing Egyptian Women: Sex, Law, and Medicine in Khedival Egypt*. Syracuse: Syracuse University Press, 2011.

Kracauer, Siegfried. "Photography." Translated by Thomas Y. Levin. *Critical Inquiry*, 19 (Spring 1993): 421–36.

Kuhn, Annette. *Family Secrets: Acts of Memory and Imagination*. London: Verso, [1995] 2002.

Kuneralp, Sinan "The Thorny Road to Modernization: Thee Ottoman Empire and the Crimean War," in *Kırım Savaşı'nın 150nci Yılı* (150th Anniversary of the Crimean War), edited by Bahattin Öztuncay, 60–65. Istanbul: Sadberk Hanım Müzesi, 2006.

Lad, Jateen. "Panoptic Bodies: Black Eunuchs as Guardians of the Topkapi Harem." In *Harem Histories: Envisioning Places and Living Spaces*, edited by M. Booth, 136–76. Durham, NC: Duke University Press, 2010.

Lancaster, Bill. *The Department Store: A Social History*. Leicester: Leicester University Press, 2000.

Lanfranchi, Sania Sharawi. *Casting off the Veil: The Life of Huda Shaarawi, Egypt's First Feminist*. London: I.B. Tauris, 2012.

Latour, Bruno. *We Have Never Been Modern*. Cambridge: Harvard University Press, 1993.

Leaman, Oliver, ed. *Companion Encyclopedia of Middle Eastern and North African Film*. London: Routledge, 2001.

Lepore, Jill. "Ahab at Home: Two hundred years of Herman Melville." *The New Yorker*, July 29, 2019.

Bibliography

Lewis, Reina. *Gendering Orientalism: Race, Femininity and Representation*. London: Routledge, 1996.

Lewis, Reina. "On Veiling, Vision and Voyage: Cross-cultural Dressing and Narratives of Identity." *Interventions: International Journal of Postcolonial Studies* 1, no. 4 (1999): 500–20.

Lewis, Reina. *Rethinking Orientalism: Women, Travel and the Ottoman Harem*. London and New York: I.B. Tauris, 2004.

Lewis, Reina and Nancy Micklewright, eds. *Gender, Modernity and Liberty: Middle Eastern and Western Women's Writings: A Critical Sourcebook*. London: I.B. Tauris, 2006.

Leyla Saz Hanımefendi. *The Imperial Harem of the Sultans: Memoirs of Leyla (Saz) Hanımefendi*. 1922. Reprinted, Istanbul: Peva Publications, 1994.

Lionnet, Françoise and Shu-mei Shih, eds. *Minor Transnationalism*. Durham: Duke University Press, 2005.

Lockman, Zachary. *Contending Visions of the Middle East: The History and Politics of Orientalism*. 2nd edn. Cambridge: Cambridge University Press, 2009.

Lott, Emmeline. *The English Governess in Egypt: Harem Life in Egypt and Constantinople*. 2 vols. London: Richard Bentley, 1866.

Lutfi, Huda "Manners and Customs of Fourteenth-Century Cairene Women: Female Anarchy versus Male Shar'i Order in Muslim Prescriptive Treatises." In *Women in Middle Eastern History: Shifting Boundaries in Sex and Gender*, edited by Nikki R. Kreddie and Beth Baron, 99–121. London and New Haven: Yale University Press, 1991.

Mahjoub, Jamal. *A Line in the River: Khartoum, City of Memory*. London: Bloomsbury, 2018.

Mahmood, Saba. *Politics of Piety: The Islamic Revival and the Feminist Subject*. Princeton: Princeton University Press, 2005.

Makdisi, Ussama. "Ottoman Orientalism." *The American Historical Review* 107, no. 3 (June 2002): 768–96.

Mallah, Narjis Mihrangiz. *Az zanan-i pishgam-i Irani: Afzal Vaziri, dukhtar-i Bibi Khanum Astarabadi*. Tehran: Shirazeh, 2006.

Marcus, Sharon. *Between Women: Friendship, Desire, and Marriage in Victorian England*. Princeton: Princeton University Press, 2007.

Massad, Joseph A. *Desiring Arabs*. Chicago: The University of Chicago Press, 2007.

Mauss, Marcel. "Techniques of the Body." *Economy and Society* 2, no. 1 (1973): 70–88.

Mbembé, J.-A. "Necropolitics," translated by Libby Meintjes. *Public Culture* 15, no. 1 (Winter 2003): 11–40.

McGuire, Meredith B. *Lived Religion: Faith and Practice in Everyday Life*. Oxford: Oxford University Press, 2008.

Melek Hanoum. *Thirty Years in the Harem: or the Autobiography of Melek-Hanoum, Wife of H.H. Kibrizli-Mehemet-Pasha*. London: Chapman and Hall, 1872.

Melman, Billie. *Women's Orients: English Women and the Middle East, 1718–1918: Sexuality, Religion and Work*. London: Palgrave Macmillan, 1992.

Méouchy, Nadine and Peter Sluglett. "General Introduction." In *The British and French Mandates in Comparative Perspectives*, edited by Nadine Méouchy and Peter Sluglett, 1–19. Leiden: Brill Publishers, 2004.

Meriwether, Margaret L. and Judith E. Tucker. *Social History of Women and Gender in the Modern Middle East*. Boulder: Westview Press, 1999.

Mernissi, Fatima. *Beyond the Veil: Male-Female Dynamics in Muslim Society*. 2nd edn. London: al Saqi Books, 1985.

Merrill, Frances and Merrill Mason. *Among the Nudists – Early Naturism*. 1931. Reprinted, Redditch: Read Books Ltd., 2013.

Mestyan, Adam. *Arab Patriotism: The Ideology and Culture of Power in Late Ottoman Egypt*. Princeton, NJ: Princeton University Press, 2017.

Micklewright, Nancy. "Women's Dress in Nineteenth Century Istanbul: Mirror of a Changing Society." PhD diss., University of Pennsylvania, Philadelphia, 1986.

Micklewright, Nancy. "Tracing the Transformation of Women's Dress in Nineteenth Century Istanbul." *Dress* 13 (1987): 33–42.

Micklewright, Nancy. "Late Nineteenth-century Ottoman Wedding Costumes as Indicators of Social Change." *Muqarnas* 6 (1989): 161–74.

Micklewright, Nancy. "Personal, Public and Political (Re)Constructions: Photographs and Consumption." In *Consumption Studies and the History of the Ottoman Empire, 1550–1922*, edited by Donald Quataert, 261–88. New York: SUNY Press, 2000.

Micklewright, Nancy. "Harem/House/Set: Domestic Interiors in Photography from the Late Ottoman World." In *Harem Histories. Envisioning Places and Living Spaces*, edited by Marilyn Booth, 239–60. Durham: Duke University Press, 2010.

Micklewright, Nancy. "Alternative Histories of Photography in the Ottoman Middle East." In *Photography's Orientalism, New Essays on Colonial Representation*, edited by Ali Behdad and Luke Gartlan, 75–92. Los Angeles: The J. Paul Getty Trust, 2013.

Micklewright, Nancy. "Picturing the 'Abode of Felicity' in 1919. A Photograph Album of Istanbul." In *Seeing the Past—Envisioning Islamic Art and Architecture: Essays in Honor of Renata Holod*, edited by D. Roxburgh, 250–78. Leiden: Brill, 2014.

Mitchell, Timothy, ed. *Questions of Modernity*. Minneapolis: University of Minnesota Press, 2000.

Mitchell, Timothy. "The Stage of Modernity." In *Questions of Modernity*, edited by Timothy Mitchell, 1–34. Minneapolis: University of Minnesota Press, 2000.

Mitchell, Timothy. *Carbon Democracy*. New York: Verso, 2011.

Moore, Jason. *Capitalism in the Web of Life: Ecology and the Accumulation of Capital*. New York: Verso, 2015.

Moore, Jason. "Capitalocene, Part I: On the Nature and Origins of our Ecological Crisis." *The Journal of Peasant Studies* 44, no. 3 (2017): 594–630.

Motlagh, Amy. *Burying the Beloved: Marriage, Realism, and Reform in Modern Iran*. Stanford: Stanford University Press, 2012. https://www.brismes.ac.uk/nmes/wp-content/uploads/2011/06/NMES2011QSNachabe.pdf (accessed on December 20, 2020).

Nachabe, Yasmine. "An Alternative Representation of Femininity in 1920s Lebanon: through the mise-en-abîme of a masculine space." *New Middle Eastern Studies Journal* (2011). Available online: https://www.brismes.ac.uk/nmes/wp-content/uploads/2011/06/NMES2011QSNachabe.pdf (accessed on December 20, 2020).

Naef, Silvia. "Visual Modernity in the Arab world, Turkey and Iran: Reintroducing the 'Missing Modern': Introduction." *Études Asiatiques: Revue de la Société Suisse – Asie* 70, no. 4 (2016): 1005.

Naeff, Judith. *Precarious Imaginaries of Beirut: A City's Suspended Now*. Cham, Switzerland: Palgrave Macmillan, 2018.

Najmabadi, Afsaneh. *Women with Mustaches and Men without Beards: Gender and Sexual Anxieties of Iranian Modernity*. Berkeley and Los Angeles: University of California Press, 2005.

Nashat, Guity. "Marriage in the Qajar Period." In *Women in Iran: From 1800 to the Islamic Republic*, edited by Lois Beck and Guity Nashat, 37–62. Urbana: University of Illinois Press, 2004.

Nava, Mica. *Visceral Cosmopolitanism: Gender, Culture and the Normalisation of Difference*. Oxford: Berg, 2007.

Necipoğlu, Gülru. *Architecture, Ceremonial, and Power. The Topkapı Palace in the Fifteenth and Sixteenth Centuries*. Cambridge: MIT Press, 1990.

Nicklas, Charlotte and Annebella Pollen, eds. *Dress History: New Directions in Theory*. New York: Bloomsbury Academic, 2015.

Niessen, Sandra, Ann Marie Leshkowich and Carla Jones, eds. *Re-Orienting Fashion: The Globalization of Asian Dress*. Oxford and New York: Berg, 2003.

Nochlin, Linda. "The Imaginary Orient." In Linda Nochlin, *The Politics of Vision. Essays on Nineteenth-Century Art and Society*, 33–59. New York: Harper and Row, 1989.

O'Grady, Lorraine. "Olympia's Maid: Reclaiming Black Female Subjectivity," 1992. In *The Feminism and Visual Cultural Reader*, edited by Amelia Jones. London and New York: Routledge Press, 2003.

Oberling, P. "The Istanbul Tünel." *Archivum Ottomanicum* 4 (1972): 217–63.

Orga, Irfan. *Portrait of a Turkish Family*. London: Victor Gollancz Ltd., 1950.

Öztuncay, Bahattin. *Vassilaki Kargopoulo. Photographer to his Majesty the Sultan*. Istanbul: Birleşik Oksijen Sanayi, A Ş, 2000.

Öztuncay, Bahattin. *The Photographers of Constantinople: Pioneers, Studios and Artists from 19th Century Istanbul*, 2 vols. Istanbul: Aygaz, 2003.

Öztuncay, Bahattin, ed. *Kırım Savaşı'nın 150nci Yılı (150th Anniversary of the Crimean War)*. Istanbul: Sadberk Hanım Müzesi, 2006.

Öztuncay, Bahattin. *Hanedan ve Kamera, Osmanlı Sarayından Portreler/Dynasty and Camera, Portraits from the Ottoman Court*. Istanbul: Aygaz, 2010.

Paidar, Parvin. *Women and the Political Process in Twentieth-Century Iran*. New York: Cambridge University Press, 1995.

Pappe, Ilan. *The Modern Middle East: A Social and Cultural History*. 2nd edn. London: Routledge, 2010.

Pardoe, Julia. "The City of the Sultan, and the Domestic Manners of the Turks, in 1836." London: Henry Colburn, 1837. Reproduced in *Gender, Modernity and Liberty: Middle Eastern and Western Women's Writings: A Critical Sourcebook*, edited by Lewis and Micklewright. London: I.B. Tauris, 2006.

Pateman, Carole. *The Sexual Contract*. Cambridge: Polity Press, 1988.

Peirce, Leslie. *The Imperial Harem: Women and Sovereignty in the Ottoman Empire*. Oxford: Oxford University Press, 1993.

Peirce, Leslie. "AHR Forum: Writing Histories of Sexuality in the Middle East." *American Historical Review* 114, no. 5 (December 2009): 1325–39.

Bibliography

Pettinger, Lynne. "Brand Culture and Branded Workers: Service Work and Aesthetic Labour in Fashion Retail." *Consumption, Markets and Culture* 7, no. 2 (June 2004): 165–84.

Philipp, Thomas. *Jurji Zaidan and the Foundations of Arab Nationalism: A Study by Thomas Philipp*, translated by Hilary Kilpatrick and Paul Starkey. Syracuse: Syracuse University Press, 2010.

Pollard, Lisa. *Nurturing the Nation: The Family Politics of Modernizing, Colonizing, and Liberating Egypt, 1805–1923*. Berkeley: University of California Press, 2005.

Povinelli, Elizabeth. *The Empire of Love: Toward a Theory of Intimacy, Genealogy, and Carnality*. Durham: Duke University Press, 2006.

Pratt, Mary Louise. *Imperial Eyes: Travel Writing and Transculturation*. London: Routledge, 1992.

Puar, Jasbir. *Terrorist Assemblages: Homonationalism in Queer Times*. Durham: Duke University Press, 2007.

Quataert, Donald, ed. *Consumption in the Ottoman Empire*. New York: State University of New York Press, 1999.

Quataert, Donald. *The Ottoman Empire 1700–1922*. Cambridge: Cambridge University Press, 2000.

Rabine, Leslie W. *The Global Circulation of African Fashion*. Oxford: Berg, 2002.

Reekie, Gail. *Temptations: Sex, Selling in the Department Store*. St. Leonards: Allen & Unwin, 1993.

Renda, Günsel. *A History of Turkish Painting*, Seattle: University of Washington Press, 1989.

Renda, Günsel, ed. *Women in Anatolia: 9000 Years of the Anatolian Woman*. Istanbul: Ministry of Culture, 1993.

Reynolds, Nancy. *A City Consumed: Urban Commerce, the Cairo Fire, and the Politics of Decolonization in Egypt*. Stanford: Stanford University Press, 2012.

Riello, Giorgio and Peter McNeil, eds. *The Fashion History Reader: Global Perspectives*. London: Routledge, 2010.

Rivière, Joan. "Womanliness as a Masquerade," 1929. In Russell Grigg *Female Sexuality: The Early Psychoanalytic Controversies*. London: Karnac Books, 2018.

Roberts, Mary. "Contested Terrains: Women Orientalists and the Colonial Harem." In *Orientalism's Interlocutors: Painting, Architecture, Photography*, edited by Jill Beaulieu and Mary Roberts, 179–204. Durham: Duke University Press, 2002.

Roberts, Mary. *Intimate Outsiders: The Harem in Ottoman and Orientalist Art and Travel Literature*. Durham: Duke University Press, 2007.

Roberts, Mary. "Nazlı's Photographic Games: Said and Art History in a Contrapuntal Mode." *Patterns of Prejudice* 48, no. 5 (2014): 460–78.

Roberts, Mary. *Istanbul Exchanges: Ottomans, Orientalists and Nineteenth-Century Visual Culture*. Berkeley: University of California Press, 2015.

Rosaldo, Renato. *Culture and Truth: The Remaking of Social Analysis*. London: Routledge, 1993.

Rose, Nikolas. *Governing the Soul: The Shaping of the Private Self*. 2nd edn. 1989. Reprinted, London: Free Association Books, 1999.

Ross, Chad. "Building a Better Body: Nudism, Society, Race and the German Nation (1890–1950)," PhD dissertation, University of Missouri-Columbia, 2003.

Rovine, Victoria L. *African Fashion, Global Style: Histories, Innovations, and Ideas You Can Wear*. Indiana: Indiana University Press, 2015.

Roxburgh, David J. and Mary McWilliams, eds. *Technologies of the Image: Art in 19th-Century Iran*. Cambridge: Harvard Art Museums, 2017.

Ruggles, Dede Fairchild, ed. Women, Patronage, and Self-Representation in Islamic Societies. New York: State University of New York Press, 2000.

Russell, Mona. "Modernity, National Identity, and Consumerism: Visions of the Egyptian Home, 1805–1922." In *Transitions in Domestic Consumption and Family Life in the Modern Middle East*, edited by R. Shechter, 37–62. Houses in Motion Conference Proceeding, 2003.

Rüstem, Ünver. "Dressing the Part: Ottoman Self-Representation in the Age of Orientalism," Paper presented at Objects of Orientalism, Clark Art Institute, Williamstown MA., 29–30 April, 2016.

Rüstem, Ünver. *Ottoman Baroque. The Architectural Refashioning of Eighteenth-Century Istanbul*. Princeton: Princeton University Press, 2019.

Ryzova, Lucie. *The Age of the Efendiyya: Passage to Modernity in National-Sakaoğlu, Necdet and Nuri Akbayar. A Milestone on Turkey's Path to Westernization: Sultan Abdülmecid*. vol. 8. Istanbul: DenizBank Publications, 2002.

Ryzova, Lucie. "'I Am a Whore but I Will Be a Good Mother': On the Production and Consumption of the Female Body in Modern Egypt." *Arab Studies Journal* XII, no. 2/XIII, no. 1 (Fall 2004/Spring 2005): 80–122.

Ryzova, Lucie. "Egyptianizing Modernity through the 'New *Effendiya*': Social and Cultural Constructions of the Middle Class in Egypt under the Monarchy." In *Re-Envisioning Egypt, 1919–1952*, edited by Arthur Goldschmidt, Amy Johnson, and Barak Salmoni, 124–63. Cairo: American University in Cairo Press, 2005.

Salmoni, Barak. "Historical Consciousness for Modern Citizenship." In *Re-Envisioning Egypt, 1919–1952*, edited by Arthur Goldschmidt, Amy Johnson, and Barak Salmoni, 164–93. Cairo: American University in Cairo Press, 2005.

Sanders, Paula. "Gendering the Ungendered Body: Hermaphrodites in Medieval Islamic Law." In *Women in Middle Eastern History: Shifting Boundaries in Sex and Gender*, edited by Nikki R. Keddie and Beth Baron, 74–95. New Haven: Yale University Press, 1991.

Sakaoğlu, Necdet, Nuri Akbayar. *Sultan Abdülmecid: A Milestone on Turkey's Path to Westernization no 8.* Istanbul: DenizBank Publications, 2002.

Scheer, Monique, "Are Emotions a Kind of Practice (and is that what makes them have a history)? A Bourdieusian Approach to Understanding Emotion." *History and Theory* 51, no. 2 (2012): 193–220.

Scheid, Kirsten. "Necessary Nudes: *Hadatha* and *Mu`asara* in the Lives of Modern Lebanese." *International Journal of Middle East Studies* 42, no. 2 (2010): 203–23.

Scheid, Kirsten. "Divinely Imprinting Prints, or, how pictures became influential persons in Mandate Lebanon." In *The Routledge Handbook of the History of the Middle East Mandates*, edited by Cyrus Schayegh and Andrew Arsan, 371–91. London: Routledge, 2015.

Scheiwiller, Staci Gem. *Liminalities of Gender and Sexuality in Nineteenth-Century Iranian Photography: Desirous Bodies.* New York: Routledge, 2017.

Schumann, Christoph. "The Generation of Broad Expectations: Nationalism, Education, and Autobiography in Syria and Lebanon, 1930–1958." In *The Making of the Arab Intellectual*, edited by Dyala Hamzah, 188–211. London: Routledge, 2013.

Semeniuk, Ivan. "Genetic study of Quebec Residents Finds Air Pollution Trumps Ancestry." *The Globe and Mail* [Online], March 6, 2018. Available online: https://www.theglobeandmail.com/news/national/genetic-study-of-quebec-residents-finds-air-pollution-trumps-ancestry/article38217989/ (accessed October 21, 2020).

Şeni, Nora. "Fashion and Women's Clothing in the Satirical Press of Istanbul at the End of the 19th Century," in *Women in Modern Turkish Society*, edited by Şirin Tekeli. London: Zed Books, 1995.

Shaarawi, Huda, "*Harem Years: The Memoirs of an Egyptian Feminist (1879-1942),*" translated and edited by Margo Badran. New York: The Feminist Press, [n.d] 1987. Reproduced in *Gender, Modernity and Liberty: Middle Eastern and Western Women's Writings: A Critical Sourcebook*, edited by Lewis and Micklewright. London: I.B. Tauris, 2006.

Shafik, Viola. *Popular Egyptian Cinema: Gender, Class, and Nation.* Cairo: American University in Cairo Press, 2007.

Shahshahani, Sohelia. *Persian Clothing During the Qajar Reign.* Tehran: Farhangsara-yi Mirdashti, 2008.

Shaw, Wendy. "Modernism's Innocent Eye and Nineteenth-Century Ottoman Photography." *History of Photography* 33 (1) (2009): 80–93.

Sheehi, Stephen. "A Social History of Early Arab Photography or a Prolegomenon to an Archaeology of the Lebanese Imago." *International Journal of Middle East Studies* 39, no. 2 (May 2007): 175–206.

Sheehi, Stephen. *The Arab Imago. A Social History of Portrait Photography, 1860–1910.* Princeton and Oxford: Princeton University Press, 2016.

Shissler, Holly. "Beauty is Nothing to Be Ashamed of: Beauty Contests as Tools of Women's Liberation in Early Republican Turkey." *Comparative Studies in South Asia, Africa, and the Middle East* 24, no. 1 (2004): 109–26.

Siraj al-Haqq Kugle, Scott. *Homosexuality in Islam.* London: Oneworld Publications, 2010.

Smalls, James. "Menace at the Portal: Masculine Desire and the Homoerotics of Orientalism." In *Orientalism, Eroticism, and Modern Visuality in Global Cultures*, edited by Julie Codell and Joan del Plato, 43–72. London: Routledge, 2018.

Smith, Karen W. *Constantin Guys: Crimean War Drawings 1854–1856.* Ohio: Cleveland Museum of Art, 1978.

Spivak, Gayatri. "Can the Subaltern Speak?" In *Marxism and the Interpretation of Culture*, edited by Cary Nelson and Lawrence Grossberg 271–313. Urbana: University of Illinois Press, 1988.

Suad, Joseph. "The Public/Private: The Imagined Boundary in the Imagined Nation/State/Community: The Lebanese Case." *Feminist Review* (Autumn 1997), 57: 73–92.

Tadmor, Naomi. "The Concept of the Household-Family in Eighteenth-Century England." *Past and Present* 151 (May 1996): 111–40.

Tahmasbpour, Mohammad Reza. "Photography during the Qajar Era, 1842-1925." In *The Indigenous Lens: Early Photography in the near and Middle East*, edited by Markus Ritter and Staci G. Scheiwiller, trans. Reza Sheikh, 57–76. Berlin and Boston: De Gruyter Inc., 2017.

Bibliography

Talbot, Michael. "Sparks of Happenstance: Photographs, Public Celebrations, and the Ottoman Military Band of Jerusalem." *Journal of the Ottoman and Turkish Studies Association* 5, no. 1 (2018): 33–66.

Tavakoli-Targhi, Mohamad. "Imagining Western Women: Occidentalism and Euro-Eroticism." *Radical America* 24 (July–September 1990 [1993]): 74–6.

Tavakoli-Targhi, Mohamad. "Refashioning Iran: Language and Culture during the Constitutional Revolution." *Iranian Studies* 23, 1/4 (1990): 77–101.

Tavakoli-Targhi, Mohamad. *Refashioning Iran: Orientalism, Occidentalism and Historiography.* New York: Palgrave, 2001.

Thompson, Elizabeth. *Colonial Citizens: Republican Rights, Paternal Privilege, and Gender in French Syria and Lebanon.* New York: Columbia University Press, 2000.

Toledano, Ehud R. *The Ottoman Slave Trade and its Suppression: 1840–1890.* Princeton: Princeton University Press, 1982.

Toledano, Ehud. *State and Society in Mid-Nineteenth-Century Egypt.* New York: Cambridge University Press, 1990.

Traboulsi, Fawwaz. "From Mandate to Independence (1920–1943)." In *History of Modern Lebanon*, edited by Fawwaz Traboulsi, 88–109. London: Pluto Press, 2012.

Troutt Powell, Eve M. *A Different Shade of Colonialism: Egypt, Great Britain and the Master of the Sudan.* Oakland: University of California Press, 2003.

Troutt Powell, Eve. *Tell This in My Memory: Stories of Enslavement from Egypt, Sudan and the Late Ottoman Empire.* Stanford: Stanford University Press, 2012.

Tucker, Judith E. *Women in Nineteenth-Century Egypt.* Cambridge: Cambridge University Press, 1985.

Tulloch, Carol. "Style—Fashion—Dress: From Black to Post-Black." *Fashion Theory* 14, no. 3 (2010): 273–303.

Tulloch, Carol. *The Birth of Cool: Style Narratives of the African Diaspora.* London: Bloomsbury, 2016.

Turkle, Sherry, ed. *Evocative Objects: Things We Think With.* Cambridge: The MIT Press, 2007.

Ulrich, Laura. *A House Full of Females: Plural Marriage and Women's Rights in Early Mormonism, 1835–1870.* New York: Alfred A. Knopf, 2017.

Vaka, Demetra (Mrs. Kenneth Brown). *The Unveiled Ladies of Stamboul.* Boston and New York: Houghton Mifflin Co., 1923.

Walker, Mary Adelaide. *Eastern Life and Scenery: With Excursions in Asia Minor, Mytilene, Crete, and Roumania.* 2 vols. London: Chapman and Hall, 1886.

Walker, Mary Adelaide. *Old Tracks and New Landmarks: Wayside Sketches in Crete, Macedonia, Mitylene, etc.* London: Richard Bentley and Son, 1897.

Warhurst, Chris and Dennis Nickson. "Employee Experience of Aesthetic Labour in Retail and Hospitality." *Work, Employment and Society* 21, no. 1 (2007): 103–20.

Watenpaugh, Keith David. *Being Modern in the Middle East: Revolution, Colonialism, and the Arab Middle Class.* Princeton: Princeton University Press, 2006.

Wigoder, Meir. "History Begins at Home: Photography and Memory in the Writings of Seigfried Kracauer and Roland Barthes." *History and Memory* 13, no. 1 (2001): 19–59.

Women's Worlds in Qajar digital archive, www.qajarwomen.org.

Woodsmall, Ruth. *Moslem Women Enter a New World.* New York: Round Table Press, Inc., 1936.

Yeğenoğlu, Meyda. *Colonial Fantasies: Towards a Feminist Reading of Orientalism.* Cambridge: Cambridge University Press, 1998.

Zaydan, Jurji. *Asir al-Mutamahdi* (Prisoner of the False Mahdi), translated by Eve Troutt Powell. Cairo: Dar al-Hilal, first published in Arabic in 1892.

Ze'evi, Dror. *Producing Desire: Changing Sexual Discourse in the Ottoman Middle East, 1500–1900.* Berkeley and Los Angeles: University of California Press, 2006.

Zemon Davis, Natalie. *The Return of Martin Guerre.* Cambridge: Harvard University Press, 1984.

Zeyneb Hanoum. *A Turkish Woman's European Impressions, edited and with an introduction by Grace Ellison.* London: Seeley, Service and Co. Ltd., 1913.

Zilfi, Madeline C. *Women and Slavery in the Late Ottoman Empire.* Cambridge: Cambridge University Press, 2010.

Zimmerman, Andrew. "The Ideology of the Machine and the Spirit of the Factory: Remarx on Babbage and Ure," *Cultural Critique*, no. 37 (Autumn, 1997): 5–29.

Zürcher, Erik J. *The Young Turk Legacy and Nation Building, From the Ottoman Empire to Ataturk's Legacy.* London: I.B. Tauris, 2010.

INDEX

Page numbers followed by 'f' and 'n' refer to figures and notes respectively.

Index

Index

Index